The Transformation of Arbitration in Africa

The Transformation of Arbitration in Africa

The Role of Arbitral Institutions

Edited by
Emilia Onyema

Wolters Kluwer

Published by:
Kluwer Law International B.V.
PO Box 316
2400 AH Alphen aan den Rijn
The Netherlands
Website: www.wklawbusiness.com

Sold and distributed in North, Central and South America by:
Wolters Kluwer Legal & Regulatory U.S.
7201 McKinney Circle
Frederick, MD 21704
United States of America
Email: customer.service@wolterskluwer.com

Sold and distributed in all other countries by:
Turpin Distribution Services Ltd
Stratton Business Park
Pegasus Drive, Biggleswade
Bedfordshire SG18 8TQ
United Kingdom
Email: kluwerlaw@turpin-distribution.com

ISBN 978-90-411-6729-3

To all users of arbitration in Africa

Editor

Emilia Onyema is a senior lecturer in International Commercial Law at SOAS, University of London. She is a Fellow of the Chartered Institute of Arbitrators and qualified to practice law in Nigeria and is a non-practising Solicitor in England and Wales. Her teaching and research cover international sales law, law and development in Africa and international commercial arbitration. She has widely published in these areas and is the author of the book, *International Commercial Arbitration and the Arbitrator's Contract* (Routledge, 2010). She holds a Ph.D. in international commercial arbitration from Queen Mary University of London.

Contributors

Mohamed Abdel Raouf is the Director of the Cairo Regional Centre for International Commercial Arbitration (CRCICA) and Associate Professor at Paris 1 Panthéon-Sorbonne. He sits regularly as arbitrator in different jurisdictions; Member of the Governing Board of the International Council for Commercial Arbitration (ICCA) and the Board of the Arbitration Institute of the Stockholm Chamber of Commerce (SCC); Vice President of the International Federation of Commercial Arbitration Institutions (IFCAI), CEDR Accredited Mediator, and arbitrator listed in the Panel of Arbitrators of the Court of Arbitration for Sport (CAS). Mohamed holds a Ph.D. in international arbitration from the University of Montpellier I, France.

Narcisse Aka is the Secretary General of the Arbitration Centre of the OHADA CCJA and teaches the law of arbitration at the OHADA Higher Regional School of Magistracy (ERSUMA). He is the former Secretary General of the Court of Arbitration, Ivory Coast Chamber of Commerce and Industry. His publications include the Commentary on OHADA Uniform Act on Arbitration Law: Practice and Institutions in Africa.

Emmanuel Amofa is the Administrator of the Ghana Arbitration Centre since its inception in 1996. He qualified as a barrister in Ghana and actively practices various forms of commercial law and arbitration in Ghana and internationally. He authored the chapter on Ghana in Boseman Lise (gen ed.) *Arbitration in Africa: A Practitioner's Guide* (Kluwer Law International 2013).

Duncan Bagshaw was the first Registrar of LCIA-MIAC and currently with Stephenson Harwood LLP in London. He is a barrister called to the Bar in England and Wales and a member of the Chartered Institute of Arbitrators.

Dalia Hussein is a legal advisor at the CRCICA and Lecturer at the Faculty of Law, Zakazik University. Dalia was an Administrative Prosecutor in Egypt, and Counsel in arbitration practice where she represented states and private parties in commercial and investment disputes before many institutions including CRCICA, ICSID and DIAC. Dalia holds a *Maîtrise en Droit* from Paris I Pantheon Sorbonne University, an LL.B. from Cairo University, an LL.M. in Private International Law and International

Commercial Law from Paris II Panthéon- Assas University, an LL.M. in Private Law from Cairo University and a Ph.D. in international arbitration from Cairo University.

Megha Joshi was appointed the first Executive Secretary/Chief Executive Officer of the Lagos Court of Arbitration (LCA) International Centre for Arbitration & ADR (ICAA) in November 2012. She has been responsible for implementing the institutional framework of the business, administration and engagement of all the stakeholders of dispute resolution services at the LCA. Megha graduated with a degree in Politics from Manchester University in 2004, after which she interned for United States Senator, Hillary Rodham Clinton in New York State and assisted the Democrats campaign in the 2004 Presidential elections.

Mahutodji Jimmy Vital Kodo is Technical advisor to the President of the OHADA, CCJA. He practised law in Paris and Nanterre (France) and served as Adjunct Professor at the University of Paris-Est Creteil, France. He holds law degrees from University of Abomey-Calavi, Benin (Master's Degree), University of Lille 2, France (LL.M.), and University of Paris-Est Creteil (LL.D). In 2008, Mr Kodo co-authored the Annotated OHADA Code, published by the Institut International de Droit d'Expression et d'Inspirations Françaises (IDEF), and L'Application des Actes Uniformes de l'OHADA, Publications de l'Institut Universitaire André Ryckmans 5 (Louvain-la-Neuve: Academia-Bruylant, 2010).

Kariuki Muigua holds Ph.D. in Law, LL.B, LL.M. (Env. Law, Nairobi), FCIArb (Chartered Arbitrator), Accredited Mediator, FCPSK, MKIM, Dip in Arb (UK) and is Advocate, Lecturer, Centre for Advanced Studies in Environmental Law and Policy (CASELAP), University of Nairobi; Chairperson, Chartered Institute of Arbitrators (Kenya Branch) 2013-2015.

Tolu Obamuroh is Associate General Counsel at the LCA. Tolu obtained his LL.M. degree at Columbia Law School in 2013. Tolu is a Weinstein Fellow and a doctoral candidate at Penn State Law School. His research is on pre-arbitration procedures and the expansion of arbitral powers in international arbitration.

Jean Alain Penda is the OHADAC Project Manager in the French West Indies and an Independent Consultant at Price Waterhouse Coopers LLP, London. Mr Penda holds an LL.B. from the University of Buea (Cameroon), an LL.M. in International Corporate and Financial Law from the University of Wolverhampton (United Kingdom), and a Ph.D. from the University of Basel (Switzerland) specializing in sales and commercial law. Penda was a Research Assistant for the Head of Private Law at the Faculty of Law, University of Basel and a Researcher for Global Sales Law, a project supported by UNCITRAL.

Bernadette Uwicyeza was the Secretary General of the Kigali International Arbitration Centre until 2015. She is currently the Centre's senior Technical Advisor. She lectures at the University of Rwanda, Kigali Independent University and the Institute of Legal

Practice and Development (ILPD). She holds a Law degree and a postgraduate Diploma in European Union Law from the University of Rennes I in France. She co-authored the book, *New Law Governing Contracts in Rwanda* (Rosenberg Publishers, Amsterdam 2013).

Summary of Contents

Table of Contents

Foreword

Several role players consisting of professionals, institutions, states, corporate and individual users, and a plethora of supportive service providers and administrative staff contribute to the management, administration and dispensation of private commercial justice through arbitration. This book is prompted by first, the growing institutionalization of arbitration and, second, a critical concern with the ability and capabilities of the centres and institutions (hereafter 'institutions') that administer the arbitration process and the adequacy or otherwise of the services they provide for arbitration users. The book therefore is a contribution to the discussion and examination of the structures, roles and functions of these institutions on the African continent.

Whether arbitration is a field of study, a system of justice, a profession, business or an industry is beside the point. Modern arbitration is all these. We know there has to be a dispute, disputing parties and arbitrators for arbitration to come alive. But alongside these key pre-requisites are the arbitration institutions that provide administrative assistance, procedural rules and guidance for the parties and arbitrators for conducting the arbitration proceedings, ensuring the integrity of the process and ultimately the arbitral award.

Several arbitral institutions already exist and more new ones are emerging as arbitration disputes and spaces expand in Africa and elsewhere. Modern arbitration institutions therefore ought not be stuck with their limited traditional roles and functions but respond to the new opportunities offered by the ever expanding arbitration world in disputes from various fields and sectors – financial, commercial, industrial, investment and business transactions, across borders. If surveys, monitors and publications by the IMF and the UNCTAD World Investment Reports are reliable, one can believe that four of the fastest growing economies in the world in 2014 are located in Africa and foreign direct investment has increased in ten years from USD 11 billion in 2002 to over USD 56.38 billion in 2013. Think of the emerging opportunities for arbitration institutions and arbitrators offered by the ongoing industrialization initiatives in the five political and economic regions of the African Union – The Arab Maghreb Union of North Africa, the Economic Community of West African States

(ECOWAS), the East African Community (EAC), the Economic Community of Central African States (ECCAS) and the Southern African Development Community (SADC) (including the Common Market for Eastern and Southern Africa (COMESA)). These initiatives are within the context of the African Union Plan of Action for Accelerated Industrial Development in Africa aimed at building an 'integrated prosperous and peaceful Africa, driven and managed by its own citizens and representing a dynamic force in the international arena'. What is needed is action and implementation.

This book on African arbitration institutions was inspired by an arbitration conference jointly convened by Dr Emilia Onyema of SOAS University of London and myself. The conference was hosted by the African Union Commission at its headquarters in Addis Ababa on 23 July 2015. It was the first of its kind on the continent, being devoted solely to the examination of the role and functions of African arbitration institutions.

Following the conference, the Contributors to this book, all of whom were participants and affiliates or representatives of arbitration institutions, were invited by the conveners to contribute to the book chapters collating the lessons from the conference relevant to the performance of arbitration institutions in their respective African countries and regions. This book is the outcome of that exercise as well as the Contributors' own insightful appraisals, suggestions and recommendations on what all of us can do better together to promote the development, transformation, effective arbitration, and the delivery of efficient arbitration services to users across the continent. The thrust of the conference deliberations, as captured and emphasized in this book, is the creation of a facilitative, supportive, and conducive cultural and infrastructural environment for the practice of arbitration in Africa in which the arbitration institutions are promoted and encouraged to play a leading role.

Dr Onyema opens the discourse with an explanatory introduction of the '*Arbitration in Africa Project*' aimed at '*creating a sustainable culture of arbitration as a mechanism for commercial dispute resolution in Africa*' – designed to examine the contribution of four stakeholders of arbitration in Africa being, the arbitration institutions, national courts, and judges, arbitration practitioners and the governments of African states. Included in the introduction are some statistics and appendix tables of arbitration institutions and national laws that regulate arbitration in Africa's fifty-four states.

The Contributors' assignment, specified in the introduction, is to examine the key research question of whether, and if so, how African arbitration institutions can ably and effectively support the transformation of arbitration in Africa. How did the Contributors go about their task?

Onyema pulls together in Chapter 1 various strands, practical concerns and issues in arbitration practice, necessitating the expansion of arbitration centres and institutions on the continent located in various cities: Abidjan, Accra, Cairo, Johannesburg, Kigali, Lagos, Port Louis, Nairobi, and Yaoundé. She expounds that, as all these institutions offer different and diversified dispute resolution services, there is need to examine the quality of those services and the contributions they are able to make for the improvement of arbitration practice in their domiciled jurisdictions; and, in view of the dearth of arbitration references on the continent, the role of arbitration institutions as major role players inside and outside Africa, is an issue of critical concern and paramount importance. The chapter discusses the general characteristics of arbitration institutions, their functions, and how they can best promote the growth and transformation of arbitration in Africa, by for instance, maintaining an online presence with accessible and modernized arbitration rules, a professionally trained staff versed in the various businesses and transactional languages on the continent.

Onyema contemplates and argues for the expansion of institutional services that will accord with the growth of arbitration business across the continent, the promotion of a legal environment likely to attract more disputants to arbitration, and consequently, an increased caseload for the institutions and other stakeholders for the benefit of all users of arbitration.

The question whether supranational arbitration institutions can contribute to the transformation of African arbitration led Dr Mohutodji Jimmy Vital Kodo and Mr Narcisse Aka to the examination of the function of the Common Court of Justice and Arbitration of OHADA (CCJA) in Chapter 2. They analyse the dualist role of the CCJA both as a supranational court and an arbitration centre within the OHADA system and highlight its contribution to the transformation agenda within OHADA. Recognizing the existence and operations of several arbitration institutions on the continent, with differing functions and capabilities, they advocate either a merger of some of those centres or the creation of fewer regional arbitration centres to eliminate the multiplication of the same functions in order, instead, to maximize their effectiveness. They opine that the CCJA would encourage and support regional centres that are well structured and equipped, and conveniently located, so as to optimize their efficiency.

Mohamed Abdel Raouf and Dalia Hussein take up the theme of convenient location in Chapter 3 with references to past practice when arbitration centres existed only in European cities, compelling African parties either to export their disputes abroad or to use the less attractive option of litigating disputes in international contracts. Noting the dynamic growth of African economies and the expansion of cross-border trade and commerce, they see the need for an increasingly visible and readily accessible market for African arbitral institutions. They pertinently explore the contribution African institutions can make for transforming arbitration on the continent, by exemplifying and examining the role of the CRCICA. The authors further discuss the impact of the AALCO vision in the creation and growth of regional centres in Africa, the need for closer co-operation and sharing experiences for the advancement of the rule of law and due process in dispute resolution. Recognizing the challenges posed by the inefficiencies, limitations and inadequate resources in the existing institutions, the authors propose the establishment of codes of conduct to regulate institutional management and promote accountability and neutrality.

The role of the East African arbitration institutions in the transformation project is pursued by Dr Kariuki Muigua in Chapter 4, taking in the institutions located in Kenya, Tanzania, Uganda, Rwanda and Burundi, being the Member States of the EAC.

The chapter outlines the legal and institutional framework of arbitration in the region, and explores the means of achieving the goals of reliable and effective arbitration as a means of attracting investment to the region and fostering user confidence in the expeditious settlement of disputes in neutral fora. This, Dr Muigua opines, is an approach that could impact positively on the transformation project.

Duncan Bagshaw follows the discussion in Chapter 5 by considering whether the collaborative relationship between the European-based LCIA and the Mauritius-based MIAC is a necessary or helpful means to ensure the success of the African-based institution. In other words, does an African arbitration institution need collaboration with a foreign institution for the former to thrive or succeed? This leads Bagshaw first, to a description of Mauritius and its legal system, the vision of Mauritius as an international dispute resolution base, the prospects of the LCIA-MIAC alliance, and what other African states may do or emulate to become attractive international arbitration hubs. The author argues that while the LCIA-MIAC partnership enhanced the credibility of the MIAC, a successful African arbitration destination required more than a mere alliance with a foreign institution, but also and, more importantly, needed modern arbitration laws, clearly defined and supportive government policy attractive to arbitration, a court with specialist arbitration trained judges and other related support services; and that although Mauritius claims to have the requisite ingredients, it still has a long way to go to be a credible venue for arbitration.

Megha Joshi and Tolu Obamuroh discuss in Chapter 6 the mission and structure of the LCA, the role of the Lagos State Government in the establishment of the LCA and critically examine the nature of that relationship. They endorse Principle 7 of the CIArb London Centenary Principles requiring the provision of functional facilities, transcription services, hearing rooms, document handling, managerial and translation services, all of which, the authors claim, the LCA provides for the use and practice of arbitration and ADR. The Lagos State Government, they assert, promotes Lagos as a favourable arbitration seat, supports the LCA's services and contribution to the development of arbitration in Africa. Despite such government support, the authors emphasize the independence of the LCA in fulfilling its mandate by providing quality service, training, and policy advocacy to beneficiaries who include the members of the Nigerian Bar Association, the Judiciary, business leaders and policy makers. The LCA also, and notably, collaborates and shares experiences with other arbitration service providers on the continent.

In Chapter 7, Emmanuel Amofa engages with the connection between national laws and arbitration centres on the model of the Ghana Arbitration Centre. Amofa places the discussion in the context of the desirable interplay between the private arbitral process and the national legal system, and examines the critical nexus between Ghana's Alternative Dispute Resolution (ADR) legislation of 2010 (Act No. 786) and the Rules and Procedures of the Ghana Arbitration Centre (GAC), and the legislative support for arbitral parties using the GAC Rules. The author, in considerable detail, takes in the history of arbitration legislations in Ghana, the salient features of the Act No. 798 and its linkages, similarities and differences with the GAC Rules, noting that their harmonious relationship makes arbitration under the GAC Rules in Ghana attractive to disputants. Amofa argues that Institutional Arbitration Rules that complement national arbitration law are more beneficial; that Court recognition and support for this complementarity assists the administration of disputes by both arbitral institutions and tribunals, and urges the court to interpret the Act liberally to reflect international best practices. Amofa submits that Ghana is an arbitration friendly jurisdiction as its Courts do not unduly interfere with the arbitral process.

The discussion of Arbitration Centres in French-speaking African Countries is taken up by Jean Alain Penda in Chapter 8, starting with the acknowledgement of the growth of African economies, the increasing demand of both domestic and international arbitration and the consequential increase in arbitration institutions.

The author notes significantly that the majority of African arbitration disputes are administered outside the continent, that fifteen out of the twenty-one francophone sub-Sahara African States are OHADA members, and brings the French-speaking African perspective into the discussion. The author expounds on the OHADA arbitration system, and the challenges of the arbitration institutions operating under OHADA. He observes that despite the existence of modern arbitration legislation, well-trained arbitrators and institutions, African arbitration practitioners are still marginalized even in disputes emanating from the continent. French-speaking Member States of the OHADA Treaty are presented as adequately equipped and sophisticated enough to deal with the huge number of arbitration references seated in the Member States and institutions, in pursuance of which African arbitration practice should trump foreign negative perceptions and bias.

The unique powers and privileges of the CCJA, its high visibility and easy access as an arbitration institution under OHADA, are rendered as making it more appealing than ad hoc arbitration. The challenges currently facing OHADA are being addressed towards the revision of the Uniform Act on Arbitration (UAA) and the CCJA Arbitration Rules, all of which should augur well for the future of the OHADA system.

The final Chapter 9, on the promotion of arbitration to serve the purposes of domestic small and medium sized enterprises (SMEs) is taken up by Bernadette Uwicyeza who argues that the institutions' pivotal role in arbitration makes them suitable for marketing and arbitrating SME disputes; that in Rwanda a company with less than USD 200,000 turnover is registrable, as an SME which, in Africa, constitute a large proportion of the domestic market that generate work for the arbitration institutions. Various issues connected with SMEs and the marketing activities of arbitration institutions are brought into the discussion in the three sections of the chapter. A case study of marketing activities and its consequences is presented, drawn from the data and experience of the Kigali International Arbitration Centre (KIAC) which was set up to assist businesses to resolve their disputes in a timely, efficient and amicable manner, without the excessive costs of litigation or ad hoc arbitration. The KIAC business initiative enjoys government support, reduces the costs of international arbitration references, making the KIAC a viable international arbitration alternative to the courts. The participation of SMEs in arbitration, it is argued, can influence other entities and groups contracting with them at the local, regional and international levels, and consequently lead to an increase in the caseload of these arbitration institutions. The author notes that mobilizing funds for their businesses remains a major challenge for African arbitration institutions, for which reason an African initiative to support and harmonize marketing activities and strategies is a necessity.

As a project compendium two significant issues need further attention and research either for a sequel or revised edition. First, government support, whether initially or continuing, for institutions like the KIAC (Kigali), LCA (Lagos), NCIA (Nairobi), MIAC (Mauritius) and CADRE (Uganda) is apparent, despite measured disclaimers or claims of institutional independence. The challenging paradox of the institutions' need for government funding (seed money) and infrastructural assistance without government involvement and interference in their functions and activities is a serious concern in international arbitration, requiring considered institutional response in the interests of confidence building, institutional independence and international outlook. On the one hand, if institutional independence is not an abstraction but a reality, then it needs demonstration. Otherwise the clearest option is to acknowledge government support openly for the arbitration institutions to work with government to deliver the needs and promises of arbitration. This problem is recognized but not addressed or adequately. In the third of the four conferences lined up in the Arbitration in Africa Project, there will be an opportunity to bring this issue into the open with a sharper focus and to examine the role of government (whether it has or should have any role) in domestic and international arbitration, in order to define a nuanced relationship between arbitration and government in the context of the independence and internationality claimed by some African arbitration institutions and arbitral tribunals. It should be possible for the institutions and users to espouse a regulatory framework for that relationship, bearing in mind the supportive roles expected from law and policy makers, the courts, the much needed infrastructure and conducive environment for the peace, safety and security that underpin national economic development, political stability and social cohesion, in the multi-complex ways that only governments can provide.

Second, the book can be enhanced by statistical data and material information on institutional workloads and output, the number of disputes registered, administered, awards rendered and voluntarily implemented, or pending review or appeal, and periodic performance evaluation reports.

The point of interest is that, as their numerical increase (some seventy-one institutions are listed) is presented as signifying increased workloads, the institutions would do well to compile and publish the statistical information useful for practitioners and researchers. The selection, compilation and publication of significant and well-written awards will facilitate and contribute to learning and research while also enhancing the qualitative profiles of the institutions able to offer such services.

The Contributors took up the challenge of their assignment admirably well and the book's nine chapters, in three thematic parts, is an enduring tribute to their insightful assessments, thoughtful appraisals, considered opinions and cumulative endeavour in delivering this important contribution to arbitration literature. The book captures the essence, substance and focal discussion points of the Addis Ababa conference. As an impressive achievement it deserves commendation in epic verse; but seeing the Contributors have delivered of themselves in fluent diction, I too may be permitted – O Muse – to conclude by commending their efforts and outstanding achievement in laudatory prose. Where there was once vacuum, there is now an illuminating and enlightening book we can all be proud of, from an African-driven initiative, in Africa, for the benefit of all who desire to expand their knowledge of arbitration and an informed appreciation of what the African arbitration institutions can do to transform arbitration in Africa.

Judge Edward Torgbor
Vice-President, LCIA Africa Users' Council

List of Abbreviations

AALCO	Asian African Legal Consultative Organization
ACA	Arbitration and Conciliation Act 1988 (Nigeria)
ACHR	African Court of Human Rights
Act 38	Arbitration Act 1961 (Ghana)
Act 798	Alternative Dispute Resolution Act 2010 (Ghana)
ADR	Alternative Dispute Resolution
ADRC	Alternative Dispute Resolution Centre
AfDB	African Development Bank
AILA	African International Legal Awareness
ALCC	Asian Legal Consultative Committee
AU	African Union
BCAM	Burundi Centre for Arbitration and Mediation
BCDR-AAA	Bahrain Centre for Dispute Resolution/American arbitration Association
BITs	Bilateral Investment Treaties
BoT	Board of Trustees
CADEV	African Centre for Law and Development
CADR	Centre for Alternative Dispute Resolution
CADRE	Centre for Arbitration and Dispute Resolution
CAG	Arbitration Centre of Guinée
CATO	Court of Arbitration, Mediation and Conciliation of Togo
CCATP	Comparative Commercial Arbitration: Theory and Practice
CCJA	Common Court of Justice and Arbitration (OHADA)
CEMACO	Centre de mediation et d'arbitrage au Congo
CIArb	Chartered Institute of Arbitrators
CIArb-C	Chartered Institute of Arbitrators, Cairo Branch

CIArb-K	The Chartered institute of Arbitrators, Kenya Branch
CIETAC	China International Economic and Trade Arbitration Commission
CMAN	Centre de Mediation et d'Arbitrage de Niamey
CMC	Citizens Mediation Centre (Lagos)
COJA	African Congress of Business Lawyers
CPAM	Centre for Permanent Arbitration and Mediation
CRCICA	Cairo Regional Centre for International Commercial Arbitration
DIAC	Dubai International Arbitration Centre
DRC	Democratic Republic of Congo
DTAs	Double Taxation Agreements
EAC	East Africa Court
EACJ	East African Court of Justice
ECOWAS	Economic Community of West African States
ERSUMA	OHADA Professional School of Magistrates
GAC	Ghana Arbitration Centre
HKIAC	Hong Kong International Arbitration Center
IBA	International Bar Association
ILFA	International Lawyers from Africa
ICC	International Chamber of Commerce
ICCA	International Council for Commercial Arbitration
ICSID	International Centre for Settlement of Investment Disputes
ICT	Information Communication Technology
IFCAI	International Federation of Commercial Arbitration Institutions
ISPRAMED	Institute for the Promotion of Arbitration in the Mediterranean
KAA	Kenya Arbitration Act, 1995
KCAB	Korean Commercial Arbitration Board
KIAC	Kigali International Arbitration Centre
KLRCA	Kuala Lumpur Regional Centre for Arbitration
KNCC	Kenya National Chamber of Commerce
KNCCI	Kenya National Chamber of Commerce and Industry
LAL	Lagos Arbitration Law 2009
LASG	Lagos State Government
LCA	Lagos Court of Arbitration
LCIA	London Court of International Arbitration

LCIA-MIAC	London Court of International Arbitration-Mauritius International Arbitration Centre
LMDC	Lagos Multi-Door Courthouse
LSARC	Lagos State Arbitration Reform Committee
MIAC	Mauritius International Arbitration Centre
MoU	Memorandum of Understanding
NCC	National Construction Council
NCIA	Nairobi Centre for International Arbitration
OHADA	The Organisation for the Harmonization of Business Law in Africa
PCA	Permanent Court of Arbitration
PPA	Power Purchase Agreement
SCC	Stockholm Chamber of Commerce Arbitration Centre
SIAC	Singapore International Arbitration Centre
SMEs	Small and Medium sized Enterprises
TAA	Tanzania Arbitration Act
TIA	Tanzania Institute of Arbitrators
UAA	Uniform Arbitration Act (OHADA)
UNCITRAL	United Nations Commission on International Trade Law
UNIDROIT	International Institute for the Unification of Private Law

Acknowledgements

The idea and concept for the research project that led to the conference from which this book was birthed came from different people who deserve acknowledgement and appreciation. I wish to thank Judge Edward Torgbor with whom all the contributors share a major interest in the development of arbitration in Africa. Edward co-convened the SOAS/AU Arbitration in Africa conference, the discussions and output of which resulted in this book. He also graciously wrote the foreword.

Special thanks to my then, Dean at the Faculty of Law and Social Science of SOAS University of London, Professor Matthew Craven and our Associate Dean for research, Professor Stephen Hopgood, who both fully supported my engagement with this conference. I also thank my students over the years whose ideas and enthusiasm for arbitration continue to inspire my research and teaching on the subject.

The General Legal Counsel of the African Union Commission, Professor Vincent Nmehielle, and his Office deserve special thanks for taking an interest in arbitration and co-hosting the conference which led to this book. To all the chairs, speakers and participants who attended the conference and shared their ideas on promoting arbitration in Africa, especially the administrators of the arbitration institutions themselves, and all our sponsors, with special mention of Chief Bayo Ojo, *SAN* of ICAMA and Mr Kamal Shah of Stephenson Harwood LLP, I say a huge African, thank you!

Any conference and book project demands huge administrative support and this is no exception. Many thanks to Ms Christine Djumpah for all the excellent work she put into organising the conference. I also thank Dr Mimi Ajibadé who pulled all the independent chapters together so they all read as one book. All the contributors to this book collectively thank all the reviewers of the chapters. Finally, this book is a reality because of the belief in the project and push I received from Ms Eleanor Taylor of Kluwer, to whom I am most grateful.

Introduction

Emilia Onyema

Africa as a continent is resource and mineral rich and an active capital importing member of the international community. Africa has also seen a growth and resurgence in intra-Africa investments by African investors with full participation by large- and medium-sized African enterprises.[1] It is obvious that disputes arise from such flow of commercial transactions within and across borders. The more such transactions increase in numbers the greater the probability of more disputes arising. The probability of disputes arising from such transactions being resolved before domestic courts is very low for the usual reasons such as distrust and lack of confidence in the local courts.[2] The effect of such distrust is dispute resolution flight, recourse to other self-help measures or a complete lack of engagement in which case the aggrieved party cuts their losses and moves on without seeking to resolve such dispute. None of these outcomes is desirable since they all contribute to frustrating growth in business which then leads to fewer investments into these countries.[3] It is therefore important that when such disputes arise there are effective and efficient mechanisms, trusted by the disputing parties, in place to resolve them. The use of arbitration as a tried and tested mechanism for the resolution of such disputes is not in question, whether within the continent or globally.[4]

1. Some of the major investors involved in intra-Africa FDI include corporations such as The Dangote Group, MTN Telecommunications, and Ecobank. See for example Ecobank, *Africa 8 Insight 6 – Intra-Africa Investments,* available at: http://ecobank.com/africa8/insight6.html#africa8_main [last accessed 6 May 2016].
2. It is interesting that the level of distrusts among African businesses of their various domestic courts is very high. It will not be too far-fetched to posit that African businesses have greater confidence in European courts than in their own domestic courts.
3. This then leads to low economic growth which feeds into weak economic and human development indices.
4. See for example, Born G.B., *International Commercial Arbitration* 1 (Wolters Kluwer, 2009); N. Blackaby et al., *Redfern and Hunter on International Arbitration* 1 (6th ed., Kluwer Law International/OUP 2015).

However, it is well acknowledged that the level of participation by African states in the global arbitral discourse is much lower than that of other regions of the world. This is despite the numbers of arbitration references African parties generate[5] or its much touted economic growth by multilateral agencies such as the International Monetary Fund and African Development Bank.[6] Such participation can be measured by the numbers of international or domestic arbitration references that hold on the continent (as seat of arbitration); the numbers of arbitrators of African origin that are appointed as members of arbitral tribunals; the numbers of African law firms/practices or lawyers that represent their clients/disputants in such references; and finally the number and caseload of arbitration institutions that administer arbitral references in the continent. Various reasons have been proffered for this state of affairs in blogs, articles and conferences;[7] and as is the unfortunate norm with issues affecting the continent, there has been (and continues to be) a lot of talk on these concerns with no remedial action put in place. It is this need for action that has prompted and motivated the conference which led to this book, both of which are part of a larger research project on the development of arbitration in Africa. These issues are currently gaining traction in various discourses on international arbitration. An example is the hosting by Mauritius of the 23rd International Council for Commercial Arbitration (ICCA) congress, which reflects ICCA's recognition of the need to engage Africa and Africans in international arbitration.[8]

I THE ARBITRATION IN AFRICA RESEARCH PROJECT

The research project is titled: 'Creating a Sustainable Culture of Arbitration as a Mechanism for Commercial Dispute Resolution in Africa'.[9] It is designed to empirically and systematically examine how four clearly identified stakeholders of arbitration in Africa can contribute to the sustainable development of arbitration in the continent. The four stakeholders are arbitration institutions;[10] national courts and judges;[11]

5. See for example data from the ICC caseload in Table 3 of the appendix.
6. See for example http://www.africaneconomicoutlook.org/en/ [last accessed 6 May 2016]. See also the African Development Bank Economic outlook for Africa available at: http://www.afdb.org/en/knowledge/publications/african-economic-outlook/ [last accessed 6 May 2016]. See also the Report from the European Parliament on Africa's economic growth available at: http://www.europarl.europa.eu/RegData/etudes/IDAN/2016/573891/EPRS_IDA(2016)573891_EN.pdf [last accessed 6 May 2016].
7. See for example the discussions by the various panels at the May 2014 ICAMA Second Arbitration Roundtable that held in Abuja, Nigeria: http://www.icama.com/about.html.
8. For details on the 23rd ICCA Congress, see: http://www.iccamauritius2016.com/ [last accessed 6 May 2016].
9. The website dedicated to this research project is available at: http://www.researcharbitrationafrica.com/ [last accessed 6 May 2016].
10. Arbitration institutions that will provide administrative services of globally recognized standards.
11. National courts that will understand the interaction between courts and arbitration and adhere to a clear policy to play a supportive role in arbitration.

arbitration practitioners;[12] and the governments of African states.[13] Part of the terms of reference of this research project is to organize focused conferences in Africa with each stakeholder community to examine these issues and also suggest possible remedial actions for their implementation. The research project is designed over a four-year period which will include publication of the output of the conferences and monitoring of the implementation of the discussions and suggestions made at the conferences. These therefore are the desired impact: increase in the number of arbitration references administered by African arbitration institutions; modernized arbitral legal frameworks; increase in the number of international arbitration references with seats in cities in the continent; increase in the numbers of domestic arbitration references; and better access to well-reasoned court judgments on arbitration related cases from the continent. These are all measurable indicators.

This book is the output of the discussions at the first conference under this research project, which focused on arbitration institutions, and was hosted by the Office of the General Counsel of the African Union Commission in Addis Ababa in July 2015.[14] This book (as did the conference) examines the role of arbitration institutions in the transformation of the law and practice of arbitration in Africa. Specifically, the book interrogates how arbitration institutions in the continent can contribute to an acceptance of arbitration as the dispute resolution of choice in appropriate cases within the continent. Such acceptance will require a cultural shift from litigation to arbitration as the preferred dispute resolution mechanism of choice for commercial disputes arising in or connected to Africa.

In a 2014 Article I noted that there are adequate numbers of arbitration institutions in the West African region so that developing a new supranational institution will only further congest an already crowded market space. I also noted that the presence of these many institutions has not realized the AALCO vision of 'greater inflow of arbitral hearings with seats in the continent'.[15] This is particularly so with those disputes with at least one African party (defined as a party registered or domiciled in an African country).[16] This conclusion as it relates to the West African region remains correct but not necessarily so for some other regions of the continent. For example in countries located in Central Africa (including the Horn of Africa) there appears to be

12. Arbitration practitioners that are duly qualified and attain a globally recognized professional standard.
13. This particularly engages legislators and the executive arms of the governments of African states to transmit a clear understanding of how they can support arbitration through creating a favourable non-legal and legal environment for arbitration to thrive. There are examples already of state support in Mauritius and Rwanda that the research will draw upon in this regard.
14. The conference was co-hosted by the Office of the Legal Counsel of the African Union Commission, Addis Ababa on 23 July 2015.
15. E. Onyema, *Regional Arbitration Institution for ECOWAS: Lessons from OHADA Common Court of Justice and Arbitration* IALR 99-111 (2014), available at soas.ac.uk/eprints while IALR is available on Westlaw.
16. E. Torgbor, *Opening up International Arbitration in Africa*, vol. 1 no. 1 LCA Dispute Resolution Journal 1-20 (2014) examined old prejudices against the appointment of qualified African as arbitrators in international dispute resolution.

fewer arbitration institutions,[17] so that (in this region) it may not be a matter of congestion but of too few qualitative arbitration institutions within the reach of disputants to administer arbitration references. It therefore follows that each region of the continent needs to be examined to determine what that region needs as it relates to the availability of arbitration institutions or centres. This will therefore not permit generalizations.

One of the key distinctions of this research project is its pan-African dimension. Discussions on Africa are usually bifurcated into French and English discourses, again linked to the continent's colonial past. Different official languages of African countries are one limitation of its integration efforts.[18] So for example Francophone African countries engage very little with Anglophone African countries on these matters.[19] It is arguable that language barriers play a major role in the discussions on arbitration in Africa with the result that French speaking African countries organize and carry out their own discussions without the English speaking countries fully participating and vice versa. This research project is therefore designed to engage all African countries which, explains why it adopts a pan-African approach. It is expected that this approach will lead to greater integration and sharing of information with the resultant effect of consistency of arbitral practice across the continent.[20]

In addition to language limitation is the recognition that most conferences on arbitration in Africa hold outside the continent and usually with very few speakers from Africa. To counter this, the conferences for this research project will all hold in various countries in Africa with a mixed group of speakers from both within and outside the continent. Each conference will be hosted by an arbitration institution or organization within Africa.[21] Finally, the conferences for this research project are primarily funded by various African organizations and international law firms with strong arbitration-related interests in Africa. These three factors have engendered a strong sense of ownership and participation by African arbitration practitioners in the conferences and as contributors to this book. It was therefore also proper and to reflect this pan-Africanism that the first conference was hosted by the African Union Commission, as the umbrella organization of African states, at their offices in Addis Ababa.[22]

17. See data on the list of arbitration institutions in Africa and their locations in Table 2 in the appendix.
18. Though, such difference is not a major limitation factor as the same can be said of other regions of the world.
19. Though as OHADA shows, there may be better coordination between Francophone and Lusophone countries.
20. The practical consequence of this decision is that the relevant conference proceedings and their outputs will be bilingual, in the French and English languages.
21. In furtherance of this, the Lagos Court of Arbitration Centre will host the second conference in the research project series on the role of courts and judges in the development of arbitration in Africa. For more details, see: http://www.researcharbitrationafrica.com/ [accessed 29 March 2016]. Well over 100 participants, speakers and chairs of panels have registered to attend this Lagos conference which will hold from 22-24 June 2016.
22. The conference at Addis Ababa on 'The Role of Arbitration Institutions in the development of arbitration in Africa' was attended by seventy participants, speakers and session chairs from all regions of Africa, England, France, and the United States of America.

II STATISTICS

Data available shows that there are arbitration institutions that administer arbitral references in various countries of the continent.[23] Table 2 in the appendix contains a list of seventy-one identifiable arbitration institutions in thirty-nine African countries.[24] There is evidence to support the allegation that most disputants (Africans and African registered companies) nominate arbitration institutions in other parts of the world to administer their disputes in preference to using arbitration institutions in the continent. For example, data from the ICC International Court of Arbitration over the sixteen year period between 2000 and 2015 show that 1,608 African parties were disputants under ICC Rules of Arbitration. Over the same period African cities were nominated as seats only ninety-four times while 431 arbitrators of African origin were appointed.[25] None of the arbitration institutions in Africa listed under Table 2 have administered disputes with similar number of African parties. The Cairo Regional Centre which is one of the busiest arbitration institutions in Africa from 2008 to 2014 administered a total of 375 cases with majority of the non-Egyptian parties from non-African countries.[26]

Research as evidenced in Table 1 in the appendix also shows that most African countries have relatively modern national arbitration laws. Forty of the fifty-four African states have arbitration laws that are post the 1985 UNCITRAL Model Law, with seventeen of these laws post 2000. There are however still states with laws from the 1900s.[27] African states have also signed up to relevant arbitration conventions, the 1958 New York and the 1965 Washington Conventions.[28]

There is also data to show that a growing number of African lawyers (and other professionals) are actively undertaking various trainings in arbitration and general ADR. An example is the relatively large number of African members of the Chartered Institute of Arbitrators. An example from data obtained from the headquarters office of the Chartered Institute of Arbitrators, shows that between January and the end of December 2015, a total of 1,563 Africans became associates (801), members (583) and

23. The International Trade Centre lists twenty-seven arbitration institutions/centres in Africa, and this is available at: http://www.intracen.org/Centres-by-geographic-area-Africa/ [last accessed 6 May 2016]. The Happs Arbitration Links lists ten arbitration institutions/centres in Africa and is available at: http://www.arbitration-links.de/00000099670ba0802/index.html [last accessed 6 May 2016]; while ICCA lists twenty-one institutions/centres at http://www.arbitration-icca.org/publications/Directory_of_Arbitral_Institutes.html#44 [last accessed 6 May 2016].
24. This effectively shows that there are no identifiable arbitration institutions in twenty-two African countries. This of course does not mean that there are no arbitration hearings taking place in those countries, especially since most of those twenty-two countries also have legislations on arbitration. The very private nature of arbitration makes it difficult to verify how many or how often ad hoc arbitration references hold in these countries.
25. For details see, *2013 ICC Statistical Report* vol. 25 no. 1 ICC Bulletin 5 (2014). The information of the 2015 data was obtained directly from the ICC Secretariat. Details of this data are contained in Table 3 in the appendix.
26. Details of these statistics are available on the Cairo Regional Centre's website at: http://crcica.org.eg/pub_annual.html [accessed 6 May 2016].
27. The oldest arbitration law is that of Swaziland of 1904. See Table 1 in the appendix for more details.
28. The information in Table 1 does not include BITs and RTAs which have arbitration as one of the dispute resolution mechanisms to which parties may have recourse.

fellows (179) of the Institute.[29] Such data very importantly shows that there are Africans trained in the art, law and practice of arbitration by the premier training organization for arbitration practitioners in the world. It is also noted that this data does not capture the several other thousands of individuals who have participated in arbitration training programmes provided by other organizations, arbitration institutions and universities. This data at least challenges the negative perception that there are none or inadequate numbers of trained individuals who can conduct arbitrations in Africa.

Various countries in the continent host domestic arbitration references which are usually held ad hoc and for which there is (understandably) lack of data on number of such references, because of the private nature of arbitration. Though there are many arbitration institutions located in various African countries, it is still difficult to access data on the number of cases they administer. This lack of access limits any credible empirical analysis of the domestic market for arbitration in Africa. Regardless of this limitation, it is obvious that arbitration institutions are one of the major stakeholders in the arbitral process. To thrive, modern arbitral practice requires functional arbitration institutions or centres available to administer arbitral referrals, whether domestic or international. The importance of arbitration institutions is well captured by the late Amazu A. Asouzu when he noted that:

> Arbitration institutions are the engines of arbitral reform and development. They spark the flame that kindles enthusiasm in the process both by governmental and private parties and users.[30]

The SOAS Addis Ababa conference focused on the role of arbitration institutions in Africa in driving this transformation agenda. This book pulls together the discussions at the conference to answer the questions that arise on the role of arbitration institutions in Africa and how they can better support the growth of the African arbitral market. The aim of the Addis Ababa conference was to:

> focus on the creation of an enduring culture for the effective administration of arbitration by institutions that meet the requirements of its users as part of the process towards the greater participation of African arbitrators, institutions and cities in the global arbitration space.[31]

The conference examined the current role and functions of arbitration institutions within the African continent. It identified the major institutions and their commonalities and differences to encourage strategic space sharing. It brought managers of various arbitration institutions in Africa together in the same room to

---

29. These are just the numbers from the Chartered Institute of Arbitrators. There are other arbitrator training organizations in various African countries whose numbers of trainees are not publicly available. In addition to these professional training providers, universities in Africa also offer academic courses on arbitration and various ADRs, and all major arbitration institutions on the Continent provide skills based training in arbitration and other ADR processes, particularly mediation.
30. A.A. Asouzu, *Arbitration in Africa: Agenda for Reform* ADR L.J. 343-436, 381 (1997).
31. The Conference Discussion Paper is available at: http://eprints.soas.ac.uk/20421/ [last accessed 6 May 2016].

deliberate on their role in the development of arbitration in the continent. It also provided space for the users of arbitration services to discuss their perceptions of the scope and quality of the services these institutions provide. Finally, participants at the conference suggested ways the institutions can improve their effectiveness towards placing the institutions at the forefront of administering dispute resolution in Africa. The outputs of these discussions are explored in the chapters of this book which hopes to contribute to increasing the visibility and viability of arbitration institutions in the administration of domestic, intra-Africa and international dispute resolution.

III APPENDIX

There are three tables in the appendix to this book. These tables provide data to clarify the common mistake in discourses on Africa of treating the continent as though it was one country without any appreciation of the diversity of peoples, customs, languages, laws and legal systems, and the impact these have on matters affecting the continent.

Table 1 is a list of fifty-four African countries and their arbitration related convention status and national law regimes. On the New York Convention, thirty-six of the fifty-four states are parties.[32] So 66.6% of the fifty-four African states listed, are New York Convention states (this is 23% of the 156 strong convention Member States worldwide). The importance of the New York Convention to the enforcement of arbitration agreements and recognition and enforcement of foreign arbitral awards (so both domestic and international awards) cannot be over-stated. It is interesting to note that the major trading states in the Continent are parties to the New York Convention; for example: Egypt, Ghana, Kenya, Mozambique, Nigeria, and South Africa. However there are important trading states that are yet to ratify the convention; for example, Angola and Ethiopia. There are also African countries such as Sudan, Somalia and Libya who, though not parties to the New York Convention, are parties to the Riyadh Convention.[33] It must be noted that there are more parties to the New York Convention, the predominant number of which are not parties to the Riyadh Convention so that participation in the Riyadh Convention should not stop these states also participating as members of the New York Convention.[34]

As it relates to the ICSID Convention, fifty of the fifty-four African states have signed and/or ratified the Convention.[35] This represents 92.6% of the Continent

32. For details on the status of the New York Convention contracting states, see: http://www.uncitral.org/uncitral/en/uncitral_texts/arbitration/NYConvention_status.html [accessed 27 April 2016].
33. The Riyadh Arab Agreement for Judicial Cooperation, 1983. The other African members of the Riyadh Convention are: Tunisia, Algeria, Djibouti (non-ICSID state), Somalia (non-New York Convention state), Libya (not party to both New York and ICSID Conventions), Morocco, and Mauritania. It is understood that Somalia is currently planning to sign the New York Convention.
34. There are twenty Member States of The Riyadh Convention all of which are also members of the New York Convention except Iraq and Yemen. The other non-African states to the Riyadh Convention are: Bahrain, Jordan, Kuwait, Lebanon, Oman, (territory of Palestine), Qatar, Saudi Arabia, Syria, and United Arab Emirates.
35. Angola, Djibouti, Libya and South Sudan have not signed the ICSID Convention.

accounting for 31.3% (50 of the 160) of all signatory states worldwide.[36] This data supports the view that as it relates to international conventions on arbitration, African states have fared reasonably well. One explanation for the larger number of African states that have signed or ratified the ICSID Convention, may possibly be because most of these states, as already stated are capital importing states and attract foreign investments from capital exporting states keen to protect the investments of their citizens. The large numbers may also have been driven by the presumption on the part of African states that signing the ICSID Convention may attract greater inflow of foreign investment. The second explanation may be the impact of the sponsoring role of the ICSID Convention by the World Bank and the bank's relationship with developing African states. But as it is well known, the ICSID Convention is limited to the arbitration of investment disputes and it is not settled that membership of ICSID plays a major role in driving foreign investment inflow.[37]

The same Table 1 also lists the national laws that regulate arbitration (domestic and international) in the fifty-four African states and only two states have no discernible law applicable to arbitration. These are: Sierra Leone,[38] and South Sudan. This means that 96.3% of African states have laws applicable to arbitration in their jurisdictions. This clearly evidences an obvious awareness of the relevance of the mechanism of arbitration and its regulation under national laws in one form or the other. Table 1 therefore is clear evidence of the engagement of African states (as it relates to having statutory framework for arbitration) with the legal basis of arbitration in their jurisdictions. There is the need to interrogate the effectiveness of the substantive provisions of these laws to determine whether they are modern in the sense that they provide for party autonomy and certain minimal requirements to ensure limited or no interference from the state, and limited or no opportunity of interference by the courts during the arbitral procedure.[39] As already noted above, some of these laws urgently need review and to be updated.

The provisions of some of the laws are predominantly based on the UNCITRAL Model Law. Examples are the arbitration laws of: Egypt, Kenya, Mauritius, Nigeria, Rwanda, Tunisia, Uganda, Zambia, and Zimbabwe. Most of the arbitration laws that were promulgated after the emergence of the Model Law (and did not adopt it) were evidently influenced by it. An example is the Ghana ADR Act 2010. Some arbitration laws are also influenced by the provisions of other national laws particularly those of the European countries with whom such states had a colonial relationship. One

36. Ethiopia, Guinea-Bissau and Namibia have signed but not ratified the ICSID Convention so that it is not in force in those three African countries. In addition, Bolivia and Venezuela denounced the Convention effective 2010 and 2012 respectively. For details on the status of ICSID contracting states, see: https://icsid.worldbank.org/apps/ICSIDWEB/icsiddocs/Documents/List%20of%20Contracting%20States%20and%20Other%20Signatories%20of%20the%20Convention%20-%20Latest.pdf [accessed 27 April 2016].
37. See for example Art. 25 of the ICSID Convention on its jurisdiction.
38. It is understood that there are some references to arbitration under Cap 25 Laws of Sierra Leone, 1960.
39. Such discussion is outside the remit of this book for information on arbitration laws of various African countries see Boseman L (gen ed.), Arbitration in Africa: a Practitioner's Guide, Kluwer Law International, 2013.

example is the OHADA Uniform Arbitration Act 1999, applicable in all seventeen OHADA Member States, with borrowings from the old French Arbitration Law of 1981.[40] It can therefore be concluded that generally speaking, as it relates to substantive laws on arbitration, African countries continue to modernize their laws. However there are still those countries where either there is no specific law governing arbitration (domestic and or international) or the relevant law is out-dated and no longer fit for purpose. I will suggest that a very helpful starting point in this process of modernization, for these countries, is the UNCITRAL Model Law (with amendments adopted in 2006), which at the very least can be used as a template.

Table 2 is the list of seventy-one known arbitration institutions or centres operating in thirty-nine African countries. This table includes (where available) information on the webpage of the institution. There is no identifiable arbitration institution operating in fifteen of the fifty-four African countries. This of course does not mean that no arbitration references take place in such jurisdictions. Neither does it mean that there is no arbitration institution in existence in such countries. All it means is that our research has not yet found any organization whose core business is the administration of arbitration disputes in those jurisdictions. The arbitration laws in these jurisdictions clearly allow and regulate (ad hoc) arbitration references.

Ascertaining with any degree of accuracy the numbers of arbitrations involving African parties, African arbitrators and African counsel is difficult because of lack of public access to such data. However Table 3 lists the number of African parties; number of African cities and number of African arbitrators as provided in the ICC statistics which is publicly available.[41] The data from the ICC is referenced because recourse to the ICC is very popular with African disputants and the data from the ICC is publicly available and easily accessible. Extrapolating from the more comprehensive ICC data, over the period between 2000 and 2015, a total of 1,608 African parties arbitrated under the ICC Rules. However these generated only ninety-four arbitrations with seat in an African country and 431 African arbitrators were appointed.[42] As a comparator, it is interesting that from the Annual Reports of the Cairo Regional Centre, it has little or no African parties (south of the Sahara) utilizing its services though it enjoys patronage from countries of the Middle East and global West. The Cairo Annual Reports show a clear link between nationality of the parties and the nationality of the arbitrators appointed, a link missing from the ICC data as it relates to Africa.[43]

Therefore, as concluded in my 2014 paper, the arbitration laws and rules of the majority of countries and institutions in the continent are reasonably modern, robust and functional. However these remain a work-in-progress, so that as arbitral practice

40. France revised its Arbitration Law in 2011. The OHADA Uniform Act on Arbitration 1999 is currently under review.
41. ICC data is published yearly in the ICC International Court of Arbitration Bulletin. The ICC published the ICC, *ICC Arbitration: A Ten-Year Statistical Overview* vol. 9 no. 1 ICC Bulletin, 51-63 (2008).
    This provided statistics on ICC caseload from 1998 to 2007.
42. Data culled from ICC Statistical Reports for the periods.
43. For the Cairo Regional Centre Annual Reports, see: http://crcica.org.eg/pub_annual.html [accessed 29 March 2016].

evolves, these laws and rules must be continually updated to meet the requirements and needs of modern arbitral practice, the disputants, and arbitration practitioners.[44] One thread of argument that runs through this book is that arbitration institutions can lead this process of evolution within the continent.

IV THE CONTRIBUTORS

This book explores how arbitration institutions can contribute to a change in the perception of users, against holding their arbitration reference in various African countries, through the transformation of the administration of arbitration in the continent. The contributors to this book examine and answer various aspects of the key research question which is whether and if yes, how, arbitration institutions in Africa can support the transformation of arbitration in Africa.[45] This question is examined in different contexts over nine substantive chapters. The book is divided into three parts. Part 1 comprises this introduction and one chapter which examine general issues on arbitration institutions and their functions in arbitration. Emilia Onyema in Chapter 1 examines the general nature of arbitration institutions and how, through the functions they perform, they can contribute to the successful administration of arbitration disputes in Africa. The chapter also critically examines how arbitration institutions can support the growth and transformation of arbitration generally in Africa. The chapter identifies certain minimum requirements which arbitration institutions should satisfy, such as maintaining an online presence through a functional website; adopting modern arbitration rules in relevant languages; employing qualified staff; and designing and implementing sensitization of local businesses to drive the growth of domestic arbitration. She then explores the idea of creating an association of African arbitration institutions, as an umbrella organization for all arbitration institutions operating within the continent. In conclusion the chapter asserts that there is opportunity for the many arbitration institutions in the continent to contribute to the transformation agenda for arbitration on the continent, however there is a lack of coordination of the many efforts employed towards achieving this collective goal.

Part two of this book is made up of three chapters which examine the role of regional arbitration institutions and how they can contribute to the transformation of arbitration, more particularly in the region in which each institution is located and more generally in Africa. In Chapter 2, Jimmy Kodo and Narcisse Aka examine the peculiarity of the dualist nature of the CCJA, as both an arbitration institution and the supra-national court of OHADA. The authors examine the question of whether this system should be replicated in other regions of the continent. Mohammed Abdel Raouf and Dalia Hussein in Chapter 3, examine the AALCO vision in the creation of the

44. Arbitration institutions in Africa are already evolving for example the 2015 LACIAC Arbitration Rules includes rules on multiparty disputes, consolidation, joinder of parties, emergency arbitrator. The Rules also annexed IBA guidelines for party representatives and arbitrators as part of the Rules and are available at: http://www.laciac.org/ [accessed 27 April 2016].

45. Each chapter was peer reviewed for quality assurance and all contributors are very grateful to each reviewer, though the contents of each chapter remain that of the author(s).

regional centres with particular reference to the Cairo Regional Centre and its impact on other arbitration institutions in North Africa and how they can better share their regional space. In Chapter 4, Kariuki Muigua examines the effectiveness of arbitration institutions in East Africa and suggests ways they can better collaborate and share their regional space to transform the law and practice of arbitration in East Africa.

Part three of this book then examines the peculiarity of certain identified arbitration institutions located in various regions of the continent in five chapters. Duncan Bagshaw, the first and immediate past Registrar of LCIA-MIAC in Chapter 5 examines whether arbitration institutions in Africa need a close collaboration with one of the more established international arbitration institutions to thrive, through the experience of the LCIA-MIAC. In Chapter 6, Megha Joshi and Tolu Obamuroh examine the practicalities of an arbitration institution supported by a state government and the impact of such support on the independence of the centre, from the experience of the Lagos Court of Arbitration Centre. Emmanuel Amofa in Chapter 7 examines the impact of the synergy between the arbitration law of a state and the rules of the arbitration located in that state and the advantages of such synergy using the Ghana Arbitration Centre as a case study. Jean Alain Penda in Chapter 8 examines how users of arbitration can better engage with arbitration centres in francophone African countries in realizing this vision of a truly pan-African agenda for the transformation of arbitration on the continent. In Chapter 9, Bernadette Uwicyeza, the immediate past Director of KIAC, examines how arbitration institutions can market their services and the arbitration process to small and medium sized enterprise in Africa with the aim of developing the domestic arbitral market. She draws particularly from the experience of KIAC in Rwanda.

V SUMMARY

This book (and the research project that underpins it) is a contribution to the discussion of the role arbitration and one of her stakeholders, arbitration institutions, can play in transforming not just the legal landscape in African countries for the resolution of commercial disputes, but the entire discourse on legal efficiency and access to justice in African countries.

PART I General

CHAPTER 1
Arbitration Institutions in Africa

Emilia Onyema

INTRODUCTION

Since the 1990s, some major cities in Africa have witnessed the emergence of new arbitration institutions or centres. Examples include Cairo, Lagos, Port Louis, Nairobi, Accra, Yaoundé, Abidjan, Johannesburg, and Kigali. The entities or organizations so described are of varying sizes and render different types of dispute resolution services. This development is by no means uniform across the continent. In some African countries it is not clear if there is any existing centre or institution dedicated to the administration of dispute resolution processes.[1] Arbitration institutions or centres are one of the major four stakeholders of arbitration in any jurisdiction so that it is important to examine the quality of service they provide and how they can contribute to transforming the legal culture of the jurisdictions they are domiciled.[2]

African countries do not yet attract high volumes of international arbitration references neither is the domestic arbitration market growing exponentially. It is this dearth of arbitration references that make it particularly important that the marketing of arbitration in Africa is clearly targeted. Arbitration institutions are of particular importance in this marketing of African states as viable destinations for arbitration. This chapter examines these issues with particular focus on the African continent. It is noted at the outset that under the arbitration laws of various African countries,

1. From our research as shown in Table 2 in the appendix, there is no discernible arbitration institution in the following African countries: Botswana, Cape Verde, Comoros, Eritrea, Equatorial Guinea, Gambia, Guinea Bissau, Liberia, Malawi, Mauritania, Namibia, Sao Tome & Principe, Seychelles, Sierra Leone, and Somalia.
2. The other three stakeholders as identified in a SOAS research project on the transformation of arbitration in Africa, are the states/government; courts and judges; and legal practitioners. For more information on the research project see: http://www.researcharbitrationafrica.com/ [accessed 9 Mar. 2016].

arbitration proceedings can be conducted either on an ad hoc or institutional basis. Ad hoc proceedings do not necessarily engage the services of arbitration institutions, though a growing number of institutions provide specialist services to ad hoc proceedings. Such services include acting as appointing authority and fundholding, all for a fee.[3] This book focuses on arbitration institutions and their functions so that it is only those functions they provide in support of ad hoc arbitration that will be referenced in addition to their functions under institutional arbitration proceedings.

This chapter sets the context for the discussions in the other chapters of this book. It examines the general nature of arbitration institutions and their functions in enabling the disputing parties perform the arbitration agreement. The involvement of arbitration institutions in the arbitral process raises several issues most of which this chapter examines. This chapter starts by clarifying the general nature of arbitration institutions (§1.01); and the generally accepted functions of arbitration institutions (§1.02); and then critically analyses how arbitration institutions operating in the continent can better support the growth and transformation of the law and practice of arbitration in Africa (§1.03).

§1.01 THE NATURE OF ARBITRATION INSTITUTIONS

Arbitration institutions are organizations or legal entities whose core function or purpose is to administer arbitration disputes referred to it. So what does administer mean? Administration refers to 'management'. Thus an arbitration institution's primary function is to manage the arbitral reference and not itself decide the substantive dispute between the parties.[4] To enable arbitration institutions perform this function, they set out the terms on which they will manage the reference in various documents that can collectively be referred to as a 'management agreement'. This agreement will usually be comprised in their arbitration rules and internal rules or statutes. These documents usually set out what and how (in relation to the arbitral reference) the institution and its constituent organs will do and act, what disputants can do, what arbitrators can do, the costs of these various activities and as is becoming more common, the level of their liability. Arbitration institutions (whether private or public bodies) organize and assist arbitration (domestic and international) proceedings by rendering various professional, administrative and secretarial services to the disputing parties and arbitrators, in the operation of the arbitration agreement.[5]

Under institutional arbitration references, arbitration institutions are much more involved in the arbitral reference than just as appointing authorities. So for example,

3. See for example, the Lagos Court of Arbitration Centre (LCA); and LCIA at: http://www.lcia.org/Dispute_Resolution_Services/LCIA_Services_in_adhoc_proceedings.aspx [accessed 9 Mar. 2016].
4. Sutton and Gill (eds), Russell on Arbitration (22nd ed., London, Sweet & Maxwell, 2003) at para. 3-046, gave the various roles of arbitration institutions to include acting as appointing authority, account holder, supervision of the arbitral proceedings, and production of arbitration rules.
5. P. Fouchard (ed.), *Relationships Between the Arbitrator and the Parties and the Arbitration Institution*, December, ICC Bulletin, paras 13, 15 (1995).

the International Chamber of Commerce (ICC) arbitration service includes an arbitration court and the secretariat, and has internal statutes for the court and its arbitration rules. Various aspects of the functions of each of the organs of the ICC can be found in the statutes and the arbitration rules. The institution in effect advertises to the public what it will do (usually, appoint arbitrators, provide procedural rules and hearing rooms, among others) and for what remuneration. It also sets out for the public what it expects users of its rules to do and how arbitration references it manages will be conducted. So effectively these documents set out clearly the basis and content of the institution's relationship with the users of the services it provides. Users are thereby fully informed of the nature of the services to expect from the institution and the cost of such services. This effectively implies that similar to any consumer, disputants are at liberty to 'shop around' for institutions that will give them best value for their money. It is this that adds the edge of competition to the provision of institutional arbitration services across the world, including for those in Africa.

This exchange of services for money and competition on a global stage makes the examination of the involvement of institutions in the arbitration provision market important. Over the years, arbitration institutions have proliferated all over the world. Entities that describe themselves as 'arbitration institutions' vary from small private enterprises to major organizations such as the ICC. It is obvious that the services rendered by the ICC with its wealth of experience and the service provided by a small enterprise will not be comparable, though they both will be described as 'arbitration institutions'. This variety of providers makes it imperative to clearly ascertain what basic requirements an arbitration institution properly so-called must satisfy. To answer this question, Werner Melis in 1991 described an arbitration institution as one which:

> Guarantees stability and functioning for the foreseeable future ... The Institution should further offer clearly described services and indicate which rules and procedures it will apply. The Institution should offer more than merely to act as appointing authorities, either under their own rules or occasionally under other rules. Their services also must include some administrative activities, and they must have permanent staff which is professionally trained for this purpose.[6]

This description of arbitration institutions is adopted in this chapter. There are two major requirements from this description which impact on arbitration institutions in Africa and are examined in greater detail in this section. These are: foreseeability of existence and availability of professionally qualified staff.

Generally a structural format for most arbitration institutions is that the institution defines its internal managerial operation and structure of command; defines its jurisdiction and its scope; and drafts its own bespoke arbitration rules.[7] In these documents the functions of the institution, the tribunal and the disputing parties are

6. W. Melis, *Function and Responsibility of Arbitral Institutions*, vol. 13 Comparative Law Yearbook of International Business 107, 109 (1991).
7. Or identify the applicable rules. These may be the UNCITRAL Arbitration Rules in toto or adapted. As this chapter will show the vast majority of arbitration institutions in Africa have modelled their arbitration rules after the UNCITRAL Arbitration Rules.

clearly defined. The institution itself, either through its registrar, court or administrator, makes all the important administrative (so non-judicial) decisions as it relates to the arbitration reference but does not itself decide the substantive dispute between the parties. This is implied into the functions of arbitration institutions (as administrators of the dispute resolution process) so that some arbitration institutions do not expressly state this fact in their rules while others do. For example the Arbitration Rules of the OHADA CCJA expressly provide:

> The Court shall not itself settle disputes.[8]

In the same fashion the Lagos Chamber for Commerce International Arbitration Centre (LACIAC) Arbitration Rules provide:

> The LACIAC Court does not itself resolve disputes but administers the resolution of disputes by arbitral tribunals in accordance with the Rules.[9]

However the Treaty (Re)Establishing the East African Community (EAC) expressly provides that the EAC Court of Justice:

> shall have jurisdiction to hear and determine any matter, (a) arising from an arbitration clause contained in a contract or agreement which confers such jurisdiction to which the Community or any of its institutions is a party; or (c) arising from an arbitration clause contained in a commercial contract or agreement in which the parties have conferred jurisdiction on the Court.[10]

The EAC Arbitration Rules implement this provision by providing that:

> Arbitrator means a Judge or Judges of the Court appointed to constitute [the] Tribunal.[11]

And on appointing arbitrators, the Arbitration Rules provide:

> The appointing authority shall appoint, from among the Judges of the Court a panel to constitute the Tribunal to conduct the arbitral proceedings, unless the parties agreed on a sole arbitrator who, in the like manner, shall be appointed from among the Judges of the Court.[12]

These provisions make it quite difficult to fit the EAC arbitration system neatly within the usual description of an arbitration institution as adopted in this chapter. For any organization or entity to be referred to as an 'arbitration institution', it should as a bare minimum, maintain legal personality under the law in which it is incorporated or under which it functions (§1.01[A]); it should maintain a publicly accessible physical

---

8. Article 2.2 CCJA Arbitration Rules, 1999.
9. Article 2.3 LACIAC Arbitration Rules, 2015. See also for the same provision Art. 2 para. 2 Kigali International Arbitration Centre Rules, 2012.
10. Article 32 of the East African Community Treaty 1999 which came into force on 7 Jul. 2000. The EAC Court of Justice was established under Art. 9 of the EAC Treaty and was inaugurated on 30 Nov. 2001. For more details on the EAC, see: http://eacj.org/ [accessed 8 Mar. 2016].
11. Rule 1(4) EAC Arbitration Rules 2012 text of which is available at: http://eacj.org/?page_id=502 [accessed 8 Mar. 2016].
12. Rule 8(1) EAC Arbitration Rules.

presence or offices (§1.01[B]); it should be adequately staffed with a team of professionally trained personnel (§1.01[C]); it should have a set of publicly available and accessible rules of arbitration (§1.01[D]); it should maintain a board or court of independent experts that will oversee the work of the management team (§1.01[E]); it should make publicly available its annual activities (§1.01[F]); and it may include some other optional value-added activities (§1.01[G]).

[A] Legal Capacity

I have argued elsewhere that arbitration institutions conclude various contracts when they accept to administer a reference.[13] To enable the institution validly enter into contracts, such entity must have legal capacity to contract. Such capacity will be governed by the law of the place where the entity is registered or under an international agreement recognized by the state where the institution is domiciled or has its physical presence. It is the responsibility of the arbitration institution to ensure its registration and ensure it fulfils all relevant requirements under the relevant law for it to conduct business. This is especially so since the institution renders defined services in exchange for a fee, which requires conclusion of enforceable contracts.

This is one requirement which almost all entities that refer to themselves as arbitration institutions may meet, even those that are housed within a law firm or another organization.[14]

In Africa some arbitration institutions are attached to a chamber of commerce, for example the Lagos Chamber of Commerce International Arbitration Centre (LACIAC).[15] Some others enjoy an independent existence and are registered as private enterprises, such as the Arbitration Foundation of South Africa (AFSA) and the Kigali International Arbitration Centre (Kigali).[16] The Asian-African Legal Consultative Organisation (AALCO) arbitration centres are international organizations with regional

---

13. See E. Onyema, *International Commercial Arbitration and the Arbitrator's Contract* 104-115 (Routledge, 2010), where I argued that the arbitration institution concludes a contract with the disputing parties either jointly or severally when it accepts to administer their dispute. In the same manner, the arbitration institution concludes a contract with the arbitrator(s) appointed under its arbitration rules. In addition to these agreements, the arbitration institution may conclude other contracts such as employment contracts with its employees, and contracts for provision of services with other entities with whom it transacts in its own name.
14. An example from Kenya is the Centre for Alternative Dispute Resolution (CADR) which is housed within the premises of the Kenya branch of the Chartered Institute of Arbitrators.
15. Others include the Algerian Chamber of Commerce & Industry, Algiers, the Arbitration, Mediation and Conciliation Centre of the Chamber of Commerce & Industry of Benin; Ouagadougou Arbitration, Mediation & Conciliation Centre of the Chamber of Commerce & Industry; Chamber of Commerce & Industry of Ivory Coast, Abidjan; MCCI Arbitration & Mediation Centre, Mauritius; Arbitration Centre of the Dakar's Chamber of Commerce, Industry and Agriculture; and South Sudan Chamber of Commerce, Industry & Agriculture, Juba.
16. The AFSA is a joint venture between organized business and legal and accounting professions. Other privately constituted institutions include, Arbitration Centre of Madagascar; Annaba Mediation & Arbitration Centre, Algeria; Centre for Extra Judicial Resolution of Disputes Angola; Burundi Centre for Arbitration & Mediation; Ghana Arbitration Centre; Dispute Resolution Centre, Nairobi; Euro-Mediterranean Centre for Mediation & Arbitration, Casablanca, Morocco;

remit.[17] AALCO currently has three regional centres for international commercial arbitration in Africa.[18] These are located in Cairo, Lagos and Nairobi.[19] There are also those institutions that administer arbitration references over disputes emanating from specific trade or economic activities, for example, the Conciliation and Arbitration Chamber of the Cotton Interprofessional Association, Benin.[20] There are those institutions, that though independent, are financially supported by a state government at least at its commencement stage such as the Lagos Court of Arbitration Centre (LCA, with support from the Lagos State Government) or supported by another international arbitration institution such as Mauritius International Arbitration Centre (MIAC, with support from the London Court of International Arbitration, LCIA).[21] There is the OHADA CCJA which is supranational and is established by a regional organization, OHADA under its Treaty.[22] The same also applies in the East African Court of Justice established under the East African Treaty.[23] Finally there are those private entities which market themselves as providers of arbitration services more generally.[24] These institutions all market themselves as administrators of both international and domestic disputes.

[B] Physical Location

Arbitration institutions need to maintain a physical presence in a defined location, with premises or offices from which they conduct business. Such premises should also be available to host arbitration hearings. So effectively, the arbitration institution should maintain a well-resourced office or secretariat with its own staff and in addition to among others, provide hearing rooms. It is important that users can attend the offices or physical location of the arbitration institution. This criterion may not be relevant to an arbitration institution that administers arbitrations purely virtually or online.

International Centre for Arbitration & Mediation, Abuja (ICAMA) Nigeria; Khartoum Centre for Arbitration, Sudan; and Zambia Centre for Dispute Resolution.

17. For more details see AALCO website at: http://www.aalco.int/Scripts/default.asp [assessed 8 Mar. 2016].
18. AALCO also has two other regional arbitration centres in Kuala Lumpur (Malaysia) and Tehran (Iran).
19. Other arbitration institutions with a regional focus include AFSA (Southern Africa) and Kigali (Eastern Africa) though these are not part of the AALCO regional centres.
20. The Conciliation and Arbitration Chamber of the Cotton Interprofessional Association centre in Cotonou, Benin Republic resolves disputes related to cotton exploitation in Benin between cotton growers, suppliers and ginners. Other similar arbitration centres include, Maritime Arbitrators Association of Nigeria (MANN); The National Construction Council, Dar es Salaam, Tanzania; Copyright Office Ghana Arbitration Centre; GICAM Arbitration Centre in Cameroun was set up by business employers for administration of business disputes.
21. Another example is the Directorate of Dispute Prevention & Resolution, Lesotho, which though independent of the government is connected to it and resolves trade disputes.
22. The CCJA was established under Art. 3 of the OHADA Treaty of 1993 (the Treaty itself was revised in 2008). See also E. Onyema, *Arbitration under the OHADA Regime*, vol. 11 no. 6 Int'l ALR 205 (2008).
23. The EACJ was established under Art. 9 of the EAC Treaty of 2000 and maintains its own set of arbitration rules under which the judges of the EAC sit as arbitrators as stated above.
24. An example is the International Centre for Arbitration and Mediation, Abuja (ICAMA) with more details available at: http://www.icama.com/ [accessed on 8 Mar. 2016].

However, in Africa there is no known arbitration institution that markets itself as providing only virtual or online dispute resolution services. Parties who use the services of arbitration institutions use hearing rooms within the premises of the institution to hold their hearings and meetings. It is not ideal for the offices of an arbitration institution to comprise of one or two rooms in an office where other business is conducted. It is important that the premises are dedicated to the business of administering arbitration references either solely or principally. This requirement impacts on the perception of arbitration users on the quality of the services such an institution will provide, and more generally to the reputation of arbitration within the wider community.[25] It is true that an ultra-modern dedicated glossy building or premises does not necessarily translate to exceptional quality of service but first impressions are important. The impressive glossy building will attract users through its doors while the institution located in one or two rooms within premises dedicated to other business, will not.

It is important to note that such premises must also be fit for purpose. The purpose here is to administer arbitration references. The premises must therefore be fitted to adequately provide for the various aspects of arbitration. This goes beyond providing two or three hearing rooms. Such rooms must be adequately equipped with state-of-the-art hearing facilities. Such facilities include microphones, stenograph, seats, video and audio recording equipment, internet connectivity, among others. Secure storage rooms for files and evidence must also be available. In addition to the physical premises, the institution should have adequate, well trained and qualified staff that will assist the users of the institution as discussed below. All the major and known arbitration institutions in Africa satisfy this criterion to varying degrees.[26]

[C] Professionally Qualified Staff

Arbitration institutions must maintain a well-trained and qualified work force in the management of arbitration disputes. A well-trained workforce for an arbitration institution includes professionals trained in the law and practice of arbitration that have a full understanding of various aspects of the arbitral process.[27] Generally, arbitration institutions in addition to providing administrative and technical staff also employ qualified lawyers who oversee the case management of the arbitral reference and assist the parties and arbitrators with executing the reference.[28] For those

25. This perception proceeds from the perception of the general public of the business of dispute resolution as a sophisticated trade with particular decorum and presentational expectations as is accorded to litigation before national courts and the lawyers that ply their trade before such courts. Such perception is equally accorded to arbitration and arbitration services providers.
26. For example among the three AALCO regional centres, the Lagos Regional Centre is in need of new premises solely dedicated to its primary function of administering arbitration. The same can also be said for the Arbitration Centre of the CCJA.
27. Examples of institutions in Africa which employ qualified lawyers who act as counsel in charge of each case to assist the parties and the members of the tribunal include the CCJA, LCIA-MIAC, LACIAC, Kigali, LCA, AFSA, Cairo and Lagos Regional Centres, and GICAM.
28. Such lawyers also are usually qualified in various jurisdictions as is relevant to the users of the services of the particular institution.

institutions that seek to administer more than domestic references, they must also have staff with relevant language skills.[29] The provision of this quality of service and staff require high cost outlays. For most arbitration institutions in Africa, access to the type of funds necessary to provide these quality of services, is a major handicap.

The predominant majority of arbitration institutions in Africa currently lack well-trained professional work force to deliver the level of support services the users of arbitration (particularly international arbitration) require from institutions. This is one major gap in the institutional arbitration administration market in Africa which the more established international arbitration institutions can better support the institutions in Africa. Such support will be in the form of sharing expertise and information and providing in-house training. Such collaborations already exist on the continent with the active engagement of the Permanent Court of Arbitration (PCA), ICSID, ICC and LCIA with partner institutions in Africa. This is also a gap which can be bridged by the participation of arbitration institutions in Africa, in the activities of organizations such as the International Council for Commercial Arbitration (ICCA) and the International Federation of Commercial Arbitration Institutions (IFCAI).[30]

As employer, the arbitration institution is fully responsible for the conduct of its employees. Under most national laws, the arbitration institution will be vicariously liable for the acts of its employees in the course of their employment. The employees of arbitration institutions have no contractual relationship with the disputing parties or the arbitrators even though the institution itself does. Some arbitration institution rules now expressly provide that their personnel or employees enjoy immunity from suit in addition to the institution itself.[31] The arbitration laws of most African states are silent on the issue of immunity of arbitration institutions, however almost all institutions exclude liability and provide for contractual immunity in their arbitration rules. An example is Article 17 of the 2015 LACIAC Arbitration Rules, which provides:

> Save for intentional wrongdoing, the parties waive, to the fullest extent permitted under the applicable law, any claim against the arbitrators, the LACIAC Court and any person appointed by the arbitral tribunal based on any act or omission in connection with the arbitration.

Another example is Article 47 of the Kigali Arbitration Rules, which provides:

> The Centre including its officers or the arbitrators shall not be liable to any person for negligence, act or omission in connection with arbitration governed by this Rules.
>
> The Centre including its officers shall not be under any obligation to make statements in connection with any arbitration governed by this Rules.[32]

---

29. Most international institutions have staff that speak various languages especially relevant, to their users.
30. For more details on ICCA see: http://www.arbitration-icca.org/about.html [accessed 8 Mar. 2016] and for more details on IFCAI see: http://www.ifcai-arbitration.org/ [accessed 11 Mar. 2016].
31. Examples are Art. 31 LCIA-MIAC Rules, and Art. 47 KIAC Rules.
32. Provisions to the same effect are also included in: Art. 16 Cairo Regional Centre Arbitration Rules; Art. 45 Lagos Regional Centre Arbitration Rules; Art. 14 CCJA Arbitration Rules; Art. 16 LCA Arbitration Rules.

The validity and enforcement of these provisions have yet to be tested before national courts in the continent. However, it is hoped that when they do come under scrutiny, national courts will give effect to them and take a robust and supportive view. Finally, arbitration institutions create opportunities for students studying a relevant subject (usually law) or recent graduates to intern with them. This provides an invaluable experience for the next generation of arbitration practitioners. It is not clear how many arbitration institutions in Africa offer this opportunity to African students though there is evidence that some institutions provide such opportunity.[33]

[D] Arbitration Rules

Arbitration institutions may produce their own bespoke set of arbitration rules or adopt other rules (an example is the UNCITRAL Arbitration Rules). Such arbitration rules form part of the arbitration agreement between the disputing parties in institutional arbitration proceedings. It is accepted that these rules are the primary procedural 'laws' applicable to the arbitration proceeding.[34] The Arbitration Rules of most arbitration institutions in Africa are modelled following the UNCITRAL Arbitration Rules. This brings some degree of harmonization and predictability to the norms governing the conduct of arbitration disputes under these institutional rules. UNCITRAL revised its 1976 Arbitration Rules in 2010.[35] This revision took account of the need for the Arbitration Rules to:

> conform to current practices in international trade and to meet changes that have taken place over the last thirty years in arbitral practice.[36]

Thus UNCITRAL recognizes the need for periodic revision of its Rules and the same is true of all major arbitration institutions in the world.[37] Some arbitration institutions in Africa have updated their arbitration rules to reflect modern developments in arbitral practice such as issues of: joinder of parties, consolidation of disputes, concurrent hearing, and emergency arbitrator procedure. A good example of a modern set of arbitration rules is the LACIAC 2015 Arbitration Rules. These rules are based on the UNCITRAL Arbitration Rules and include provisions on joinder of parties, consolidation of hearings, emergency arbitrator rules, fast track arbitration, rules for online dispute resolution, and detailed provisions on cost. These Rules also incorporate as annexes the IBA Guidelines on Party Representation in International Arbitration (2013)

---

33. One example is the Cairo Regional Centre.
34. Effectively the *lex arbitri* comprises the arbitration agreement, arbitration rules and the law of the seat of arbitration.
35. For more details see: http://www.uncitral.org/uncitral/en/uncitral_texts/arbitration/2010 Arbitration_rules.html [accessed 11 Mar. 2016].
36. See para. 5 of the Preamble to the 2010 UNCITRAL Arbitration Rules.
37. For example, ICC revised its 1997 Arbitration Rules in 2012; LCIA revised its 1998 Arbitration Rules in 2014 while CIETAC latest Arbitration Rules came into effect on 1 Jan. 2015, and Singapore is in the process of revising its current 2013 Arbitration Rules which will come into effect in 2016.

and the IBA Guidelines on Conflicts of Interest in International Arbitration (2014).[38] The LCIA-MIAC Arbitration Rules closely align with the LCIA Arbitration Rules. The LCIA in 2014 revised their Arbitration Rules to provide for emergency arbitrator procedure and rules of conduct for legal representatives. LCIA-MIAC is yet to revise her rules. The Kigali International Arbitration Rules are available in three languages and include provisions on joinder of parties, multiparty disputes, consolidation of disputes, and emergency arbitrator.[39] The Cairo, Lagos and Nairobi Regional Centres Rules are based on the UNCITRAL Rules with modifications and the Cairo Arbitration Rules are in both the English and Arabic languages.[40] Interestingly the LCA Arbitration Rules apply to both institutional and ad hoc arbitration.[41]

Some arbitration institutions are yet to update their arbitration rules as frequently as they should in response to the market.[42] This effectively means that parties submitting their disputes to such institutions may need to make supplementary provisions for those issues not covered under such rules. However such frequent revision of rules creates a tension that requires careful balancing. This is the tension between predictability and certainty of the provision of the rules and innovation in the revision of the rules which may bring with it some degree of uncertainty (at least before the new provisions become embedded). Such uncertainty may also creep in with the revision of the rules because parties would generally nominate the particular arbitration institution in its arbitration agreement which is usually concluded some time before the dispute arises. In such situation (which is the majority of cases) parties may have been aware of a different version of the arbitration rules to the one their reference may become subjected. To forestall such uncertainty and surprise, it is important that disputants are either given the choice to arbitrate under the old or new rules; or the current rules should expressly provide that the new rules govern all such references under the institutional rules. For example, the preamble to the LCIA-MIAC Arbitration Rules provide in relevant part:

> Where any agreement, submission or reference provides in writing and in whatsoever manner for arbitration under the rules of the LCIA-MIAC Arbitration Centre … the parties shall be taken to have agreed in writing that the arbitration shall be conducted in accordance with the following rules … or such amended rules as … may have adopted hereafter to take effect before the commencement of the arbitration.[43]

---

38. The LCIA Arbitration Rules 2014 are available at: http://www.laciac.org/?page_id=169 [accessed 11 Mar. 2016].
39. The Kigali Arbitration Rules 2012 are available at: http://www.kiac.org.rw/IMG/pdf/-3.pdf [accessed 11 Mar. 2016].
40. For the Cairo Regional Centre Arbitration Rules see: http://crcica.org.eg/arbitration_rules.html [accessed 11 Mar. 2016].
41. Preamble to the Lagos Court of Arbitration Centre Arbitration Rules 2011 (revised in 2013).
42. An example is the OHADA CCJA Arbitration Rules adopted in 1999 are currently under revision.
43. See Art. 7 KIAC for very similar provision.

For LACIAC, reference to its arbitration rules is a reference to the 2015 Arbitration Rules 'as amended from time to time'.[44]

[E] Independent Management Board

The role of the independent board or court or council is to make decisions on some functions or tasks assigned to the Institution in the arbitration rules and its internal statutes. Such functions generally include, confirming or appointing arbitrators; deciding arbitrator challenge applications; scrutinizing the arbitral award, and in some cases fixing the fees of the members of the arbitral tribunal.[45] The performance of these important tasks by an 'independent' organ of the Institution reassures the disputing parties of the quality and consistency of the standards applied in the decision-making exercise. This independent board or court of the institution also oversees the general operation of the institution and its management and provides strategic leadership and oversight for the institution. All major arbitration institutions in Africa have such an independent board or court. In most of these institutions the membership of such board or court includes both nationals of the states they are domiciled and foreigners. Furthermore in most of these institutions, the names of the members of their board or court are publicly available.[46]

[F] Publication of Annual Data

In this present age, it is practically inconceivable that any service provider, such as an arbitration institution, will not have an online presence. Such presence has become a sine qua non for any business enterprise or service provider. However, there are still quite a number of arbitration institutions in Africa without an online presence. This makes knowledge about their existence and the services they offer very difficult.[47] An online presence, which all major arbitration institutions in Africa have, ensures information about the institution and the services they provide are publicly available and easily accessible. Such accessibility will attract users both within and outside the arbitration institution's location. Table 2 in the Appendix to this book provides a list of seventy-one arbitration institutions in thirty-nine African countries. Interestingly of the

---

44. See Art. 2.1 LACIAC Arbitration Rules 2015. Article 1 of the LCA Arbitration Rules refers to 'these Rules' only.
45. See for example Art. 1 of the ICC Rules on the function of its International Court of Arbitration; Art. 3 LCIA Rules on the function of its Court and Registrar; Art. 2 CIETAC Rules on the function of its Arbitration Court and its Chairman; Art. 2 of Kigali Rules on its Board of Directors, General Secretariat and General Secretary; Art. 1 LACIAC Rules on the LACIAC Court.
46. For example the Kigali Centre Board of Directors available at: http://www.kiac.org.rw/spip.php?rubrique43 [accessed 11 Mar. 2016]. The LCIA Court performs this role for LCIA-MIAC for which see: http://www.lcia-miac.org/about-us/organisation-structure.aspx [accessed 11 Mar. 2016]. For the LACIAC Court, see: http://www.laciac.org/?page_id = 130 [accessed 11 Mar. 2016].
47. It goes without saying that if the wider public are unaware of the existence of a particular institution, it will be very difficult for them to access or even use such institution's services.

seventy-one arbitration institutions listed in Table 2, forty-eight have their own dedicated website.

However, it is one thing for an arbitration institution to have a dedicated website and another on the quality of the information provided by the institution on its website. Most of the arbitration institutions in Africa with an online presence do not provide qualitative information on the services they provide, while for some institutions, the information on their websites are out-dated and inaccurate.[48] An example of relevant qualitative information which should be easily accessible on the websites of arbitration institutions is their annual statistics or reports. The annual reports of both the Cairo and Lagos Regional Centres are easily accessible on their websites.[49] In comparing the annual reports of these two AALCO Regional Centres, Cairo by far provides more qualitative and detailed information and data which is very useful to users of arbitration including the researches and the researchers on the subject. In the same category is the Kigali Centre which also provides detailed qualitative report on their website.

There is no gainsaying the fact that to attract business, arbitration institutions in Africa must each maintain a website that provides current information on their services and activities, including their annual reports or statistics with enough details of the business they transacted in each reporting circle. Such online presence will ensure their existence is well known and information of their experience of administering arbitration references is easily accessible to enable users assess their suitability to administer their arbitration reference.[50] This view therefore means that it is not enough for arbitration institutions in Africa to operate a website, but such website must be user friendly, attractive, easy to navigate and contain qualitative and relevant information for (particularly prospective) users of their services, and the general public.

[G] Additional Services

Arbitration institutions may provide other services that, though not central or core to their management or administration of arbitration references, may promote the use of the mechanism of arbitration in resolving disputes. Thus though not core, such services will assist with the generation of arbitration references and create a supportive environment for dispute resolution to thrive. Such non-core services can be categorized into educational, (these will include the provision of arbitration related training, conferences, workshops and seminars with or without a fee for the dissemination of

48. It is fair to note that there appears to be a generational divide on this issue so that the more modern arbitration centres such as LACIAC and Kigali have more user friendly websites with very useful information that is easy to navigate. This is not the situation with the better websites of most other arbitration institutions in Africa.
49. See for Lagos Regional Centre Reports: http://www.rcicalagos.org/annual_reports.html [accessed 11 Mar. 2016]; and for Cairo Regional Centre Reports see: http://crcica.org.eg/pub_annual.html [accessed 11 Mar. 2016].
50. An example of the effect of lack of information is the Happ's Arbitration Links which provide weblinks to arbitration institutions in various regions of the world. For Africa it lists only ten arbitration institutions: http://www.arbitration-links.de/00000099670ba0802/index.html [accessed 5 Apr. 2016].

information on arbitration) (§1.01[G][1]); informational, (the provision of arbitration related information from its particular jurisdiction to the general public) (§1.01[G][2]); and relational, (lobbying government agencies on arbitration related matters such as responding to relevant government consultation papers) (§1.01[G][3]).

[1] Educational Services in Arbitration

Training of arbitration practitioners in various African countries is thriving. An example is the numbers of Africans that participate in the training programmes of the Chartered Institute of Arbitrators.[51] According to data obtained from the Chartered Institute of Arbitrators between January and December 2015, a total of 1,563 Africans attained various categories of its membership with a total of 801 associate members, 583 full members and 179 fellows, from Kenya (459), Mauritius (54), Nigeria (807), South Africa (59), Zambia (62), Zimbabwe (17), and a minority (105) that have no Chartered Institute of Arbitrators branch affiliation. This data is important considering the core function of the Chartered Institute of Arbitrators is to provide:

> training and education for arbitrators ... This gives users confidence that the very best people are helping to resolve their dispute.[52]

It is important to note that training in the law and practice of arbitration is provided by various organizations and institutions in various African countries and that the data above is only from one of such providers. This effectively means that the number of Africans that have completed one or more training programmes in arbitration will be much higher than these. However, this data is useful to show that the argument that Africa lacks skilled arbitration practitioners is without any evidential basis.

As is well known, there is no requirement for a prospective arbitration appointee to have gone through any specific arbitration related training before being appointed as arbitrator. This view is also supported by the silence on the point under most arbitration laws and rules. Some arbitration laws and rules set out certain generic criteria such as, any person the parties trust or any person that meets the qualifications prescribed by the parties, as an individual that can be appointed as arbitrator.[53] In more developed jurisdictions also, there is no evidence that a specific arbitration related qualification (such as membership or fellowship of the Chartered Institute of Arbitrators) is a prerequisite for individuals wishing to be appointed as arbitrator to possess, neither is there evidence to link the possession of such 'qualifications' to appointment as arbitrator. This, however, is not the situation in some (primarily English speaking) African countries. In some of these countries such as Nigeria, the possession of the

51. There are several other arbitration training providers in various African countries but the Chartered Institute of Arbitrators is the best known across English speaking Africa.
52. See: http://www.ciarb.org/about [accessed 11 Mar. 2016].
53. For example, Art. 11(5) of the UNCITRAL Model Law refer to nationality, qualifications, independence and impartiality as criteria to be taken into account in appointing an arbitrator. See also Art. 30 of the CIETAC Arbitration Rules 2015 for similar considerations.

qualification of 'Fellow' or 'Chartered Arbitrator' of the Chartered Institute of Arbitrators is almost a prerequisite for an individual to be considered for appointment as arbitrator. This 'requirement' has helped to drive the demand by individuals for arbitration training on the continent and also provides a degree of quality assurance for users of arbitration. It must also be acknowledged that as it relates to arbitration, the quality and procedural expertise of arbitrators improve with practice and as they garner experience in the field. Arbitration institutions or organizations linked to institutions (an example is xx with the Chartered Institute of Arbitrators, Kenyan branch) in various African countries provide training in arbitration (and alternative dispute resolution processes generally). In providing these training in arbitration (which are usually paid), arbitration institutions earn some much-needed income and disseminate information and knowledge on arbitration.

In addition to providing dedicated training in arbitration (and other ADR processes), institutions also organize workshops and conferences at which current issues in arbitration (and ADR) are discussed, ideas are exchanged and arbitration practitioners use the opportunity to network. On this point, the PCA continues to engage with arbitration institutions in the continent and assist with capacity building and knowledge sharing. ICSID also maintains some partnership agreements with some institutions in the continent with joint training provisions.[54] In this regard, the work of the Africa International Legal Awareness (AILA)[55] and the International Lawyers from Africa (ILFA)[56]organizations must be mentioned as both organizations are prominent players in the provision of (arbitration related and general legal) training for law professionals on the continent in collaboration with law firms within and outside the African continent. The provision of these training and capacity building opportunities should reassure those arbitration users who remain sceptical of the availability of expertise for arbitration work within the continent. It is important to recognize in this context that some African countries (especially those with very small economies) may lack necessary arbitration related expertise. However, across the continent there are very well trained and skilled arbitrators with very active practices in Africa. These individuals are also available to sit anywhere within or outside the continent. To assist with finding such individuals for example, AILA publishes a directory of African nationals from various countries with expertise in various legal fields.[57]

Arbitration institutions generally have access to arbitration practitioners who can contribute to the practical learning of students studying arbitration or related subjects at various institutions of higher education. Such contribution can be through a mentoring scheme organized by the institution but performed by those arbitration practitioners who are either its members or use its services. The mentoring scheme may be targeted at young arbitration practitioners who are seeking to gain experience. On the part of the arbitration institutions, they can create internship positions for students (and graduates) of arbitration and related subjects to give such students (and

54. One example is with the Lagos Regional Centre.
55. For more information, see: http://www.aila.org.uk/ [accessed 11 Mar. 2016].
56. For more information, see: http://www.ilfa.org.uk/home [accessed 11 Mar. 2016].
57. See AILA website at: https://www.aila.org.uk/page-1381080 [accessed 29 Apr. 2016].

graduates) exposure to the practical dimension of the subject. These mentoring and internship schemes are important in growing the next generation of arbitration practitioners from the continent. Some arbitration institutions on the continent offer these additional opportunities. An example is the LCA which operates both schemes.

[2] Informational Services

There is a dearth of accessible information on arbitration experts and equally importantly arbitration related court decisions in various jurisdictions in Africa. It is therefore proposed in this chapter that arbitration institutions can step into this gap and provide the full text or, at the very least, summaries of such court decisions, or a link to their online repository (if available online). In addition, arbitration institutions can provide the full text of arbitration laws (or link to the repository of such laws if available online) of the jurisdiction they are located on their website. Another useful information, that is not publicly available, are lists of arbitration practitioners in the jurisdictions where each arbitration institution is located. Such lists can also be uploaded onto the websites of arbitration institutions and these various websites can create links to each other. Such links to information on the website of a sister institution in another African country will assist greatly in the free movement of arbitration services across the continent. Another important data that will be useful to the public is a calendar of arbitration related events in various parts of Africa. Such a calendar has become necessary with the growing number of arbitration conferences and related events holding in the continent each year. Such a coordinated calendar will assist with avoiding date clashes and duplication of events. It will also greatly improve communication of these events across the continent and will hugely boost intra-Africa discussions and sharing of arbitration related experience.

[3] Relational Services

As African countries embrace some form of democracy with separate legislative organs, and proposed laws are debated with public consultation, it is important that arbitration institutions as stakeholders in arbitration can effectively contribute to this process. They can make representations and contribute or drive discussions on the emergence of arbitration related laws. This is a very important task because effective arbitration laws promote the perception of the wider arbitration environment as supportive which in turn produces greater caseload for institutions with increased arbitration users. Furthermore, as arbitration institutions operating in Africa talk to each other and collaborate, they will develop an arbitration-focused lobby (including arbitration practitioners) that can influence governmental actions positively in favour of the promotion of arbitration and related services in various African countries.

§1.02 THE FUNCTIONS OF ARBITRATION INSTITUTIONS IN AFRICA

Arbitration institutions in Africa effectively perform the same functions as arbitration institutions anywhere in the world. This section examines some of these functions by reference to the arbitration rules of various institutions in Africa. The first point to note is that these institutions make administrative decisions over matters identified in their arbitration rules and other internal guidelines (collectively referred to as Rules in this section).[58] An example from Article 29 of the LCIA-MIAC Arbitration Rules 2012 provides:

> The decisions of the LCIA Court with respect to all matters relating to the arbitration shall be conclusive and binding upon the parties and the Arbitral Tribunal. Such decisions are to be treated as administrative in nature and the LCIA Court shall not be required to give any reasons.

On its part the OHADA CCJA Arbitration Rules in Article 1 provides:

> The decision it (CCJA Court) takes with a view to ensuring the proper setting in motion and satisfactory termination of arbitral proceedings and those linked to the scrutiny of the award are of administrative nature.[59]

This section examines some of the functions of arbitration institutions: to check correct submission of disputes to it (§1.02[A]); to act as appointing authority under ad hoc references (§1.02[B]), to appoint arbitrators (§1.02[C]), and to determine applications challenging arbitrators (§1.02[D]).

[A] On Submission of the Dispute under Its Rules

An arbitration institution may be empowered by its Rules to make a prima facie decision that the parties' submission to it is in accordance with their arbitration agreement. Such a decision is an important step for the arbitration institution to take before accepting to administer the dispute. Most arbitration institutions customarily will satisfy themselves (before accepting a request for arbitration) that there exists a prima facie arbitration agreement referring to its arbitration rules. If the institution is not satisfied it may reject the request for arbitration.[60] The decision of the arbitration institution on this issue does not deprive the arbitral tribunal (when constituted) of the

58. The Quebec Court of Appeal pronounced on the administrative nature of decisions made by arbitration institutions in *Centre Canadien d'Arbitrage Commercial v. Garantie des Baltiments Residentiels Neuf de l'APCHQ Inc*, Case No. 2005 QCCA 728 of 17 Aug. 2005. See also *Societe Opinter France v. Sarl Dacomex* Rev Arb 1987 at 475 (decision of French Supreme Court).
59. Provisions to the same effect are contained in the arbitration rules of all the other arbitration institutions in Africa.
60. For example in *Ceskolowenska Obchodni Bank AS (Cecobank) v. ICC* (1986) Rev Arb (1987) 367 No. 1 Medt & Mid. East Arb Qtly 3 (1987), the court held that the ICC Court's administrative decision on the existence of an arbitration agreement is not binding on a national court or the arbitrators. In this case, the ICC Court declared there was no arbitration agreement between Cecobank and Bank Mediterranee Sarl. Cecobank sued to compel the ICC to form a tribunal, and for damages for breach of contract.

power to determine the existence and scope of the arbitration agreement.[61] Such 'preliminary' decision by the arbitration institution primarily ensures the arbitration proceeding commences and the arbitral tribunal is constituted. An example of the provision of one major arbitration institution in Africa on this issue is Article 7 paragraph 4 Kigali Arbitration Rules:

> The Centre (Kigali International Arbitration Centre) shall decide whether and to what extent the arbitration shall proceed if and to the extent that the Centre is prima facie satisfied that an arbitration agreement under the Rules may exist...
>
> In all matters decided by the Centre under Article 7 para 4, any decision as to the jurisdiction of the Arbitral tribunal, except as to parties or claims with respect to which the Centre decides that the arbitration cannot proceed, shall then be taken by the Arbitral tribunal itself.[62]

As already mentioned above, accepting a reference triggers the commitment from the arbitration institution to the disputants to render the various services involved in the administration of their submission to arbitration in accordance with its Rules, in exchange for a fee. Thus the legitimate expectation of arbitration institutions is that the disputing parties will pay their notified fees as and when due. This expectation makes it imperative that parties are clearly informed of the rate of fees payable, in what currency, how and when this should be paid. Arbitration institutions provide information on cost of arbitrating under their rules usually on their website and this may also include a cost calculator[63] and as part of their Rules.[64] Arbitration institutions revise their published range of fees from time to time. Most arbitration institutions require the payment of a deposit towards these fees by the disputing parties, in an amount determined by it before the arbitration commences followed by additional payments as the arbitral proceeding progresses. This is an important service arbitration institutions render so that arbitrators can confidently proceed with the reference in the knowledge that the arbitration institution is in-pocket to pay their fees when this becomes due.

The high cost of international arbitration is currently very topical[65] and raises a question whether African arbitration institutions can leverage on this concern of disputants to attract more users to their services which comparatively are far less expensive. I very much doubt that cost alone will increase arbitral traffic in this desired

61. Such decision may be taken as part of the determination by the arbitral tribunal of its jurisdiction pursuant to the doctrine of competence-competence recognized under the arbitration rules of all arbitration institutions in Africa.
62. Article 7.2 para. 3 KIAC Arbitration Rules.
63. Some arbitration institutions provide a cost calculator on their website where parties can input an amount of claim and find out the likely cost of making such a claim. For example Cairo Regional Centre maintains a cost calculator on its website. See: http://crcica.org.eg/feescalc.html [accessed 11 Mar. 2016].
64. The effect of stating cost of the arbitration in the Rules is to bind the disputants. See for example Ch. 6 of Kigali Rules, and Ch. V LACIAC Rules.
65. As an example of the importance of this issue, LCIA very recently, on 3 Nov. 2015 published its 'cost and duration data' to aid disputants in making 'smart and informed' choices of comparative institutions. See: http://www.lcia.org//News/lcia-releases-costs-and-duration-data.aspx [accessed 11 Mar. 2016].

direction. This is primarily because the cost factor does not feature in reasons why disputants stay away from African seats and institutions. However if a supportive arbitration environment is created in African states, then the cost factor may become a relevant topic to which African jurisdictions will be included as it relates to international arbitration.

On the domestic front, litigating before national courts in the vast majority of African countries is not an expensive enterprise. This is primarily because as in every other jurisdiction disputants basically pay court fees, which in African jurisdictions are quite reasonable. In addition to low court fees, disputants do not pay for hearing rooms or pay for the services of arbitration institutions as they would be required to do in arbitration. The fees they pay for legal advice and representation will usually be comparable in both arbitration and litigation. However in some jurisdictions, the winning party may be better off in arbitration for recouping its expenses in prosecuting the arbitral reference than in litigation.[66] The impact of this situation is that certain disputants in Africa may find litigating before national courts cheaper (cost wise) than arbitrating the same dispute. However litigation is disadvantaged by the delays and appeal mechanism currently plaguing most African jurisdictions. The fact that there is no 'appeal' in arbitration and final awards can only be challenged on very limited grounds is a major incentive to domestic entities to opt for arbitration instead of litigating their dispute. This in effect may mean that the additional cost burden of arbitration is evened out by the faster resolution of the dispute.[67]

[B] Act as Appointing Authority

Generally, arbitration institutions accept to act as appointing authority in ad hoc arbitration references for a fee. As appointing authority, arbitration institutions assist the arbitral process by appointing arbitrators. Institutions perform this function in support of arbitration references not under their Rules. For those references under their Rules, such institutions effectively perform some of the same functions as the appointing authority.[68] The disputing parties could leave the appointment of all or some of the arbitrators to the arbitration institution (as appointing authority). The arbitration institution in this capacity maybe equally empowered to decide on arbitrator challenge applications,[69] and assist with the appointment of a replacement arbitrator.[70]

Though an arbitration institution can conceivably refuse designation as appointing authority (since it is not bound by such a designation), it is very doubtful that any

66. A major example is in Nigeria where costs awarded by the courts do not bear any semblance to the costs expended by any of the parties.
67. This benefit is lost where after the final award has been rendered the parties then commence full-blown litigation in an attempt to enforce the award.
68. It is interesting to note that Art. 7 LACIAC Arbitration Rules expressly provide that 'The LACIAC Court shall be the appointing authority in all arbitral proceedings conducted under these Rules'.
69. Article 12(1) UNCITRAL Arbitration Rules.
70. Article 12(2) UNCITRAL Arbitration Rules.

arbitration institution will refuse to so act.[71] This is primarily because the arbitration institution will be paid for performing such service. However if per chance the nominated appointing authority refuses to accept such nomination, the parties may agree to nominate another appointing authority. It is argued that in addition to being paid for its services, acting as appointing authority is an important function for arbitration institutions to perform in ad hoc references. The presence of an arbitration institution which has acquired experience in appointing arbitrators and determining arbitrator challenge issues reassures the disputing parties that these tasks will be performed by an independent entity with requisite experience of making such decisions. Moreover, such assistance brings into ad hoc references some of the experience and expertise used in institutional references. It also promotes closer collaboration between both types of arbitral proceedings. Finally, such interaction provides a much-needed window into the numbers of ad hoc proceedings taking place in the jurisdiction. Therefore, there are several other reasons, apart from fees, which call for support for arbitration institutions to act as appointing authority in ad hoc proceedings.

[C] Appoint Arbitrators

The appointment of arbitrators is one of the most important and principal functions of any arbitration institution. However, the arbitration rules of institutions only provide general guidelines of the considerations such institutions take into account when performing this task of appointing arbitrators.[72] Aspiring arbitrators will very much welcome more information on the standards or criteria which arbitration institutions apply in making their selection. Arbitration institutions generally maintain lists of arbitrators from which they select arbitrators. Almost all the major arbitration institutions in Africa also maintain such lists or panels of arbitrators from which they select appointees when they make appointments.[73]

In appointing arbitrators under institutional Rules, parties are given the right to directly or indirectly appoint or nominate appointees for the appointment of the institution. LCIA-MIAC following the lead of LCIA Arbitration Rules expressly provides that, 'The LCIA Court is empowered to appoint arbitrators'.[74] However under the arbitration rules of almost all the other major arbitration institutions, the disputing parties can make such appointments. For example Article 8 of the Arbitration Rules of

71. Article 6(2) UNCITRAL Rules provides in part, '... or if the Appointing Authority agreed upon refuses to act'.
72. The rules give general guidelines, e.g., on nationality, conditions in the arbitration agreement, impartiality and independence, and qualifications determined by the parties, but the final determining factor(s) are not made public.
73. For example Annex 3 to the Kigali Rules provides the criteria for its panels of arbitrators. Kigali maintains two panels: one for domestic arbitrators and one for international arbitrators. Both lists are published on its website.
74. LCIA-MIAC Arbitration Rules, Art. 5.5 Ch. 3 of the Kigali Arbitration Rules also empower the parties to nominate arbitrators for appointment by the Kigali Centre.

the Cairo Regional Centre expressly empowers the parties to appoint the arbitrators failing which the Cairo Regional Centre will appoint such arbitrators.[75]

Arbitrators appointed under the Arbitration Rules of these institutions offer their services for a fee. In the vast majority of cases, these arbitration institutions fix the rates of fees and reimbursable expenses arbitrators sitting under their rules are paid. There is usually a scale of fees the arbitrators are notified of when they accept appointment.[76] For example under LACIAC Arbitration Rules, the LACIAC Court has the exclusive right to fix the arbitrators' fees,[77] while under the Kigali Rules, it is for the arbitration tribunal to 'specify in the final award the total amount of the costs of the arbitration' and apportionment among the parties.[78] For the Lagos Regional Centre, this is a task to be shared between the arbitral tribunal and the Director of the Centre.[79] This is different from the provision of the Cairo Regional Centre Arbitration Rules which leaves it to the arbitral tribunal to fix the cost of the arbitration in the final award.[80] There are also differences on how the fees of the arbitrators are calculated under the different arbitration rules. For some it is ad valorem[81] while for others it is on a time-spent basis.[82]

The arbitration institution notifies the disputing parties of the remuneration payable to the arbitrators though payment of this sum is made through the arbitration institution to the arbitrators. This results in the arbitrators not looking directly to the parties to pay their fees and reimbursable expenses following the publication of the award. There is a clear link with the movement of the award and fees in this transaction. The arbitrator effectively transfers the final award to the arbitration institution in exchange for their fees. This scheme as currently designed raises a question on what happens where the arbitration institution has not been placed in funds by the parties so that when the arbitral tribunal transfers the final award to the institution, it is unable to pay the fees of the arbitrators. In such a scenario, who will be liable for the fees of the arbitrator? Some institutional rules expressly provide that liability for the fees of the arbitrator lie with the parties. An example is the Kigali Rules which in this regard provides:

> The Secretariat may from time to time direct parties to make further advances towards costs of the arbitration incurred or to be incurred *on behalf of or for the benefit* of the parties.[83] [Emphasis added].

By virtue of this provision the Kigali Centre acts as agent of the parties (as disclosed principals) for the payment of the fees of the arbitrators. Therefore, the

75. See also to the same effect, Art. 11 of LACIAC Arbitration Rules; Art. 11 Lagos Regional Centre Arbitration Rules.
76. See for example, Arts 10 and 24 CCJA Arbitration Rules.
77. See Art. 45 LACIAC Arbitration Rules.
78. See Art. 42 Kigali Arbitration Rules.
79. See Art. 41 Lagos Regional Centre Arbitration Rules.
80. See Art. 42 Cairo Regional Centre Arbitration Rules.
81. For example under LACIAC, Art. 45 Arbitration Rules; and Kigali, Art. 45 Arbitration Rules.
82. For example under LCIA-MIAC Schedule of Costs Annex to the Arbitration Rules.
83. Article 42 para. 5 Kigali Arbitration Rules.

parties remain liable for such fees and can conceivably be sued by the arbitrator for payment of their fees.

[D] Decide Challenges to Arbitrators

Arbitration institutions determine arbitrator challenge applications emanating from arbitration proceedings conducted under their rules and when they act as appointing authority in ad hoc proceedings. Most arbitration rules provide that the decision of the institution on such application is final.[84] Depending on the law of the seat of the arbitration, a disputing party may still reserve its right to challenge the decision of the arbitration institution while continuing to participate in the arbitration proceedings.

When the arbitration institution sustains an arbitrator challenge, it appoints a replacement arbitrator or repeats the prior arbitrator appointment procedure. The arbitration institution also appoints a replacement arbitrator when the arbitrator withdraws, becomes incapable of continuing with his mandate, de jure or de facto.[85] Under some institutional arbitration rules, a truncated tribunal may continue with the arbitral proceedings and make a final award.[86] Under those Rules where the truncated tribunal cannot proceed without the appointment of a replacement arbitrator, the 'new' tribunal may repeat the hearings or continue from where the 'old' tribunal stopped. These will all depend on the agreement of the parties and also as a practical issue, of the stage of the arbitral hearing at which the truncation occurred.

It is evident that these are the same tasks performed by arbitration institutions located in any part of the world and so are of a generic nature. However, the quality of the service provided and the cost of such service provision will differ.

§1.03 CONTRIBUTION TO THE TRANSFORMATION OF ARBITRATION IN AFRICA

This section examines how arbitration institutions operating within the continent can contribute to or support the transformation of arbitration in Africa. This is a transformation from the current position of a pre-litigation disposition by disputants to an environment where the predisposition will be in favour of arbitration as the dispute resolution of choice instead of litigation. The analysis starts from the premise that arbitration institutions are one of the major stakeholders in the use and promotion of

84. For example Art. 13 Cairo Regional Centre Arbitration Rules; Art. 15 Lagos Regional Centre Arbitration Rules empowers the Centre or appointing authority (where parties already agreed to one) to make the decision; Art. 14 LACIAC Arbitration Rules empowers the LACIAC Court to make the decision; Art. 19 Kigali Arbitration Rules empowers the Kigali Centre to make the decision.
85. Article 14 Cairo Regional Centre Arbitration Rules; Art. 16 Lagos Regional Centre Arbitration Rules; Art. 11 LCIA-MIAC Arbitration Rules; Art. 15 LACIAC Arbitration Rules; and Art. 20 Kigali Arbitration Rules.
86. See for example: Art. 21 Kigali Arbitration Rules; Art. 16 LACIAC Arbitration Rules; Art. 12 LCIA-MIAC Arbitration Rules; Art. 15 Cairo Regional Centre Arbitration Rules; Art. 17 Lagos Regional Centre Arbitration Rules.

arbitration as a dispute resolution mechanism. As a stakeholder, arbitration institutions have a major interest in the development of the legal environment in African countries to support arbitration particularly, as the primary function of such institutions is to administer or manage arbitration references. The lucrative nature of arbitration business in terms of financial income is borne out by the increase in both numbers and geographical spread of arbitration institutions in Africa as evidenced in Table 2 in the appendix to this book.

As evidenced in Table 2 in the appendix, most African countries can boast of the existence of at least one arbitration institution within their jurisdiction while the larger economies in the continent have multiple institutions dedicated to administering arbitration references. In each region of the continent there is at least one major arbitration institution with international reputation that attracts major international references. Examples are Cairo Regional Centre in North Africa; Kigali Centre in East Africa; ADR Africa/AFSA and LCIA-MIAC in Southern Africa; Ghana Arbitration Centre, Lagos Regional Centre and LCA Centre in West Africa; with GICAM and OHADA CCJA serving the francophone/OHADA countries.

However the existence of these many arbitration institutions in countries of Africa has not deepened the acceptance or development of arbitration nor improved the otherwise negative perception by foreign disputants of arbitrating in Africa. It is true that there are major structural challenges which, regardless of how efficient an arbitration institution may be, go beyond the capacity of these institutions to fix.[87] This however does not mean that there is no role for arbitration institutions to play in transforming the legal environment in African countries. Therefore it is not too early to examine how these centres/institutions can better support the growth of arbitration in the continent. This section examines how arbitration institutions can contribute to the transformation of arbitration in Africa, through sensitization activities targeted at local businesses (§1.03[A]), transparency of their services (§1.03[B]), closer collaboration between African arbitration institutions (§1.03[C]), and explores the idea of these institutions forming themselves into an African Arbitration Association (§1.03[D]).

[A] Sensitization of Domestic Businesses

By growth, it is meant not just increase in numbers of disputes being arbitrated (though this is very important and a measurable growth indicator) but equally important, is achieving a cultural shift in the choice of dispute resolution mechanism, so that arbitration becomes the dispute resolution mechanism of choice for disputants, especially those emanating from commercial transactions. The direct effect of this shift will lead to greater numbers of domestic, intra-Africa and international disputes being

87. Such structural deficiencies affect the quality of the laws and rules on arbitration; the role of judges in creating a supportive environment for arbitration to thrive; security of lives and property in African countries; infrastructure deficits; and lack of a 'rule of law' culture. SOAS University of London Project on the development of arbitration in Africa aim to contribute to some of the resolution of some of these issues with the goal of transforming the legal environment for arbitration to thrive in Africa. For the project website, see: http://www.researcharbitrationafrica.com/ [accessed 11 Mar. 2016].

arbitrated within the African continent. The push for this growth will have a direct impact also on the increase in the use of African lawyers in advising commercial clients in both transactional and advocacy roles. It will also directly impact the choice of seats of arbitration in African countries. Such pro-African choice may also lead to an increase in the numbers of arbitration related disputes adjudicated by national courts within Africa. All of these transformations will open up the African arbitral market and lead to greater acceptance and understanding of the arbitral process within the continent. Such acceptance will in turn contribute to the drive for 'African voices' to be included in the formulation and development of global arbitral jurisprudence, practice, norms, laws and rules.

Arbitration institutions are usually the first independent agency that disputing parties approach when a dispute arises. It is therefore massively important that these institutions provide such disputants with an excellent service that is also good value for money. It is obvious that if disputants are given excellent service they will return to use the same services if the need arises in the future. There is empirical evidence in support of this correlation from research conducted by the Kigali International Arbitration Centre.[88] In addition satisfied customers provide the best advertisement or marketing for a service and will propagate the information to their colleagues, peers, customers and clients through experiential evidence. This is particularly true in Africa where there is still a strong sense of community and greater reliance on personal or experiential information or recommendation.

Information gathering, dissemination and sharing is one major service which arbitration institutions on the continent can provide to users (primarily commercial parties regardless of size) on the continent. They can do this through outreach programmes with information offices available to businesses where such businesses are located. For example, Kigali operates a one-stop office for all enquiries on arbitration. This office explains what arbitration is, the process, the output, enforcement and annulment processes to members of the public who may become future clients.[89] With such outreach programmes, when a business is negotiating a contract, it already has some basic information about the process of arbitration and the importance of including an enforceable dispute resolution clause in the contract. The application of such basic knowledge (through the inclusion of an arbitration clause in the contract) will ensure that disputes arising under that contract will be referred to arbitration.[90] In addition, such businesses will be most likely to include submission to the rules of the institution that informed them of the process in the first instance. So the institution may get more business by way of parties adopting its arbitration rules. However of greater importance is the inclusion of an arbitration clause in the contract in the first place since without an arbitration agreement, the institution will not have the dispute to manage nor will arbitrators have disputes to determine.

88. For more details see Ch. 9 below by Bernadette Uwiyceza on the Kigali International Arbitration Centre.
89. *Ibid.*
90. The arbitration laws of the vast majority of African states require their courts to either stay proceedings or reject a claim which is covered by an arbitration agreement.

Sensitization of commercial parties is particularly important because of the nature and size of most businesses in the continent. Such businesses do not just straddle the informal economy versus formal economy divide but are usually very small in size. Their size means they have little money to spend on legal advice and usually conclude their business transactions without such legal advice. This therefore puts greater pressure on the need to inform these businesses of arbitration before they conclude contracts of a commercial nature.

Arbitration centres or institutions of whatever size and specialist focus, can easily engage in such outreach programmes with businesses operating in the communities in which they are located. If each arbitration institution on the continent provides such outreach programmes, it will serve for a better-informed constituency which may lead to greater numbers of cases for administration by institutions. It will certainly lead to better informed and drafted arbitration clauses. This clearly implies that since such constituency will primarily be domestic, the caseload it will generate may also be predominantly domestic. This will still achieve the goal of changing the dispute resolution culture of commercial entities in Africa from a litigation focus. In addition, as the arbitral domestic market grows, the experience and knowledge of administering such references by arbitration centres, will improve and this will infect their administration of international references when they are seated in Africa.[91] Therefore there is great merit in arbitration institutions in Africa targeting domestic arbitration references (in addition to international references). The domestic market will almost always generate more cases than the international market especially with the stiff competition from other more international well known, older and better-experienced arbitration institutions jostling for the same business.

Experience of the ability to effectively administer arbitration references can always be gained from administering domestic disputes, and this experience can then be transferred to administering international disputes. It is interesting that many arbitration institutions in Africa market themselves as 'international' and actively seek to attract international cases. However it is not realistic to expect to receive such references if the institution cannot show or does not have any experience of administering arbitration disputes in the first place. This is simply because such disputes are usually very high value with too much at stake for parties to entrust its management to an institution whose track record they are not confident about. Such expectation, it is argued, is misplaced. It is preferable for these arbitration institutions to deploy their marketing efforts instead to the domestic market, without neglecting the international market.[92] The need to look inwards and grow the domestic market is even stronger

91. An example from China on the value of the domestic arbitral market shows a steady increase in the number of domestic references from 2006 with a dip in 2012 as evidenced in CIETAC statistics. Between 2006 and 2015, CIETAC administered a total of 13,492 arbitrations of which 4,396 were foreign while the vast majority of 9,096 disputes were purely domestic. See for details: http://www.cietac.org/index.php?m=Page&a=index&id=40&l=en [accessed 5 Apr. 2016]. This again confirms that, for most arbitration institutions, the bulk of references will come from the domestic market.
92. To compete in the international market a fully functioning, well designed and updated website will be an invaluable tool, if not a prerequisite.

because there is not enough international business for all the institutions in the world. This therefore means that these arbitration institutions in Africa will need to step out to engage the local businesses around then and to generate the business.

As mentioned above the arbitration administration providers market in Africa is congested in some jurisdictions and very thin in others. In those jurisdictions where arbitration institutions abound (such as South Africa, Egypt and Nigeria) there must be strategic space sharing and marketing to ensure that the higher goal of changing the dispute resolution culture of businesses with their choice of dispute resolution mechanism is achieved.

[B] Transparency

As mentioned above, some arbitration centres operating in Africa do not have their own dedicated website or an online presence, while of those institutions with a presence online, most do not provide adequate information relevant to disputants or interested parties seeking out arbitration centres to investigate either with a view to using or even just for research purposes. In comparison to the well-known international arbitration centres, such as the ICC, SIAC, LCIA, and CIETAC, that provide relevant information on their websites, are user friendly and easy to navigate, institutions in Africa clearly need to do more.

Most arbitration institutions in Africa maintain a panel of arbitrators though their arbitration rules do not limit the selection of arbitrators from such panels. Some arbitration institutions publish the names of the individuals on their list while others do not.[93] For example, the OHADA, CCJA publishes its list of neutrals,[94] Cairo Regional Centre publishes two lists of arbitrators in Arabic and English,[95] and the Kigali Centre also publishes two lists: one for domestic arbitrators and the other for international arbitrators.[96] For some other institutions, a comprehensive and updated list of the arbitrators on their panels is not made publicly available. It is clearly better to publish such lists where they are used by the arbitration institution.

The Lagos Regional Centre lists the criteria against which it accepts prospective arbitrators to be listed on its panel. Kigali provides the criteria for selection onto her panels in its arbitration rules and from time to time advertises a call for application for enlistment onto the panels. A question on why such institutions should publicize the basis of their selection exercise may be raised, especially in light of the characterization of such decisions as administrative and so not open to challenge; and the fact that the more established arbitration institutions do not characteristically publish such information. Two issues need to be addressed in answering this question. The first issue is that African arbitration centres need to make a more concerted effort to establish

93. For example the Lagos Regional Centre maintains a list of arbitrators but such list is not publicly available on their website.
94. For the current list, see: http://ohada.org/phocadownload/LISTE_ARBITRES_2015.pdf [accessed 11 Mar. 2016].
95. See: http://crcica.org.eg/arbitrators.html [accessed 11 Mar. 2016].
96. See: http://www.kiac.org.rw/spip.php?rubrique25 [accessed 11 Mar. 2016].

themselves unlike those institutions that are already established and well known, tried and tested.[97] The second issue relates to the perception of the fairness of the selection process. This has some bearing on the user's trust of the managers of the centres. This clearly is a reputational issue. African centres need to build the reputation of fairness, integrity and professionalism, and this can be evidenced through a greater degree of transparency than the practice among the more established international arbitration institutions in other continents.[98]

Such transparency also extends to arbitrator challenge issues. In this situation a clear statement of the benchmark instrument against which such decisions are made will be satisfactory. For example, a clear statement that the institution in making arbitrator challenge decisions applies the IBA Guidelines on Conflicts of Interest in International Arbitration will reassure foreign disputants whose lawyers will be familiar with the Guidelines. LACIAC has gone further by incorporating this IBA Guidelines into its Arbitration Rules.[99] Such express declaration reassures users, clarifies their expectations and further builds standards coalesced around international best practice.[100] It also reassures international users that domestic and (usually parochial) standards will not be adopted by the institution in making such decisions, even as appointing authority. This will make the institution more attractive to users.

As part of the supportive environment for arbitration to thrive, is the role of African courts and judges in supporting arbitration references connected to their jurisdiction. It has been noted that this is the primary stakeholder that is not currently aligned to the vision of transforming the African arbitral landscape.[101] Arbitration institutions on the continent fully appreciate the impact of the perception of a weak judiciary in attracting primarily international disputes. Some of the major arbitration institutions in Africa engage with the judiciary in their location through workshops and organizing training on arbitration law and practice to the judges; an outreach which is very useful in ensuring that these decision makers had a robust appreciation of arbitration and its complimentary nature to litigation.

One major gap which remains is the lack of access to the full text of arbitration related judgments made by judges in Africa. It is through the reasoning and decisions of judges in cases that their attitude towards arbitration can be assessed. This makes access to such decisions very important. As already mentioned above, arbitration institutions in these various African countries are well placed to bridge this gap by

---

97. In addition the individuals listed on the panels of international arbitration institutions are also well known around those circles and also recycle themselves around the various institutions.
98. The baggage of the poor perception of the continent in general also extends to arbitration institutions operating within the continent.
99. Annex II to the LACIAC Arbitration Rules 2015. The LCA Rules on their part refer to the IBA Guidelines as well.
100. This remains the view even with the recent English High Court decision and pronouncement on the weaknesses of the IBA Guidelines in *W Limited v. M SDN BDH* [2016] EWHC 422 (Comm). It must be noted that the comments of the judge in this case was on the basis of English law.
101. See the Discussion Paper for the 2nd SOAS Arbitration in Africa conference titled *Rethinking the Role of Courts and Judges in Supporting Arbitration in Africa* which will be hosted by the Lagos Court of Arbitration, 22-24 Jun. 2016 at: http://www.researcharbitrationafrica.com/ [accessed 11 Mar. 2016].

making such judgments publicly available on their websites. There is a new project recently launched by Leyou Tameru known as 'International Arbitration Africa' (I-Arb). This is an online platform which provides information on arbitration in Africa and Africa related arbitration judgments from various jurisdictions.[102]

[C] Closer Intra-Africa Collaboration

As already noted, arbitration institutions operating in Africa are of varying sizes and have different degrees of arbitration administration experience. Most of these institutions are however very small in size and have very little verifiable arbitration management experience. Some of these institutions do not have collaborative relationships with other more established international arbitration institutions, while the few major institutions are growing in size and have collaborative relationships with other international arbitration institutions. These same major institutions in Africa engage with the global arbitration community through attendance (including as speakers/moderators) at various conferences and events, and in the promotion of their institutions. The access these major institutions have to arbitration expertise and information far outweighs those of the smaller institutions in the continent. There is therefore the need for greater collaboration among institutions within the continent, and especially those located in the same country or region of the continent.

Such collaboration and engagement can be achieved through information sharing and exchange of expertise. An example is engaging speakers from the various institutions (large and small) at conferences. It can also be through organizing targeted intra-Africa (or intra-country) workshops for continuous professional development and sharing of knowledge and experience. In addition to such exchanges, the major institutions must be willing to better engage the smaller institutions in this regard. The larger institutions can also establish contacts with the smaller centres (especially those within their geographical area) and be willing to share information, best practice and advice with them.

For this idea to thrive, it calls for a collaborative relationship between the institutions which in the long run will benefit all arbitration stakeholders. Such collaboration may also lead to the possibilities of mergers with, and even take-overs of, the smaller institutions. The possibility of such mergers is more promising in the larger economies/jurisdictions with several business hubs/cities where the services offered by the major institutions can then be located closer to the users. This may also require the major institutions to set up franchises or branches in different parts of a particular country or different countries within a region. Such spread will assure disputants of access to the same quality of service provided by the major institutions without the additional cost of physically going to the city the institution's offices are located.[103]

In countries with several arbitration institutions, such institutions may also consider setting up a dispute resolution village or hub where they can all set up their

102. For more information, see: http://www.iarbafrica.com/about-us [accessed 11 Mar. 2016].
103. The arbitration rules of these arbitration institutions clearly allow arbitration references under their rules to be held at any place though that is not the reality in practice.

offices. An example is provided by the LCA.[104] It is important that arbitration institutions in Africa think creatively and organically how find the best ways to maximize their potential in the environment in which they operate. It is such domestication of services that will set them apart from institutions in other jurisdictions. This means in effect that reproducing the norm in other jurisdictions may not be appropriate for the legal environment in African countries for her arbitration institutions to thrive.

[D] Proposal for an Association of African Arbitration Institutions

The need for collective progression and expertise leads to the question of whether arbitration institutions on the continent should form themselves into a formal association or group whose sole purpose will be the promotion of expertise in the administration of arbitration (and other ADR) processes. Such an association will of necessity be of a pan-African nature to engage all arbitration institutions operating within the continent to which membership will be open. This is not my original idea but one that was mooted at the Addis Ababa conference on arbitration institutions in 2015 by the General Counsel of the African Union Commission, Professor Vincent Nmehielle, in his welcome address to the conference participants.[105] Though the logistics for such association will need to be carefully thought out, the key issue at the outset is the umbrella organization (which ideally should have a pan-African nature) that will take ownership of such an association. The natural organization for such a role is the African Union as the pan-African umbrella of almost all African countries.[106]

The benefits of such association are not difficult to appreciate. The primary benefit will be the standardization of practice and process in the provision of the service of administration of dispute resolution processes across the continent. Members of the association will share experience and knowledge and assist each other in their development. At the continental level, the association can act as a lobby group on all arbitration related issues that cut across different states and regions of the continent. Such matters usually will require governmental action and the association can lobby Heads of Governments and relevant Ministers, who make such decisions. For the international arbitral community, such an association should be welcomed and supported as it will provide an umbrella organization through which they can engage with the arbitration institutions across the continent.

The association will also benefit from a relationship with the ICCA which is an umbrella international non-governmental organization for arbitration practitioners,

104. For more details see Ch. 4 below by Megha Joshi and Tolu Obamuroh on the Lagos Court of Arbitration Centre.
105. The conference titled, *The Role of Arbitration Institutions in the Development of Arbitration in Africa* and was organized by SOAS and hosted by the Office of the General Counsel of the African Union Commission on 23 Jul. 2015. The conference papers are available at: http://eprints.soas.ac.uk/20421/ [accessed 10 Mar. 2016].
106. The current membership of the African Union comprises fifty-three African countries with the exception of Morocco, see: http://www.au.int/en/AU_Member_States [accessed on 10 Mar. 2016].

academics, institutions and other stakeholders (such as judges) with an interest in promoting settlement of disputes.[107] ICCA and her members can provide technical support with training, collaborations, information gathering and sharing with arbitration institutions in Africa through such an association.

The association will also be connected to and maintain a collaborative relationship with the IFCAI which aims:

> to establish and maintain permanent relations between commercial arbitration institutions, foster a broad exchange of information on all aspects of arbitration and conciliation, encourage the responsible use of these dispute resolution techniques, and facilitate the exchange of information on member organisation services.[108]

For now, there are very few African arbitration institutions that are members of IFCAI. As at the end of December 2015, only Cairo Regional Centre and Sharm El Sheikh International Arbitration Centre, both in Egypt, are members of IFCAI from Africa.[109] Clearly all arbitration institutions operating in Africa (particularly those who describe themselves as international) ought to belong to this association whose aims squarely fit into the needs of institutions on the continent. IFCAI states that its membership is open to 'organizations involved in commercial arbitration in its various forms'. As already mentioned, this is a proposal which needs to be explored further by all arbitration stakeholders in Africa.

CONCLUSION

This chapter examined arbitration institutions as one major stakeholder in arbitration in Africa. It explored the role arbitration institutions can play in transforming arbitration in Africa and concludes that there is a growing increase in the number of arbitration institutions operating in the continent who can fully contribute to transforming the legal environment for arbitration to thrive in various African countries. It examined various services arbitration institutions offer and those they can also offer and recognized that these are all very demanding tasks but which will all assist in transforming the legal environment in African countries to one that is supportive of arbitration as the dispute resolution mechanism of choice in commercial disputes. This chapter clearly argues that a supportive legal environment will lead to more disputants choosing to resolve their disputes through the mechanism of arbitration and this will lead to an increase in the caseload of the arbitration institutions in Africa. Therefore the engagement of arbitration institutions in transforming arbitration in Africa will be beneficial to them as well as the wider arbitration community.

107. For more details on ICCA, see: http://www.arbitration-icca.org/ [accessed on 5 Apr. 2016].
108. For more details on IFCAI see: http://www.ifcai-arbitration.org/ifcai-members/ [accessed 5 Apr. 2016].
109. See for the 2015 IFCAI membership list: http://www.ifcai-arbitration.org/ifcai-members/ [accessed 5 Apr. 2016].

PART II Regional Arbitration Institutions in Africa

CHAPTER 2

The CCJA as a Regional Arbitration Institution

Mahutodji Jimmy Vital Kodo & Narcisse Aka

INTRODUCTION

This chapter discusses the arbitration institution operating under the auspices of the Common Court of Justice of OHADA to answer the question whether supranational arbitration institutions are required for the transformation agenda for arbitration in Africa. This chapter will examine the function of the CCJA in the context of OHADA (§2.01); the arbitration remit of the CCJA (§2.02); some thoughts on the role of a supranational arbitration institution in the transformation of arbitration in its region (§2.03).

§2.01 CCJA IN THE CONTEXT OF OHADA

The Organisation for the Harmonization of Business Law in Africa (OHADA) was created by Treaty on 17 October 1993, signed by fourteen African Heads of States in Port Louis, Mauritius, with the primary aim of encouraging the inflow of foreign investments into the OHADA area. The OHADA Treaty is now in force in seventeen African countries.[1] Membership of OHADA, according to the Treaty, is open to all

1. In the order of date of ratification, OHADA Member States are: Bissau Guinea (15 Jan. 1994), Senegal (14 Jun. 1994), Central African Republic (13 Jan. 1995), Mali (7 Feb. 1995), Comoros (20 Feb. 1995), Burkina-Faso (6 Mar. 1995), Benin (8 Mar. 1995), Niger (5 Jun. 1995), Ivory Coast (29 Sep. 1995), Cameroon (20 Oct. 1995), Togo (27 Oct. 1995), Chad (13 Apr. 1996), Congo (28 May 1997), Gabon (2 Feb. 1998), Equatorial Guinea (16 Apr. 1999), Guinea (5 May 2000). See the table in *OHADA: Traité et Actes uniformes commentés et annotés, Juriscope,* 2e éd., 2002; ISSA-SAYEGH, J., POUGOUE, P.-G., & SAWADOGO, M. F. (2002). *OHADA: Traité et Actes uniformes commentés et annotés* (2è ed.). (JURISCOPE, Ed.) Bruxelles: Bruylant. The latest

states, whether or not members of the African Union (AU), the current successor to the Organisation of African Unity mentioned in the Treaty.[2] All but one of the current OHADA Member States' legal systems follows the civil law tradition. Cameroon is the only OHADA jurisdiction whose legal system follows both the civil and common law traditions.

In OHADA Member States, the Treaty creates a dualist legal system, where national laws coexist with the business legislations of the OHADA regime.[3] OHADA laws however supersede national laws covering the same subject. The limited subject matter jurisdiction of OHADA necessarily affects only business laws and their procedure. Though the word 'harmonisation' is used in the title of OHADA, its laws, in reality, adopt a unification of laws method. According to Yakubu, harmonization integrates community law within the framework of national laws. It can be effected by replacing pre-existing national laws with new laws, or by setting a framework within which non-identical national laws must be oriented to reach a common goal.[4] It can be argued therefore that the law-making body of OHADA has used these two techniques of harmonization, since a new set of laws has been created and segments of non-conflicting national legislation covering the same issues are still applicable. Once adopted, OHADA Uniform Acts become directly applicable in its Member States so that they form an integral part of the national legislation of the Member States without the necessity of any enactment by national parliaments.[5] The Uniform Acts created

---

country to ratify the Treaty is Democratic Republic of Congo: The Law N° 10/002 on adhesion of Democratic Republic of Congo to OHADA was promulgated on Thursday 11 Feb. 2010; source: http://www.lobservateur.cd/index.php?option=com_content&view=article&id=1197:adhesion-de-la-rdc-a-lohada&catid=45:economie&Itemid=65 [accessed 5 Apr. 2016].

2. Article 53 of OHADA Treaty. This expressly means that membership of OHADA is also open to non-AU states subject to the consent of existing members.
3. By virtue of Art. 2 of the Treaty, 'Business law' in the OHADA system refers to:

> Business Law regulations concerning Company Law, definition and classification of legal persons engaged in trade, proceeding in respect of credits and recovery of debts, means of enforcement, bankruptcy, receiverships, arbitration. Also included are the following laws: Employment law, Accounting law, Transportation and Sales laws, and any such other matter that the Council of Ministers would decide, unanimously, to so include as falling within the definition of Business Law.

   Unofficial translation of the treaty, taken from: http://www.ohada.com/traite.php?newlang=english&categorie=1 [accessed 5 Apr. 2016].
4. For more details, see J. A. Yakubu, *Community laws in International Business Transactions*, in C. Dickerson (ed.), *Unified Business Law for Africa: Common Law Perspectives on OHADA*, 4 (GMB Publishing London, 2009). Although harmonization is mentioned in the Treaty, OHADA in fact unifies business laws, and the word 'harmonisation' was used instead of 'unification' consciously and for political reasons.
5. As at April 2016, there are nine Uniform Acts in force under the OHADA Treaty and these are: the Uniform Act Relating to General Commercial Law (17 Apr. 1997, revised 15 Dec. 2010); Uniform Act Organizing Securities (17 Apr. 1997, revised 15 Dec. 2010); Uniform Act Relating to Commercial Companies and Economic Interest Group (17 Apr. 1997, revised 30 Jan. 2014); Uniform Act Organizing Collective Proceedings for Wiping Off Debts (10 Apr. 1998, revised

pursuant to the Treaty automatically and directly repeal all pre-existing legislation contrary to them and supersedes any future legislation on the covered areas.[6]

The Common Court of Justice and Arbitration (CCJA) is one of the key institutions of OHADA.[7] The CCJA is a supranational Court created to ensure the uniform interpretation and application of the Uniform Acts to further ensuring consistency in the unification of business laws across the OHADA Member States. The jurisdiction of the CCJA includes giving advisory opinions to the Permanent Secretary, Member States or a national court on OHADA related cases; hearing appeals on OHADA laws from national courts;[8] and providing administration services for arbitration references based on the Uniform Act on Arbitration.[9] As an appellate Court, the CCJA has the power to render final decisions in the cases brought before it. The CCJA exercises the same powers as national Supreme Courts of the Member States of OHADA as it relates to OHADA legislation.[10] Therefore, the CCJA has final and exclusive jurisdiction on OHADA law, and its decisions have the status of finality (res judicata) and are immediately enforceable in each Member State.[11] As already mentioned, the CCJA does not have jurisdiction to grant penalties for offences or over criminal liabilities.[12] The CCJA can also overrule its prior decisions where there is a clerical error or misrepresentation.[13]

---

10 Sep. 2015); Uniform Act Organizing Simplified Recovery Procedures and Measures of Execution (10 Apr. 1998); Uniform Act on Arbitration (11 Mar. 1999, currently under revision); Uniform Act organizing and harmonizing Company Accounting Systems (22 Mar. 2000, currently under revision), the Uniform Act on Contracts for the Carriage of Goods by Road (22 Mar. 2003) and the Uniform Act on Relating to Cooperatives Companies (15 Dec. 2010).

6. Article 10 of OHADA Treaty. For an application by the CCJA, see CCJA, N° 043/2005, 7-7-2005: Aziablévi YOVO et autres c/ Sté TOGO TELECOM, recueil de Jurisprudence de la CCJA, n° 6, juin-décembre 2005, p. 25.- Le Juris-Ohada n° 1/2006, p. 8. See also comments of Filiga Michel SAWADOGO in Ohadata D-07-16; and Ohadata J-06-32 available at www.ohada.com [accessed 5 Apr. 2016].
7. The other institutions of OHADA created by the Treaty are the Conference of Heads of State and Government, the Council of Ministers, the Permanent Secretary and the Regional School of Magistracy.
8. Such appeals are from the Courts of Appeal of Member States or lower courts for first and last resort decisions. There is no appeal from Supreme Courts of Member States to the CCJA; however, they can refer OHADA-related cases to the CCJA.
9. Article 14 of OHADA Treaty.
10. This explains why the Supreme Courts of OHADA Member States lack jurisdiction over matters on OHADA law. Additionally, the CCJA can perform de novo review where needed.
11. Article 20 of OHADA Treaty. See also CCJA N° 059/2005, 22-12-2005: BIAO-CI c / Sté IPN, Recueil de jurisprudence de la CCJA, n° 6, juin-décembre 2005, p. 38, Ohadata J-06-36 available at: www.ohada.com [accessed 5 Apr. 2016].
12. The subject-matter jurisdiction (jurisdiction ratione materiae) of the CCJA is limited. The CCJA can determine criminal issues only when such issues are connected to cases brought before it. The CCJA cannot issue penalty orders. Member States have exclusive jurisdiction to issue and enforce penal sanctions according to domestic criminal laws according to Arts 5 and 14(3) of OHADA Treaty. On this see CCJA, 3ème ch., n° 188/2015, 23-12-2015; P. n° 129/2012/PC du 24-09-2012: ADAMA COULIBALY c/ Procureur Général près la cour d'appel d'Abidjan, COULIBALY Dramane, Ohadata J-16-181 available at: www.ohada.com [accessed 5 Apr. 2016].
13. A clerical error or scrivener's error is an error resulting from a minor mistake or inadvertence, in writing or copying something on the record, and not from judicial reasoning or determination according to B. A. Garner (ed.), *Black's Law Dictionary* (9th ed., West Publishing, 2009). For example, the CCJA corrected a wrong date in its decision: CCJA, n° 015/2003, 1-7-2003: CI-TELCOM devenue Côte d'ivoire TELECOM c/ Sté PUBLISTAR, Le Juris-Ohada, n° 3/2003,

§2.02 ARBITRATION UNDER THE CCJA

The arbitration system under OHADA is twofold: there is a Uniform Act governing general arbitration proceedings where the seat of the arbitral tribunal is in any of the seventeen Member States,[14] and an institutional arbitration under the auspices of an Arbitration Centre that is part of the CCJA itself. The latter is governed by a different set of rules and the Uniform Act on Arbitration does not apply to it.[15] This section examines the institutional arbitration of OHADA under the auspices of the CCJA. It examines the nature of the CCJA as an arbitration institution (§2.02[A]) and its benefits and challenges (§2.02[B]).

[A] CCJA as an Arbitration Institution

The mission of the arbitration centre of the CCJA is to provide, in compliance with the Regulation on Arbitration, an arbitral solution to contractual disputes where the conditions set by the Treaty are met.[16] These conditions are that there must be a contract, to be performed or that is being performed totally or partially in one of the seventeen Member States of OHADA, or at least one of the parties is domiciled within the geographical area of OHADA; there must be a valid arbitration agreement.[17] This section briefly discusses the regulatory framework for CCJA arbitration (§2.02[A][1]),

juillet-septembre 2003, p. 38; Recueil de jurisprudence CCJA, n° 2, juillet-décembre 2003, p. 43; Ohadata J-04-109 available at: www.ohada.com [accessed 5 Apr. 2016]. The CCJA also overruled a decision which wrongfully ordered a winning party to pay costs in CCJA, Arrêt rectificatif n° 018/2007, 26-4-2007: OPCVN c/ SONIBANK, en presence de la CCA-Etat du Niger, Elhadj N. A., Recueil de Jurisprudence n° 9, Janvier-Juin 2007, p. 96; Ohadata J-08-235 available at: www.ohada.com [accessed 5 Apr. 2016]. An example of interpretation is of Art. 32 of the Uniform Act Organising Simplified Recovery Procedures and Measures of Execution in CCJA, n°2/2001, 11-10-2001: Epoux Karnib c/ SGBCI, Recueil de jurisprudence CCJA, n° spécial, janvier 2003, p. 37; Le Juris Ohada, n° 1/2002, janvier-mars 2002, p. 24. Penant n° 841, p. 538, Ohadata J-02-06, overruled by CCJA, N° 012/2003, 19-6-2003: SEHIC HOLLYWOOD S.A. c/ SGBC, Le Juris Ohada 3/2003, juillet-septembre 2003, p. 18; Recueil de Jurisprudence CCJA, n° 1, janvier-juin 2003, p. 13; Oadata J-04-104; available at: www.ohada.com [accessed 5 Apr. 2016].

14. Uniform Act on Arbitration of 11 Mar. 1999.
15. The CCJA clearly established, that the institutional arbitration mechanism under its auspices is governed exclusively by Arts 21-26 of the OHADA Treaty, the Regulation of Arbitration of the CCJA, the Rules of the CCJA on arbitration (Règlement intérieur de la CCJA en matière d'arbitrage), their annexes and the arbitration fees schedule of the Court in force at the date of the start of the arbitral proceedings. See, CCJA, ass. plén., n° 45, 17-7-2008: SONAPRA c./ SHB, Le Juris-Ohada, n° 4/2008, p. 60, Ohadata J-09-83, available at: www.ohada.com [accessed 5 Apr. 2016]. The CCJA has consistently maintained this position on the issue. See for examples, CCJA, Ass. plén., n° 102/2015, 15-10-2015; Req. n° 059/2014/PC, 27-03-2014: Léopold EKWA NGALLE, Mrs Hélène NJANJO NGALLE, Société Anonyme LEN HOLDING, Société International Business Corporation SA c/ Société Nationale d'Hydrocarbures (SNH), Personnel SNH, Ohadata J-16-95. CCJA, Ass. plén., n° 103/2015, 15-10-2015; Req. n° 093/2014/PC, 21-05-2014; Rec. n° 100/2014/PC, 30-05-2014: Société Benin Control SA c/ Etat du Bénin, Ohadata J-16-96. CCJA, Ass. plén., n° 139/2015 du 19 novembre 2015; Rec. n° 130/2014/PC du 25/07/2014: République de Guinée c/ GETMA International, Ohadata J-16-132, available at: www.ohada.com [accessed 5 Apr. 2016].
16. Article 2 of Rule on Arbitration.
17. Article 21 of OHADA Treaty.

certain provisions of CCJA arbitration rules (§2.02[A][2]), and grounds for annulment of CCJA arbitral awards (§2.02[A][3]).

[1] Regulatory Framework

In addition to Articles 21-26 of the OHADA Treaty, CCJA arbitration is also governed by the: Regulation on Arbitration before the CCJA, with its two Annexes, contained in Decision N° 004/99/CCJA of 3 February 1999 on Arbitration Fees and Decision N° 004/99/CM of 12 March 1999 approving the former one; the Rules of the CCJA on Arbitration; and the relevant provisions of the Regulation of proceedings before the CCJA.[18]

Pursuant to Article 1 of the Regulation on Arbitration, the CCJA, in its capacity as an arbitration institution, performs 'administrative duties' within the framework set by Article 21 of the OHADA Treaty. The decisions made by the Court in this regard, for the organization and smooth running of arbitration proceedings are administrative decisions, which do not have any res judicata effect. Such decisions are discretionary and need not be reasoned or justified, and cannot be appealed. It is important to emphasize the fact that the Court itself does not settle disputes submitted to CCJA arbitration, only the appointed arbitrators do.

[2] CCJA Arbitration Rules

To trigger arbitration under the CCJA Arbitration Rules, parties must have concluded a valid arbitration agreement. This refers to an agreement signed by duly authorized persons.[19] All signatories to the agreement are bound by it and it should refer any dispute to arbitration. Any court or judge seized of a matter covered by such agreement shall decline jurisdiction and refer the dispute to arbitration as agreed by the parties.[20] The CCJA has also admitted the possibility of an unwritten arbitration agreement.[21]

The seat of the arbitration can be freely agreed by the parties in the arbitration agreement or at a later stage. When the parties have not chosen the seat of the arbitration, the Court fixes the seat in a decision before transmitting the case file to the arbitral tribunal. If it becomes necessary, the appointed arbitrators can change the seat after consulting the parties.[22] There is no specific provision requiring the seat of the

18. See *Règlement n° 001/2014/CM du 30 janvier 2014 modifiant et complétant le Règlement de procédure de la Cour Commune de justice et d'Arbitrage du 18 avril 1996, et entré en vigueur le 4 février 2014 – J.O. OHADA n° spécial du 04-02-2014, pp. 228-240.*
19. For companies, it would be the Secretary or the person having the power to represent the company.
20. Article 23 of OHADA Treaty. This provision excludes situations where interim measures are sought under the agreement.
21. CCJA, Ass. plén., n° 020/2013, 18-4-2013: Société Inter Africaine de Distribution dite IAD c/ 1) Compagnie Malienne pour le Développement des Textiles dite CMDT; 2) Groupement des Syndicats de Producteurs de Coton et Vivriers du Mali dit GSCVM, Recueil de jurisprudence n° 20, vol. 2, janvier – décembre 2013, p. 104-109, Ohadata J-15-20, available at: www.ohada.com [accessed 5 Apr. 2016].
22. Article 10 of Regulation on Arbitration.

arbitration to be within the geographical area of OHADA, though this is highly recommended.[23] Practically, parties can agree a seat in a Member State of OHADA and ask the Court's authorization to hold hearings in a different location. Such place can be outside the geographical area of OHADA, since in this case, the juridical seat would not have been moved.

In appointing arbitrators, the parties can appoint a sole or three-member panel of arbitrators.[24] When there is a panel of three arbitrators, each party appoints one arbitrator of its choice and the two appointed arbitrators appoint the third, who usually serves as the chairperson of the panel. In case of disputes regarding the appointment of the arbitrators, the CCJA has the power to appoint the arbitrators. To assist the CCJA with its arbitrator appointment function, it maintains a list of arbitrators, which is reviewed on a yearly basis. In appointing their arbitrators, parties are free to choose arbitrators from outside the list of the Court. However, when the Court appoints arbitrators, it chooses from the list. The Court confirms for appointment all arbitrators nominated by the parties. In appointing arbitrators, the Court takes into account, the nationality of the parties and their place of residence, as well as those of their counsel and the arbitrators, the issues at stake in the dispute and possibly the law chosen by parties. When necessary, the Court may request expert advice before appointing the arbitrators.[25] No appeal may be filed against a decision made by the CCJA on the challenge of the nomination or appointment of an arbitrator.[26]

All appointed arbitrators must be and remain independent toward parties throughout the arbitral proceeding. Upon accepting their mission, the arbitrators must disclose to the Secretary General of the Court any fact or circumstance likely to affect his impartiality, including any bias or personal or financial interest in the result of the proceedings, as well as any past or current relationship with parties or their counsels.[27] The arbitrators can decide on their jurisdiction at any time in the arbitral proceedings, in accordance with the principles of Kompetenz-Kompetenz.[28]

Arbitrators sitting under the CCJA Arbitration rules can make interim orders to investigate, preserve or protect the rights of the parties.[29] Such interim measures can be granted exequatur by the Court if necessary.[30] Pursuant to Article 19 of the Regulation on Arbitration, the arbitral tribunal has the power to exercise its discretion in deciding what appropriate interim measures to order.[31]

---

23. This is to avoid jurisdictional challenge.
24. In most cases, a panel of three arbitrators is appointed.
25. Article 3 of Regulation on Arbitration.
26. Article 4 of Regulation on Arbitration. For a case clearly stressing this point, see CCJA, Ass. plén., n° 102/2015, 15-10-2015; Req. n° 059/2014/PC, 27-03-2014: Monsieur Léopold EKWA NGALLE, Madame Hélène NJANJO NGALLE, Société Anonyme LEN HOLDING, Société International Business Corporation SA c/ Société Nationale d'Hydrocarbures (SNH), Personnel SNH, Ohadata J-16-95, available at: www.ohada.com [accessed 5 Apr. 2016].
27. Article 4 of Regulation on Arbitration.
28. Article 21 of Regulation on Arbitration.
29. Article 19 of Regulation on Arbitration.
30. Article 10.5 of Regulation on Arbitration.
31. See CCJA, Ass. plén., n° 098/2014 du 30 octobre 2014; P Rec. n°128/2012/PC du 20/09/2012: SCP PYRAMIDION c/ Agence d'Exécution des Travaux d'Infrastructure du Mali dite AGETIER-Mali, Ohadata J-15-189, available at: www.ohada.com [accessed 5 Apr. 2016].

After the hearings, the arbitral tribunal produces its award. Before the award is notified to the parties, the arbitrators must submit it to the Court for scrutiny. This is a formal review (not on the merit) process. The Court scrutinizes all awards including those settling jurisdictional issues, partial and final awards. In this scrutiny process, the Court can only suggest formal amendments to the text, if needed, and then provide some guidelines to the arbitrators on cost awards and sets the fees of the arbitrators.[32]

[3] Annulment of CCJA Awards

One of the most important features of CCJA is the interaction between its functions as a supranational court and as an arbitration institution. This section discusses the jurisdiction of the CCJA to annul awards made under its arbitration institution rules. After the arbitral award is notified to the parties, the losing party may challenge the award before the CCJA. At this stage, the Court will no longer be acting under its arbitral jurisdiction but under in its judicial role. When the enforcement of an arbitral award is challenged before it, the Court presides in plenary session.[33] The Regulation on Arbitration provides four grounds on which a CCJA arbitral award may be annulled. These are where: there was no valid arbitration agreement, the arbitrators ruled outside the scope of their mission, there was no adversarial proceeding, and the award violates international public policy.[34] Where any one of these grounds is proved, the CCJA will annul the arbitral award.

The consent of a party to refer a dispute to institutional arbitration under the auspices of the CCJA cannot be presumed. Nothing in the legal framework of the CCJA allows presumption of a party's consent to arbitration. This is such a fundamental basis of CCJA arbitration that a party's lack of objection to the arbitration cannot be construed as a waiver of the requirement of express consent. In a challenge where the defendant alleged verbal consent but provided no evidence of the verbal consent, and the arbitral tribunal proceeded to assert jurisdiction, the CCJA held that the arbitral tribunal acted without a valid arbitration agreement and its award was annulled.[35]

A CCJA award will be annulled where equity and proper administration of justice are not observed. This is to avoid denial of justice and subsequent legal uncertainty, since an arbitral tribunal necessarily hears and settles a dispute that will not be heard any state court. This is on the fact of the dispute being covered by an arbitration agreement which basically removes jurisdiction from national courts.[36]

32. Article 23 of Regulation on Arbitration.
33. This is different from the panel (usually of three judges) that perform the administrative functions assigned to the Court under its Arbitration Regulations.
34. Article 30.6 of Regulation on Arbitration.
35. CCJA, Ass. plén., n° 039/2014 du 17 avril 2014; Rec. cont. val. sent. arb. n° 095/2013/PC du 26/07/2013: Etat du Mali c/ Société CFAO, Ohadata J-15-130, available at: www.ohada.com [accessed 5 Apr. 2016].
36. CCJA, Ass. plén., n° 020/2013, 18-4-2013: Société Inter Africaine de Distribution dite IAD c/ 1) Compagnie Malienne pour le Développement des Textiles dite CMDT; 2) Groupement des Syndicats de Producteurs de Coton et Vivriers du Mali dit GSCVM, Recueil de jurisprudence n° 20, vol. 2, janvier – décembre 2013, pp. 104-109, Ohadata J-15-20, available at: www.ohada.com [accessed 5 Apr. 2016].

The CCJA will also annul an arbitral award where the arbitrators fail to comply with their mission as contained in the arbitration agreement. The mission of the arbitrator is also contained in the claims and demands of the parties, as presented in the record of the arbitral proceedings.[37] Where an arbitral tribunal was asked to decide whether there was a wrongful termination of a contract, and after analysing the contract decided that the defendant did not breach the contract, the CCJA held that arguments of the parties and the evidence presented showed that the arbitral tribunal complied with its mission.[38] It is however noted that the mere breach by the arbitrators of their mission is not enough to review the merits of the dispute. This only allows the CCJA to check whether the arbitrators have complied with their mission on the grounds upon which the award is challenged since, the arbitrators have a discretion in assessing the facts of the case.[39]

The arbitral award can also be annulled where the adversarial process is not followed by the arbitral tribunal. Compliance with the principle of adversarial proceedings requires that each party is allowed, not only to present his own evidence and arguments, but also to respond to the facts and evidence presented by the other party. Adversarial proceedings do not however require that the arbitrator allow the same time to all parties for the same demands. The CCJA has held that the refusal to appoint an expert cannot constitute a breach of the principle of adversarial proceedings.[40] In the same position is the situation where a party having agreed the schedule of proceedings, failed to produce its evidence within the allocated time.[41] Also, where in a majority decision, the minority arbitrator appended his dissenting opinion to the award signed by the two arbitrators; there was no breach of the adversarial proceeding.[42] Finally, the arbitral award may be set aside if it violates international public policy,[43] but not for violation of the law or conflicting reasons in an award.[44]

---

37. Article 15 Regulation of Arbitration.
38. CCJA, Ass. plén., n° 098/2014 du 30 octobre 2014; Rec. n° 128/2012/PC du 20/09/2012: SCP PYRAMIDION c/ Agence d'Exécution des Travaux d'Infrastructure du Mali dite AGETIER-Mali, Ohadata J-15-189, available at: www.ohada.com [accessed 5 Apr. 2016].
39. CCJA, Ass. plén., n° 033/2015 du 23 avril 2015; Rec. n° 011/2014/PC du 24/01/2014: ETAT DU MALI c/ Société Groupe TOMOTA S.A., Ohadata J-16-33, available at: www.ohada.com [accessed 5 Apr. 2016].
40. CCJA, Ass. plén., n° 033/2015 du 23 avril 2015; Rec. n° 011/2014/PC du 24/01/2014: ETAT DU MALI c/ Société Groupe TOMOTA S.A., Ohadata J-16-33, available at: www.ohada.com [accessed 5 Apr. 2016].
41. CCJA, Ass. plén., n° 098/2014 du 30 octobre 2014; P Rec. en cont. de val. de sent. Arb. n°128/2012/PC du 20/09/2012: SCP PYRAMIDION c/ Agence d'Exécution des Travaux d'Infrastructure du Mali dite AGETIER-Mali, Ohadata J-15-189, available at: www.ohada.com [accessed 5 Apr. 2016].
42. CCJA, Ass. plén., n° 098/2014 du 30 octobre 2014; P Rec. en cont. de val. de sent. Arb. n°128/2012/PC du 20/09/2012: SCP PYRAMIDION c/ Agence d'Exécution des Travaux d'Infrastructure du Mali dite AGETIER-Mali, Ohadata J-15-189, available at: www.ohada.com [accessed 5 Apr. 2016].
43. CCJA, Ass. plén., n° 098/2014 du 30 octobre 2014; P Rec. en cont. de val. de sent. Arb. n°128/2012/PC du 20/09/2012: SCP PYRAMIDION c/ Agence d'Exécution des Travaux d'Infrastructure du Mali dite AGETIER-Mali, Ohadata J-15-189, available at: www.ohada.com [accessed 5 Apr. 2016].
44. CCJA, Ass. plén., n° 102/2015, 15-10-2015; Req. n° 059/2014/PC, 27-03-2014: Monsieur Léopold EKWA NGALLE, Madame Hélène NJANJO NGALLE, Société Anonyme LEN HOLDING,

[B] Benefits and Challenges of CCJA Arbitration

This section briefly discusses the benefits (§2.02[B][1]) and challenges (§2.02[B][1]) of the dualist nature of CCJA in two sections.

[1] Benefits of CCJA Arbitration

There are usually several advantages of institutional arbitration, such as reference to a pre-established set of arbitration rules to guide the arbitral proceeding; and provision of a list of individuals with requisite expertise to act as arbitrators and from which parties may choose their arbitrators. One of the common benefits of institutional arbitration is the predictability of costs. Any party planning to submit a claim to the arbitration centre of the court will have an overview of the costs the procedure will incur, both in terms of administrative fees[45] and arbitrators' fees, depending on the amount of the claim. The CCJA maintains a fee schedule which is publicly available.[46]

In the interest of the parties, the fees and expenses of the arbitrators are exclusively set by the Court in compliance with the fee schedule of the Regulation on Arbitration and any separate agreement between the arbitrators and the parties is null and void.[47] The Court strictly complies with these rules on fees. It recently annulled an award rendered by a panel of three arbitrators who deliberately ignored the fee schedule, on the ground that the panel has not complied with its mission.[48] In its decision, the Court noted that the rules governing the fees for institutional arbitration are intended to ensure that parties who have agreed to submit their disputes to arbitration by the Court, pay fees that are proportional to the actual value of their disputes and that are determined on a scale known in advance, stressing again the predictability of costs.[49] It is worth noting, however, that under exceptional circumstances and if necessary, the Court (and only the Court) may authorize an increase in fees of the arbitrators and decide the amount.[50]

Société International Business Corporation SA c/ Société Nationale d'Hydrocarbures (SNH), Personnel SNH, Ohadata J-16-95, available at: www.ohada.com [accessed 5 Apr. 2016].

45. Administrative fees are the fees payable to the Court itself for managing the arbitral proceedings.
46. The Fee Schedule is available upon demand from the Arbitration Centre of the CCJA. It will also be available on the revised official website of OHADA, the release of which is expected for 1 May 2016. See also Barthélemy Mercadal, Mahutodji Jimmy Vital Kodo et al., *Code Pratique Francis Lefebvre OHADA: Traité, Actes uniformes et Règlements annotés* 126-127 (2nd ed., Editions Francis Lefebvre, 2014).
47. See on Art. 9 of the Regulation on Arbitration Decision N° 004/99/CCJA of 3 Feb. 1999 on CCJA Arbitration Fees, an Annex to the Regulation on Arbitration. See CCJA, Ass. plén., n° 139/2015, 19-11-2015; Rec. n° 130/2014/PC du 25/07/2014: République de Guinée c/ GETMA International, Ohadata J-16-132, available at: www.ohada.com [accessed 5 Apr. 2016].
48. CCJA, Ass. plén., n° 139/2015, 19-11-2015; Rec. n° 130/2014/PC du 25/07/2014: République de Guinée c/ GETMA International, Ohadata J-16-132, available at: www.ohada.com [accessed 5 Apr. 2016].
49. *Ibid.*
50. Article 24.3 of Regulation on Arbitration.

Since 2010 when the revised OHADA Treaty came into force,[51] all the four official languages of the Member States (French, English, Spanish and Portuguese) became the working languages of OHADA.[52] The new Article 42 of the Treaty provides that before their translation into English, Spanish and Portuguese, all the documents already published in French are fully enforceable, and where there is a difference between the French version and one of the other languages, the French version will prevail. The Treaty and some of the Uniform Acts have been unofficially translated into the English language and is widely used.[53] This situation raises some organizational and conceptual problems, because of prevalence of French in the Treaty.[54] Although the Court has already ruled that documents submitted by a party in any of the four official languages are valid.[55]

The most distinguishing part of CCJA arbitration is the ease of enforcement of its awards. This is because once the CCJA grants exequatur of the award it is valid in all seventeen Member States of OHADA. This is not the same position with arbitral awards made under the Uniform Arbitration Act (UAA). Such UAA awards are still subject to the regular enforcement proceedings at both national and regional courts.[56]

[2] Challenges of CCJA Arbitration

The CCJA also faces various challenges in performing its duties, such as organizational and financial weaknesses. However, there is a recurring issue linked to its dual nature.

51. Newsletter of OHADA of 4 Mar. 2010 at: www.ohada.com/newsletter.php?news = 04032010-848# [accessed 5 Apr. 2016].
52. Article 42 of the 2008 revised version of OHADA Treaty.
53. While this paper was being finalized, we were notified of the launch of the official translation of OHADA laws into the English language.
54. As Martha Simo Tumnde puts it:

> Implicitly, any document in English or any other language would be a translation from French to English or Spanish or Portuguese. Most of the texts in translation have been criticised for being literal, inadequate and rather nebulous. They are simply approximations, and in many cases there are no legal equivalents in English. There is a need for co-drafting of future OHADA Uniform Acts in order to avoid translation. Furthermore, it would be desirable to have a co-revision team to work together on the existing Uniform Acts. This team should employ contextual meanings of terminologies and the adaptation approach to translation. Member States should develop an OHADA lexicon of words, phrases and concepts. This would go a long way clarifying the misunderstandings of legal jargons and terminologies.

M. S. Tumnde, *OHADA as Experienced in Cameroon: Addressing Areas of Particular Concern to Common Law Jurists*, in C. Dickerson Moore (ed.), *Unified Business Law for Africa: Common Law Perspectives on OHADA*, *supra*, 72 (GMB Publishing, 2009).
55. See CCJA, 3ème ch., n° 31, 6-12-2011: Sté TRIGON ENERGY LTD c/ BANQUE COMMERCIALE DU SAHEL (BCS SA), Juris Ohada, 2011, n° 4, oct.-déc., n° 4, p. 28, Ohadata J-13-12, where the Court ruled that an English document submitted to the Court by a party cannot be set aside because it has not been translated into French.
56. It is worth remembering that a challenge to an award governed by the Uniform Act on Arbitration will go through the national judicial system (first instance and appeal, depending on each Member State's internal judiciary) before reaching the CCJA for a final appeal that will be binding and enforceable in all the seventeen Member States.

The Court if too often 'accused' of being judge and party when it comes to arbitration. Some commentators, such as Maury, argue that the Court should not act as arbitration centre and then as court of justice when CCJA awards are challenged.[57] With regard to this alleged bias of the CCJA, a careful reading of the provisions of the Regulation on Arbitration[58] and the Rules of Arbitration,[59] clearly show that the Court: administers arbitral proceedings and creates restricted panels in charge of arbitration;[60] takes administrative decisions in that capacity, devoid of any res judicata effect; does not itself settle disputes;[61] and that processes have been designed to prevent members of the Court from being directly involved in arbitration proceedings. It follows from the foregoing that the Court, as a judicial body ruling on challenges to arbitral awards, is different from the Court as an arbitration Centre organizing and administering arbitral proceedings. Various high courts within OHADA Member States recognize this distinction of the CCJA.[62]

§2.03 CCJA AS A SUPRANATIONAL ARBITRATION INSTITUTION

This section examines whether the model of the CCJA Arbitration Centre should be adopted in other regions of Africa. This is in the light of the African Union Commission General Counsel's call for a pan-African continental Court of Arbitration for Africa.[63] There are several arguments in favour of establishing regional centres on the model of the CCJA (§2.03[A]); but some conditions will need to be met and some challenges will need to be overcome for such initiative to be efficient (§2.03[B]).

57. F. Maury, *Guinée. Ces honoraires qui coûtent très chers à GETMA*, Jeune Afrique. Online: http://www.jeuneafrique.com/mag/292443/economie/guinee-honoraires-coutent-tres-cher-a-getma/ [accessed 9 Mar. 2016]. For more details, see F. Maury, *Port de Guinée. la condamnation de la Guinée annulée*, available at: http://www.jeuneafrique.com/283427/societe/port-de-conakry-la-condamnation-de-la-guinee-annulee/ [accessed 9 Mar. 2016]. See also, Affaire GETMA-Guinée. Les arbotres respondent, available at: http://www.jeuneafrique.com/285543/societe/affaire-getma-guinee-les-arbitres-repondent/ [accessed 9 Mar. 2016].
58. For example, Art. 1 and Art. 2 of the Regulation on Arbitration.
59. For example, Arts 2.5, 2.6, 3.1, and 3.2 of the Rules of Arbitration.
60. Usually there are two panels of three judges of the Court.
61. Not only the Court does not rule on the merits of arbitration cases, but it does not even interfere with the arbitrators, even when it performs the formal review of the draft of arbitral awards before they are signed and notified to the parties. Pursuant to Art. 29.5 of the Regulation on Arbitration, the Court reviews the cases and rule on the merits only where a challenge to an award has been successful (i.e., when the award has been annulled) and only if both parties ask for that de novo review.
62. See the following decisions: *Cass. ass. plén. 6-11-1998, Guillotel c/ Sté Castel, 2e espèce, JCP.1998.II.10198 rapport P. Sargos; D.1999.1.concl. J.-Fr. Burgelin*; CEDH *25 juillet 2000, Tierce c/ Saint-Marin, D. 2001.339 et chron. C. Goyet, Remarques sur l'impartialité du tribunal, D. 2001.328; Cass.* 1e civ. 11-3-2009 n° 08-12.149, de Premont: D. 2009.880.som. obs. X. Delpech; GP 2009.1309 note G. Huchet; PA 2009 n° 144 p. 20 note C. Tse; JCP E 2009.1781.chr. n° 10 obs. C. Seraglini.
63. This call was made at the SOAS/AU Addis Ababa arbitration conference on 'The Role of Arbitration Institutions in the Development of Arbitration in Africa', 23 Jul. 2015.

[A] Justification for CCJA-Type Arbitration Institutions in Africa

The main reasons for creating dispute resolution centres on the model of the CCJA within the continent can be drawn from the advantages of institutional arbitration generally, the CCJA's unique exequatur system and the far-reaching scope of its jurisdiction.

As already mentioned above, the most important benefit of the CCJA arbitration system is the ability to seek enforcement of the award before the CCJA and with that one order pursue execution in all Member States. This makes the arbitration system cost and time effective. Creation of one or more similar systems on the continent, whether at regional level such as for ECOWAS or with a wider scope on the continent will be more than useful in attracting more users for such dispute resolution centres.

It will also be more reassuring to investors operating on the continent since there will be fewer jurisdictions involved in the arbitral process. It will save time and money for an investor to know that when a dispute arises, they will be dealing with one arbitration centre, with a unique arbitration system and an award coming out of that system will be enforceable in a wide geographical area after a simple exequatur process.

The second reason is that following the OHADA model, the CCJA is not a national court system, but a regional one. The judges serving on the Court are not regarded as national judges representing or serving the interests of the country of which they are citizens. This can be an additional warranty of their independence. For maximum effectiveness, the decisions from such a regional court must have res judicata effect.

[B] Conditions to Be Satisfied

We have identified seven issues for consideration in the creation of CCJA-like arbitration centres, for further examination.

First, appropriate measures must be in place to ensure enforcement of the decisions of such a centre. This is because one recurring issue in most African jurisdictions when it comes to efficiency of justice is enforcement of decisions and awards. Second, there must be a valid exequatur system recognized by many countries available. This is of utmost importance in order to create an efficient supranational jurisdiction in Africa. There are some legislations, such as the General Judicial Cooperation Convention, known as the Tananarive Convention, of 12 September 1961, which governs relations of judicial cooperation between African States. It is not clear whether such conventions still apply within the continent. Thus, it would be important to create a clear judicial cooperation mechanism, at least by an exequatur such as the one of the CCJA where once an award is final and is granted exequatur of the President of the Court; it can be enforced in any Member State with no further proceedings. Third, it may be useful to link such regional courts with the African Court of Human Rights (ACHR), after all African States will have ratified the Court's Protocol. This is because of the universal scope of the ACHR jurisdiction.[64] Doing so may make it possible for a party to seek and obtain remedies where a regional court takes too long before rendering a decision in a case submitted to it. Fourth, such regional centres/courts must operate in the many official languages used across African countries.[65] Fifth, such centre must have capable and well-qualified personnel. For arbitration centres to succeed on the Continent there is need for careful selection and training of all the people involved: arbitrators, attorneys, employees of the arbitration centres as well as judges that are likely to review arbitral awards. It would therefore be appropriate to design a training programme that would encompass all aspects of arbitral proceedings, taking into account peculiarities of all major legal systems for all these persons. It may also be necessary to include a mandatory requirement in their rules that at least one arbitrator of each tribunal (where parties have chosen three arbitrators) shall be an African professional. Sixth, the centres must also be properly equipped with state-of-art facilities. Arbitration is a business that needs to be properly marketed and require these to compete in the current international arbitral market. Finally, such centres must be properly and sustainably funded, at least at the outset until they reach the stage of financial autonomy.

CONCLUSION

This chapter analysed the dualist nature of the CCJA as a supranational court and arbitration centre within the OHADA area. It highlights the contribution of CCJA arbitration to the transformation of arbitration within OHADA and notes that there are currently many arbitration centres on the African continent, some countries hosting several of them. It may therefore be useful to merge some centres or to create few regional arbitration centres. In choosing that course, this chapter suggests that the CCJA of OHADA may be a good source of inspiration in the creation of such regional centres, provided that appropriate measures are taken in their design and location, so as to avoid simply duplicating centres that may not be operated efficiently.

---

64. See: http://www.achpr.org/about/afchpr/ [accessed 7 Apr. 2016].
65. It is important to stress on the language issue since it is still not solved in all jurisdictions. For example, although OHADA has now four official languages (English, French, Portuguese and Spanish), French is still the dominant language and no official translation of the Uniform Acts and the Treaty exist; unofficial translations of some of those statutes do exist, however and are being used. We have been informed that an official translation of the statutes into English has been ordered by the Permanent Secretary of OHADA and is currently being done. Also, there seems to be steps toward effective use of OHADA official languages since the consultant that has just been selected by the Permanent Secretary to revise the arbitration rules of OHADA (both institutional and ad hoc) with funding of the World Bank has undertaken to translate the draft of the revised texts into the four official languages, this requirement having been included in the terms and conditions of the agreement with the Permanent Secretary. It is expected that future new legal instruments of OHADA would be drafted in all the four languages.

Chapter 3
The Cairo Regional Arbitration Centre

Mohamed Abdel Raouf & Dalia Hussein

INTRODUCTION

Prior to the establishment of new regional arbitral institutions in Africa, the users from the continent had very few available arbitral fora to which disputes arising out of their business transactions could be referred. Such fora were located in main European cities, usually one in which at least one of the parties to the said transaction was located. The location of the arbitration was usually not where the contract was performed. In other words, while some of the parties to business transactions involving parties from Africa were located in jurisdictions where reputable arbitral institutions already existed, African parties had no option but to offer litigation before their national courts, which, was not considered appropriate in the context of international contracts. This situation resulted in a sort of imbalance especially during the negotiation phase of business transactions. As African economies continued their dynamic economic growth, largely driven by cross-border trade and investment, the prospects of an increasing number of disputes became inevitable and hence the need to make institutional arbitration available and easily accessible. At the same time, the world witnessed a rising trend towards regionalism in arbitration. This was in light of the expansion of arbitration as an acceptable means to resolve commercial disputes.

This chapter examines the question of how regional arbitration institutions in Africa can contribute to the transformation of arbitration in the continent. It will examine the role of the Cairo Regional Centre for International Commercial Arbitration (Cairo Regional Centre) in this transformation agenda. This general question will require the examination of how these institutions can gain the confidence of users of arbitration and serve particularly the needs of African users drawing from the experience of the Cairo Regional Centre. To answer these questions, this chapter will discuss the vision of the Asian-African Legal Consultative Organisation (AALCO) of creating regional centres for arbitration in Africa (§3.01); the growth of arbitration under the Cairo Regional Centre (§3.02); and the need for closer cooperation and sharing of experience between African arbitral institutions (§3.03). This chapter concludes that, on the basis of the experience of the Cairo Regional Centre, arbitral institutions play a significant role in the promotion and development of arbitration as a means for dispute settlement and as a way to enhance the rule of law in Africa.

§3.01 AALCO AND ITS REGIONAL ARBITRAL CENTRES IN AFRICA

The trend towards regionalism mentioned above was confirmed by a survey conducted in 2010 by the Queen Mary School of International Arbitration.[1] The survey found that, in addition to the importance of the legal infrastructure in the choice of the place of arbitration, the location, language, culture, knowledge of the applicable procedures and connections with lawyers in the jurisdiction (what we may call 'familiarity') are major factors in the success, and therefore, the necessity, of regional institutions. In a continent with multiple cultures, languages, religions, legal systems and ethnicities, the establishment and the role of regional arbitration institutions is of major importance.

Before this trend towards regionalism became noticeable, the AALCO, originally known as the Asian Legal Consultative Committee (ALCC),[2] understood the necessity of creating arbitral institutions in two major continents of the world which lacked, at the time, regional institutions. In 1978, AALCO, within its programme in the economic field, launched its Integrated Scheme for the Settlement of Disputes in Economic and Commercial Transactions. Pursuant to that Scheme, AALCO decided to establish regional arbitration centres under its auspices, which would function as international institutions with the objectives of promoting international commercial arbitration in the Asian-African regions and providing for the conduct of international arbitrations under the auspices of such centres. It was at this time that the Kuala Lumpur Regional

1. Queen Mary University of London School of International Arbitration and White & Case LLP, 2010 *International Arbitration Survey: Choices in International Arbitration* 17, (2010) available at: http://www.arbitration.qmul.ac.uk/docs/123290.pdf, [accessed on 20 Apr. 2016].
2. AALCO was constituted on 15 Nov. 1956. It is considered to be a tangible outcome of the historic Bandung Conference, held in Indonesia, in April 1955. Seven Asian States, namely Burma (now Myanmar), Ceylon (now Sri Lanka), India, Indonesia, Iraq, Japan, and the United Arab Republic (now Arab Republic of Egypt and Syrian Arab Republic) are the original Member States. Later, in April 1958, in order to include participation of countries of the continent of Africa its name was changed to Asian-African Legal Consultative Committee (AALCC). At the 40th Session, held at the Headquarters of AALCC in New Delhi, in 2001, the name of the Committee was again changed to its current name, the Asian-African Legal Consultative Organization. AALCO membership is currently composed of forty-seven Asian and African States. These countries are: Arab Republic of Egypt; Bahrain; Bangladesh; Brunei Darussalam; Botswana; Cameroon; Cyprus; Democratic People's Republic of Korea; Gambia; Ghana; India; Indonesia; Iraq; Islamic Republic of Iran; Japan; Jordan; Kenya; Kuwait; Lebanon; Libya; Malaysia; Mauritius; Mongolia; Myanmar; Nepal; Nigeria; Oman; Pakistan; People's Republic of China; Qatar; Republic of Korea; Saudi Arabia; Senegal; Sierra Leone; Singapore; Somalia; South Africa, Sri Lanka; State of Palestine; Sudan; Syria; Tanzania; Thailand; Turkey; Uganda; United Arab Emirates; and Republic of Yemen. Among the purposes and objectives of AALCO as stipulated in Art. 1 of its Statutes is to serve as an advisory body to its Member States in the field of international law and as a forum for Asian-African co-operation in legal matters of common concern.

Centre for Arbitration (KLRCA) and the Cairo Regional Centre for International Commercial Arbitration (Cairo Regional Centre) were established in 1978 and 1979, respectively. Subsequently, three other centres were established under the auspices of AALCO in Lagos (Nigeria), Tehran (Islamic Republic of Iran) and Nairobi (Kenya). The respective host governments recognize the independent status of the regional centres like an international organization and accord to them relevant privileges and immunities.

Owing to AALCO's vision, the creation of arbitration centres in Africa made institutional arbitration accessible to African users. Over the past decade, the reluctance of such users to resort to arbitration has dramatically changed. The number and size of international commercial arbitration cases involving African parties has also increased. This is the case not only before the centres located in Africa, but also under the auspices of those existing in Europe. This confirms the positive impact of the emergence of reliable arbitration centres on increasing the confidence of users in arbitration in general and institutional arbitration in particular. Despite the foregoing, the majority of arbitrations that involve at least one African party still take place in arbitration centres located outside the continent, and the choice of African arbitrators is very limited. For example, while the number of African parties involved in arbitration cases before the ICC and the LCIA increased over the last decade, the number of cases administered by some African institutions remains very few.[3] Despite these figures, the IBA report released in September 2015 notes that regional arbitral institutions in Africa are expected to expand over the next five to ten years, if they succeed in gaining the confidence of users, get the needed experience, and of course, if the legal framework in the states where they are located is favourable to arbitration.[4]

§3.02 THE GROWTH OF ARBITRATION UNDER THE CAIRO REGIONAL CENTRE

This section examines the growth of arbitration under the Cairo Regional Centre. It gives a brief background of the Centre (§3.02[A]); its arbitration rules (§3.02[B]); neutrality and transparency of its arbitral process (§3.02[C]); affordability and predictability of its costs (§3.02[D]); and how the Centre ensures diversity and fair representation of the countries in its region in its activities (§3.02[E]).

3. J. Bentham & B. Woodd-Walker, *The Rise of Arbitration in Africa* (Simmons & Simmons, Power Point Presentation dated 10 Dec. 2015), available at: http://www.elexica.com/~/media/Files/Training/2015/12%20December/The%20Rise%20of%20Arbitration%20in%20Africa.pdf [accessed 9 Apr. 2016] stated. 'The number of African parties involved in ICC arbitrations has more than doubled in 10 years. The number of Africa-related cases in the LCIA has risen from 2 in 2004 to 30 in 2013.' This is a contrast to the number of cases administered by African institutions: 'The Kigali International Arbitration Centre registered 13 cases between June 2013 and June 2014, The Cairo Regional Centre for International Commercial Arbitration reports a new record for purely international cases in 2014, but none appear to involve cases from sub-Saharan Africa'. See also IBA Report, *The Current State and Future of International Arbitration: Regional Perspectives- IBA Arb 40 Subcommittee*, 20-21 Sep. 2015.
4. IBA Report, *The Current State and Future of International Arbitration: Regional Perspectives- IBA Arb 40 Subcommittee*, 12, 20 Sep. 2015.

[A] Brief Background of the Cairo Regional Centre

The Cairo Regional Centre was established in 1979 through an international agreement signed between the Egyptian Government and AALCO.[5] The Centre is an independent non-profit international organization enjoying all the privileges and immunities of an independent international organization in Egypt and is endowed with juridical personality. The objectives of Centre as announced by AALCO during the Doha Session in 1978 are to: promote international commercial arbitration in the Asian and African regions; provide arbitration services; render assistance in the conduct of ad hoc arbitrations, particularly those held under the UNCITRAL Arbitration Rules; coordinate and assist the activities of existing arbitral institutions in the two regions; and assist parties in the enforcement of arbitral awards.

The Centre is governed by a Board of Trustees (BoT) whose current composition reflects its nature as both an international and regional organization.[6] The management of the Centre reposes in its Director who is its duly authorized representative. The Director runs its activities and carries out the tasks assigned thereto under the Arbitration Rules of the Centre. The Director is supported by the Deputy Director, legal advisors, and the following departments: the Dispute Management Department; the Conferences and External Relations Department; the Financial and Administrative Departments; and the Information Technology Department. The Centre also has an Advisory Committee which is appointed by the Director from among the BoT members as well as other eminent African, Asian and European specialists and experts in arbitration.[7]

The Cairo Regional Centre provides a system for dispute settlement for parties engaged in trade, commerce and investment. It provides case management services and administers international and domestic arbitrations and other ADR mechanisms according to its Rules.[8] The Centre also provides administrative and technical assistance to parties involved in ad hoc arbitrations; advises disputants on dispute resolution processes; organizes conferences and seminars on dispute resolution including relevant publications; conducts academic and empirical research and studies in dispute resolution, and maintains a comprehensive library for materials in arbitration and general ADR. To ensure the excellent conduct of these services, the Centre has developed and renovated both its hearing and conference centres with a panoramic view of the Nile.[9]

5. Copy of the Agreement is available at: http://www.crcica.org [accessed 19 Apr. 2016].
6. The BoT consists of a chairman and twenty eminent members currently from Egypt, Saudi Arabia, Jordan, Lebanon, Qatar, Germany, United Kingdom, Spain, France, Japan, Somalia and Nigeria. For further details see: http://crcica.org.eg/boardoftrustees.html [accessed 20 Apr. 2016].
7. The Advisory Committee currently has fifteen members from France, Jordan, Lebanon, Switzerland/Iraq, and Egypt. For further details see: http://crcica.org.eg/org_advisorycommittee.html [accessed 20 Apr. 2016].
8. The Centre has Arbitration Rules and a separate set of Rules for Mediation.
9. The new hearing centre includes three hearing rooms (with one named after the late Dr Mohamed Aboul-Enein, the former Director of the Centre), two break-out rooms, two lounges, one technical room, one translation room, one reception and one terrace. The conference centre includes one auditorium (named after Dr Esmat Abdel Meguid, the former Secretary-General of the League of

[B] Cairo Regional Centre Arbitration Rules

The arbitration rules of an arbitral institution are undoubtedly its main product based on which users decide to arbitrate under its auspices. The more familiar the users are with such rules, the easier the selection is made. The Cairo Regional Centre has also systematically updated its Arbitration Rules to bring it in conformity with developments in international arbitration practice. This section will briefly discuss the salient features of the latest Arbitration Rules of the Centre which has been in force since 2011. It is important to note that arbitration under the auspices of the Centre is of a flexible, simplified nature, allowing for expeditious and inexpensive resolution of disputes.

The Arbitration Rules of the Centre grant the parties a great deal of autonomy in, *inter alia*, the conduct of the proceedings of arbitration, in the choice of the arbitrators, the place and language of the arbitration and the applicable laws to the dispute. From its establishment, The Centre adopted, with minor modifications, the 1976 UNCITRAL Arbitration Rules[10] which has been through five amendments leading up to the current Arbitration Rules which became effective on 1 March 2011.[11] The current Rules are based on the revised 2010 UNCITRAL Arbitration Rules, with minor modifications which takes into account the Centre's role as an arbitral institution and an appointing authority. This 2011 Arbitration Rules serves four basic purposes. First, it guarantees collegial decision-making with respect to several vital procedural matters, including the ability of a proposed arbitrator to reject his or her appointment, as well as the removal and the challenge of arbitrators. Second, it seeks to modernize the Rules and to promote greater efficiency in arbitral proceedings. Third, it fills in a few gaps that have become apparent over the years. Finally, it adjusts the original tables of costs to ensure more transparency in the determination of the arbitrators' fees.

Article 6 of the Rules makes it possible for the Centre to decide (upon the approval of the Advisory Committee) not to proceed with an arbitration if it manifestly lacks jurisdiction over the dispute. Such decision will be taken prima facie following the respondent's response to the notice of arbitration.

Article 7 of the Rules retains the default position of having three arbitrators if the parties fail to agree on the use of a sole arbitrator. However, it provides more flexibility. Specifically, the Centre may now appoint a sole arbitrator if one of the parties requests appointment of a sole arbitrator provided the appointment of a sole arbitrator is 'more appropriate' in the circumstances of the case. Pursuant to paragraph 5 of Article 8 of the

---

Arab States and the honorary Chairman of the BoT), three break-out rooms, one reading room, one lounge and a refreshment area. For more details see Cairo Regional Centre Annual Report, 2015, p. 6 available at: http://crcica.org.eg/publication/annual/pdf/English/15/CRCICA_ANNUAL_REPORT_2015.pdf [accessed 20 Apr. 2016].

10. UNCITRAL Arbitration Rules, approved by the UN General Assembly by Resolution No. 31/98 of 15 Dec. 1976. This was revised in 2010 with text available at: https://www.uncitral.org/pdf/english/texts/arbitration/arb-rules-revised/arb-rules-revised-2010-e.pdf [accessed 20 Apr. 2016].
11. Cairo Regional Centre Arbitration Rules of 1998 was modified in 2000, 2002, 2007 and 2011.

Rules, the Centre may (upon the approval of the Advisory Committee) reject the appointment of any arbitrator due to the lack of any legal or contractual requirement or past failure to comply with his or her duties. The arbitrator in question and the parties should be given the opportunity to express their views before this decision is taken. Article 10 of the Rules regulates the appointment of arbitrators in multiparty arbitrations. It provides that, where multiple parties are unable to agree upon the constitution of the tribunal, any party may request the Centre to constitute the tribunal. In such circumstances, the Centre may revoke any appointment already made and appoint or reappoint each of the arbitrators and designate one of them as the presiding arbitrator. Pursuant to Article 12 of the Rules, an arbitrator may, at the request of a party and by virtue of a decision from an impartial and independent tripartite ad hoc committee to be composed by the Centre from among the members of the Advisory Committee, be removed in the event that he or she fails to act or in the event of a de jure or de facto impossibility of performing their functions, or in the event that they deliberately delay the commencement or the continuation of the arbitral proceedings.

Article 13 of the Rules includes an innovation according to which a timeline is added for disposing of any arbitrator challenges.[12] Paragraph 2 of Article 14 of the Rules provides for a particularly noteworthy change. Under the said paragraph, in exceptional circumstances the Centre can deprive a party of its right to appoint a substitute arbitrator and may either appoint the substitute arbitrator itself or, after the closure of the hearings, authorize the other arbitrators to proceed with the arbitration and make any decision or award. This new provision was included to deal with 'strategic' resignations. It is the first time the Rules have permitted truncated tribunals.

Article 17 of the Rules now permits the joinder of third parties to arbitrations if they are parties to the arbitration agreement. Under Article 26 of the Rules, the tribunal's powers relating to interim measures are amplified so as to include injunctive relief and preservation of evidence. It also sets out the test for the grant of interim measures, and highlights costs and damages consequences in the event that interim measures are subsequently found to have been unjustified. Finally, Article 35 of the Rules relates to the law applicable to the merits and refers to 'the rules of law' and not just 'the law', which potentially enables the parties to specify, for example, the UNIDROIT Principles of International Commercial Contracts.

This very brief review shows that the 2011 Rules confers more powers upon the Advisory Committee in order to allow for more neutrality and fairness in the arbitral process.

12. The old Rules only provided a deadline for raising the arbitrator challenge. Under the current Rules, if within fifteen days the appointing party does not agree to the challenge or the challenged arbitrator does not withdraw, then the challenging party may elect to pursue its challenge. In such event, the challenge shall be finally decided by an impartial and independent tripartite ad hoc committee to be composed by the Centre from among the members of the Advisory Committee.

[C] Neutrality and Transparency of Arbitration under the Cairo Regional Centre

The Cairo Regional Centre has taken various steps to enhance the neutrality and the fairness of its arbitration process. For example, the 2011 Rules as shown above conferred upon the Advisory Committee powers over several issues to insure that decisions over these issues are taken by an independent collegial committee rather than solely by the Director of the Centre. Such issues mentioned above [B] include requests not to proceed with an arbitral case and rejection of the appointment of arbitrators. The power of the Advisory Committee under the Rules to decide the challenge and removal of arbitrators was recently challenged before the Cairo Court of Appeal. The Court accepted this competence and suggested that the tripartite committee's decisions have a judicial nature.[13]

To enhance transparency, the Centre publishes the main legal principles contained in arbitral awards rendered under its auspices in the Journal of Arab Arbitration. It also publishes its awards in an anonymized form. To date, six volumes of the awards made under the auspices of the Centre have been published in the Arabic language and four volumes in the English language. The Centre also publishes a quarterly online newsletter on its website.[14] It also issues Practice Notes with respect to the interpretation and application of some of the articles of its Arbitration Rules. The Practice Notes also serve as a guide to the users of its Arbitration Rules and help enhance the predictability of the Centre's arbitral process.[15]

The Centre recently also published a Note on the main trends deduced from the decisions of the Tripartite Ad Hoc Committees in matters of challenge and removal of arbitrators.[16] The Note includes a summary of seventeen requests for challenge of arbitrators and five requests for removal of arbitrators under the 2011 Arbitration Rules. The Note also included the grounds of the requests as well as the decisions issued by the Committees. Such information provides useful guidance to users of arbitration under the Rules of the Centre on the considerations applied in upholding or rejecting such requests.

[D] Affordability and Predictability of the Costs of Arbitration under Cairo Regional Centre

Subject to the specifics of each institution, the arbitration costs of an institutional arbitration are generally comprised of the registration, administrative and arbitrators' fees. All arbitration institutions are mindful to offer their users an affordable system of dispute resolution that would maintain their current users while attracting more users

13. Cairo Court of Appeal, Decision in Appeal No. 42/ 131J dated 14 Dec. 2014. This position was not yet confirmed by the Cour de Cassation, the highest court of Egypt in civil, commercial and criminal matters.
14. For details see: http://crcica.org.eg/pub_newsletter.html [accessed 20 Apr. 2016].
15. The Practice Notes are available in the following link: http://www.crcica.org.eg/publication/PDF/CRCICA_Arbitration_PRACTICE_NOTES2014_EN.pdf [accessed 20 Apr. 2016].
16. Journal of Arab Arbitration, Volume 24, June 2015, pp. 9-44.

and arbitrators to accept appointments. As demonstrated in the 2013 empirical study of the School of International Arbitration on 'Corporate Choices in International Arbitration: Industry Perspectives', one of the most important factors affecting the selection of any dispute settlement mechanism, especially arbitration, is costs.[17] The study shows that, across all sectors, costs were a very important issue, as arbitration is often considered to be more costly than other available alternatives. While, overall, arbitration remains the preferred dispute resolution mechanism for transnational disputes, concerns were expressed over the related issue of costs in international arbitration proceedings, which, however, is not usually a deterrent to initiating such proceedings.[18]

The emergence of new arbitration centres in Asia and Africa was a logical reaction to the concerns of users of arbitration of its rising costs. Whilst the costs of legal representations and experts constitute the highest percentage of total arbitral costs, the emergence of new competitors in different jurisdictions has definitely contributed to the reduction of such costs. For example, resorting to a reliable arbitral institution in North Africa for the settlement of a dispute involving a North African party and arising out of a contract governed by the law of a North African State would be less expensive than referring the same dispute to an arbitral institution in the USA, Europe or Asia. Most probably, counsel and the arbitrators will be from North Africa and the costs of legal representation and other relevant expenses would therefore be reduced.

In the current 2011 Rules, the Centre has implemented a significant change in the way it determines arbitrators' fees. Arbitrators' fees under the previous versions of the Rules were regarded as low. In their study comparing the costs of various arbitral institutions published in Global Arbitration Review in 2010[19] Louis Flannery and Benjamin Garel found the Centre to be by far the most affordable of six worldwide institutions for cases of various values.[20] The fees have now been increased to reflect the legitimate expectations of parties and arbitrators. The current Rules abolish the impractical distinction between fees in international and domestic cases. They clarify that the sum in dispute, based on which both administrative and arbitrators' fees are determined, shall be the aggregate value of all claims, counterclaims and set-offs. They fix ascending flat rate fees for disputes under USD 3 million in value, and allow the Centre greater discretion to determine fees for disputes of higher value, within certain boundaries. An arbitration costs calculator is now available on the Centre's website.

The new section on costs has thus far helped the Centre in attracting more cases of all sizes, while not depriving the parties of their right to select the best international arbitrators. It is worth noting that one of the two authors of the above-mentioned study

17. Queen Mary University of London School of International Arbitration, *Corporate Choices in International Arbitration: Industry Perspectives* (2013), available at: http://www.arbitration.qmul.ac.uk/docs/123282.pdf, [accessed 19 Apr. 2016].
18. *Ibid.*, p. 21.
19. See: www.globalarbitrationreview.com/news/article/28915/arbitration-costs-compared/ [accessed 20 Apr. 2016].
20. This Study compared the fees payable under the following Centres: DIAC, HKIAC, ICC, ICAC (Russia); SCC; and the Swiss (Chambers of Commerce) Arbitration Centres.

calls the adoption by the Centre of the new costs schedules a 'smart move' that will not deter current users of the Centre and 'will certainly persuade more arbitrators to accept appointments, which, in the mid and long term, will help the Centre's image and reputation'.[21] After updating the costs comparisons tables in their study to factor in the changes to the Centre's costs regime, the authors conclude that the Centre remains the least expensive institution for smaller disputes (from USD 100,000 to USD 1 million in value) and that it is also the least expensive institution for cases in the USD 500 million to USD 1 billion range, although significantly more expensive than it used to be. The authors also consider the costs in mid-size cases to be 'in the same range as its most affordable competitors'.[22]

[E] Diversity and Fair Representation of Regions in Cairo Regional Centre Arbitrations

Arbitral institutions understand the conservative nature of parties in choosing arbitrators and consider it appropriate in light of the parties' interests in eliminating unpredictability from arbitral decisions. However, given that there are currently no plans within arbitral institutions to move from the predominant system of party appointments, which is viewed as one of the most attractive features of international arbitration, if parties are not willing to take risks in this respect, institutions, whether global, regional or local, do have opportunities to introduce new arbitrators in appropriate cases, especially in small quantified claims.

As pointed out earlier, the majority of cases involving an African party are still decided under the auspices of institutions located outside the continent. African arbitrators are underrepresented in these proceedings. In a continent with multiple cultures, languages, religions, legal systems and ethnicities, ensuring the diversity of arbitrators and enhancing the capabilities of the less-represented arbitrators is a major and important role that arbitral institutions can (and must) play. When arbitral institutions have sufficient experience and are sincerely keen to conduct the necessary reforms, the risk they run in trying to expand the pool of arbitrators they appoint is, at least, a calculated one, if any, and does not, therefore, warrant abandoning the efforts of diversification. As rightly noted by Professor Gaillard in his 2014 Freshfields lecture on the *Sociology of Arbitration*, arbitral institutions are doing their best to appoint newcomers and promote diversity, but it is the parties who resist change.[23] Indeed, the nominating parties and their counsel prefer to minimize risks and to select tested

21. Global Arbitration Review available at: www.globalarbitrationreview.com/news/article/29328/all-change-cairo [accessed 20 Apr. 2016].
22. *Ibid*. For current Fee scales for arbitrators, see CRCICA's Rules at: http://crcica.org.eg/rules/arbitration/2011/cr_arb_rules_en.pdf [accessed 20 Apr. 2016].
23. Emmanuel Gaillard, *Freshfields Lecture on Sociology of Arbitration* (26 Nov. 2014), available at: http://embed.buto.tv/kQJnL#play [accessed 20 Apr. 2016]. In that connection, Lise Bosman noted in a recent article the efforts of the PCA in supporting African countries in arbitration related matters especially its role of appointing authority as designated under the arbitration laws of several African countries, L. Bosman, *The PCA's Contribution to International Dispute Resolution in Africa*, vol. 25 Stellenbosch Law Review 308 (2014).

arbitrators with whom they are familiar. In similar vein, Edward Torgbor refers to 'old prejudices against the appointment of qualified Africans as arbitrators' in international dispute resolution.[24]

The first step a regional institution may take, in the authors' view, is to provide training for arbitrators in the region through conferences, seminars and workshops. Cooperation with other regional institutions as well as international institutions and associations such as the ICC, the LCIA and the Chartered Institute of Arbitrators (CIArb) will deepen the exposure of African arbitrators and counsel and introduce them to the larger world of international arbitration. In addition, institutions may include African arbitrators in their directing bodies and arbitrators' lists. Whenever invited or obliged by its Rules to appoint an arbitrator on behalf of parties, an institution may suggest qualified African names. Since May 2011, the Cairo Regional Centre launched a progressive educational ladder of four successive courses on arbitration. The programme known as 'Comparative Commercial Arbitration: Theory and Practice' (CCATP) is held annually. It covers the main pillars of arbitration, which are: the arbitration agreement, the arbitral tribunal, the arbitral procedures and the arbitral award. The programme, in its four modules, is intended to provide the ideal platform to support the development of professional knowledge and experience in arbitration. The initiative is developed in cooperation with the Chartered Institute of Arbitrators, Cairo Branch (CIArb-C). What is unique about the tutorial teaching method adopted for on the courses is that the tutors have both common law and civil law backgrounds and they lecture together instead of separately, to give participants a wide interactive legal exposure.

The course subjects comprise a highly comprehensive collection of laws, rules, conventions, arbitral principles, international guidelines and references, extracts from specialized arbitration journals and most recent court judgments, of twenty-one arbitral awards designed especially for the programme. Decisions and Guidelines by eminent international institutions in different jurisdictions are also included as relevant. Most interestingly, the tutorials are based on three different mock cases, each of which is separately tailored for each module. A sample structure of a final award in an institutional arbitration is also given to participants as guidance and for use in their professional practice. In 2015, the Centre was approved as a Recognized Course Provider of the training courses leading to qualification for membership of the CIArb.[25] This is clearly an important step towards the training of aspiring arbitrators from the region and the widening of their exposure and experience.[26]

Furthermore, the Centre organizes annually, solely or in cooperation with various prominent institutions, seminars and conferences that address and discuss

24. E. Torgbor, '*Opening up International Arbitration in Africa*', vol. 1 LCA Dispute Resolution Journal 1 (2014).
25. This CIArb accreditation is for its Modules 1 (Law of Obligations and Civil Evidence) and 2 (Law of Arbitration). See The Centre's Annual Report, 2015, p. 6.
26. The Centre also renders similar services for other ADR mechanisms such as mediation, for which see its Annual Report, *ibid*.

emergent issues related to arbitration, ADR, trade and investment.[27] The Centre also holds monthly lectures on arbitration and various economic and investment-related topics which are organized in cooperation with the CIArb-C. Through these programmes the Centre helps to promote the knowledge and use of arbitration and ADR in the region. These events also show the importance of cooperation between the Centre and other international institutions and not only the regional ones, which is a key element for the success of arbitration and arbitration institutions in Africa.

§3.03 THE IMPORTANCE OF COOPERATION BETWEEN ARBITRAL INSTITUTIONS

Among the misperceptions about institutional arbitration is that the interaction between arbitral institutions is only a competitive one aimed at gaining the largest share of relevant markets, rather than a cooperative one aimed at developing the best conditions for international arbitration and its legitimacy. When surveyed about the nature of their interaction during the ICCA 2014 Congress in Miami, representatives of eight arbitral institutions, from Europe, Asia, Africa and Latin America[28] confirmed that if there is to be competition among arbitration institutions, it should have the single goal of improving each institution's services with a view to better catering to the needs of its users.[29] Nassib Ziadé noted:

> Since there is no need to fight over the same pool of users, arbitration institutions can lend each other resources and expertise without harming themselves. In this spirit of harmony, there are various cooperation agreements among arbitration institutions, and it is not uncommon for the hearings in a particular arbitration proceeding to take place in the facilities of a sister institution. More broadly, arbitral institutions can and should cooperate in fostering academic study of the field, and in evaluating and cultivating arbitrators, particularly rising stars from emerging and frontier economies.[30]

---

27. Such institutions include the International Institute for the Unification of Private Law, World Trade Organisation, the Organization of Economic Cooperation and Development, World Intellectual Property Organization, the Stockholm Chamber of Commerce, the International Federation of Commercial Arbitration Institutions, the United Nations Commission on International Trade Law, the Institute for the Promotion of Arbitration and Mediation in the Mediterranean, the Arab Union of International Arbitration, and the Bahrain Centre for Dispute Resolution.
28. The survey respondents are: John Beechey, President, International Chamber of Commerce; Brooks Daly, Deputy Secretary-General, Permanent Court of Arbitration; Meg Kinnear, Secretary-General, International Centre for Settlement of Investment Disputes; Richard W. Naimark, Vice President, American Arbitration Association, in charge of the International Centre for Dispute Resolution; Sundra Rajoo, Director, Kuala Lumpur Regional Centre for Arbitration; Mohamed Abdel Raouf, Director, Cairo Regional Centre for International Commercial Arbitration; Frederico José Straube, President, Centre for Arbitration and Mediation of the Chamber of Commerce of Brazil-Canada; Adrian Winstanley, Director General, London Court of International Arbitration (1997-2014); Nassib G. Ziadé, Chief Executive Officer, Bahrain Centre for Dispute Resolution.
29. See Nassib Ziadé, *Arbitral Institutions Can Do More to Foster Legitimacy: True or False?* vol. 18 ICCA Congress Series 667 (2015).
30. Nassib Ziade, *supra*, at p. 690.

Sundra Rajoo on his part indicated that:

> [F]ostering cooperation between institutions allows for development of initiatives that one centre could not undertake on its own. One example of this is the development of Asian Domain Name Dispute Resolution that is a joint effort between the KLRCA, CIETAC, HKIAC and KCAB. On a smaller scale, cooperation facilitates the promotion of arbitration generally through the organization of conferences and other events.[31]

Finally Richard Naimark noted:

> [A]rbitral institutions must conduct themselves with dignity if they are to be viewed with credibility as purveyors of justice. Competition should be measured, thoughtful, collegial and even friendly. In a sense, institutions should model responsible behaviour while still spurring each other to improve and adapt appropriately. Joint conferences and cooperative projects greatly benefit our field and mutual credibility.[32]

Through their joint events, activities and publications, arbitration centres have introduced in their respective jurisdictions important guidelines and soft laws like the IBA Rules on the Taking of Evidence in International Arbitration, the IBA Guidelines on Party Representation in International Arbitration and the IBA Guidelines on Conflict of Interest in International Arbitration.[33] Such texts were even made available in languages other than the English language primarily due to the efforts of local experts and arbitral institutions. Such cooperation also includes guidelines addressed to national judges, such as the 'ICCA Guide to the interpretation of the 1958 New York Convention', which has been translated into Arabic by the joint efforts of both the BCDR-AAA (Bahrain Centre for Dispute Resolution) and the Cairo Regional Centre. Among the other examples of successful cooperation between arbitral institutions is the Institute for the Promotion of Arbitration and Mediation in the Mediterranean (ISPRAMED), which was set up in 2009 in Milan as a non-profit organization focusing on the creation of a network among the most representative arbitral institutions of both sides of the Mediterranean basin.[34] The ISPRAMED Network aims at fostering the exchange of best practices and elaborating common principles in the management of arbitral proceedings. For this purpose, ISPRAMED concluded in 2012 a Memorandum of Understanding with six ADR centres from six States in Europe, Asia and Africa.[35] The ADR centres involved in the Network have adopted international standards of management and share practices and principles, which they jointly develop. They also promote the culture of ADR in their local business and legal communities. So far, seven ADR centres, members of the Network, have jointly issued a Report on the independence

31. *Ibid.* Sundra Rajoo, 692.
32. *Ibid.* Richard Naimark, 691.
33. For these IBA texts see: http://www.ibanet.org/Publications/publications_IBA_guides_and_free_materials.aspx [accessed 20 Apr. 2016].
34. For more details about ISPRAMED, the members of its Network, projects and activities, http://www.ispramed.it/ [accessed 20 Apr. 2016].
35. These states are Algeria, Egypt, Italy, Lebanon, Morocco, Tunisia, and Turkey.

and impartiality of arbitrators[36] and another Report on the criteria for the selection of arbitrators.[37]

Arbitration institutions in Africa can also follow the example of the ISPRAMED network, to help them share experience, promote best practice and strengthen their capacities in administering arbitrations. A Report recently mandated by the Africa Development Bank (AfDB) set forth many criteria to assess the efficiency of institutional arbitration. Among the criteria, the most important are: need to have a modern set of arbitration rules, supportive courts at the seat of arbitration, party autonomy, open list of qualified arbitrators, capability of staff of the institution, ease of enforcement of arbitral awards, limited state intervention, neutrality of the venue, especially with a state party. The Report also examined the following criteria which are specific to arbitration institutions:

- whether the Centre provides a fully independent and neutral arbitration based on the applicable procedures, and if the Centre is reasonably free from impact of domestic procedural law when the contract involves a public body of the country the Centre is located;
- whether there is a general public perception (of practitioners / lawyers / judges / interested bidders etc.) of the neutrality of the Centre which fulfils the AfDB's requirements;
- the capacity of the Centre to discharge its responsibility by examining the competency of the arbitrators that the Centre uses, the cost of procedure, and by reviewing recent performance of the Centre.

This AfDB Report assessed the following three centres: *La Cour Commune de la Justice et d'Arbitrage* (CCJA) in Côte d'Ivoire, the CRCICA in Egypt, and the Mauritius International Arbitration Centre (LCIA-MIAC) in Mauritius[38] and concluded that they include the best arbitration centres across the African continent and can readily be recommended for use by parties from both the African continent and elsewhere.[39] The conclusions from the AfDB Report confirm that the emergence of reliable and credible arbitration institutions in Asia and Africa has contributed to the creation of an enduring culture for the effective administration of arbitration by such institutions that meet the requirements of its users as part of the process towards the greater participation of Asian and African arbitrators, institutions and venues in the global arbitration space. It

36. The Report was prepared with the scientific support of Professor Charles Jarrosson and is available on ISPRAMED's website at: http://www.ispramed.it/root/network/ [accessed 20 Apr. 2016]. The Report provides in a few principles and practices the data and information collected by ISPRAMED Network members on the impartiality and independence of arbitrators, to guide their decision making on the subject.
37. Both Reports were also published in the Journal of Arab Arbitration, Volume 25, December 2015, pp. 9-32 and are available at: http://www.ispramed.it/root/network/ [accessed 20 Apr. 2016].
38. Werner Jahnel, *Assessment Report of Arbitration Centres in Côte d'ivoire, Egypt and Mauritius*, available at: http://www.afdb.org/fileadmin/uploads/afdb/Documents/Procurement/Project-related-Procurement/Assessment_Report_of_arbitration_centres_in_C%C3%B4te_d%E2%80%99Ivoire__Egypt_and_Mauritius.pdf, [accessed 20 Apr. 2016].
39. *Ibid.*, 47.

is also worth noting that the 2016 ICCA Conference will be held in the African continent (Mauritius) for the first time.[40]

CONCLUSION

The future of institutional arbitration is not without challenges. The growth of institutions, that are well managed, adequately resourced, and largely transparent in their operations, is a positive development for international arbitration and for enhancing the rule of law in Africa. However, the reputation and legitimacy of institutional arbitration may be tarnished by institutions that have neither the expertise nor resources to administer arbitrations properly. This probably justifies some self-policing, the establishment of codes of conduct for institutions, to guarantee good governance, accountability and neutrality by arbitral institutions. Cooperation between arbitral institutions in Africa in order to achieve these goals, is, therefore, a must.

40. The 2016 ICCA Congress will hold in Mauritius from 8-11 May. The authors are also aware of an initiative to create a Working Group on African arbitral practice and hope that this initiative will be endorsed by the ICCA Governing Board.

CHAPTER 4
Arbitration Institutions in East Africa

Kariuki Muigua

INTRODUCTION

This chapter examines the role of arbitration institutions located in East Africa in transforming arbitration in the region. It discusses the successes and challenges of the identified arbitration institutions. This discussion is necessitated because of the importance of international arbitration and its ever growing popularity in Africa and across the world. This chapter also highlights some of the emerging trends in arbitration in the region and makes suggestions on how arbitral institutions can contribute to the transformation of arbitration in East Africa.

The scope of this chapter is therefore limited to arbitration in Kenya, Tanzania, Uganda, Rwanda and Burundi, being the Member States of the East African Community (EAC). This chapter starts with a brief outline of the legal and institutional framework for arbitration in these countries (§4.01) and examines their effectiveness in transforming arbitration in the region (§4.02). Some suggestions on achieving the goal of effective arbitration practice in the region (§4.03) are explored.

§4.01 DISPUTE RESOLUTION PROCESSES IN EAST AFRICA

Increased globalization has brought about the need for effective and reliable mechanisms for management of commercial disputes as well as other general disputes involving parties from different jurisdictions thus resulting in the emergence of transnational dispute management mechanisms. The mechanisms now universally and primarily used for dispute management are negotiation, mediation, arbitration and conciliation.[1] In my opinion these mechanisms work best when a well-resourced, neutral and credible organization administers the process.[2] This section focuses on arbitration as one of the most preferred dispute resolution mechanisms and its administration by arbitration institutions in East African countries.

Arbitration is now regarded as the preferred mechanism for settling international disputes.[3] Peter Cresswell once argued that international arbitration should grow in tandem with the globalization of trade.[4] Arbitration has thus gained popularity over time amongst members of the business community due to its advantages over litigation. One of the most outstanding benefits of arbitration over litigation is its transnational applicability in international disputes with minimal or no interference by national courts. This lack of interference by domestic courts boosts the confidence of parties in their pursuit of justice in a forum of their choice. However, it is arguable if this advantage of arbitration can be seen in some East African countries. I have argued elsewhere that even when an African state has become a party to the relevant treaties,[5] there might still be the perception that its courts cannot be relied upon to apply their texts correctly or in good faith.[6] As it relates to Kenya, I have also noted that parties to arbitration agreements have used court intervention to delay and frustrate arbitral proceedings.[7] John McLaughlin has also argued that traditional litigation before a national court can be a costly, time-consuming, cumbersome and inefficient process, which obstructs, rather than facilitates, the resolution of business disputes.[8] Finally, William Kirtley has observed that among the primary advantages of international arbitration are its finality and the relative ease of enforcement of arbitral awards

1. There are other adjudicative (e.g., adjudication) and non-adjudicative (e.g., early neutral evaluation) processes along with various combinations of these processes (e.g., med-arb).
2. The same sentiments are echoed in, A. Dutta, *Origin of Alternative Dispute Resolution System in India* 87, available at: https://www.academia.edu/4371674/ORIGIN_OF_ALTERNATIVE_DISPUTE_RESOLUTION_SYSTEM_IN_INDIA [accessed 8 Apr. 2016]. See also Art. 33 of the United Nations Charter, 24 Oct. 1945, 1 UNTS XVI.
3. Susan D. Franck, *The Role of International Arbitrators*, 1 and available at: https://international-arbitration-attorney.com/wp-content/uploads/Microsoft-Word-ILW-ILSA-Article.docsfranck2.pdf [accessed on 7 Apr. 2016].
4. Peter Cresswell, *International Arbitration: Enhancing Standards* 10, 10-13 (The Resolver, Chartered Institute of Arbitrators, 2014). See also Court's comment in the American case of *Mitsubishi Motors Corp. v. Soler Chrysler-Plymouth, Inc.*, 473 U.S. 614 (1985) where the Court stated that:

> the expansion of [American] business and industry will hardly be encouraged if, notwithstanding solemn contracts, [we] insist on a parochial concept that all disputes must be resolved under [our] laws and in our courts.... We cannot have trade and commerce in world markets and international waters exclusively on our terms, governed by our laws, and resolved in our courts.

5. Such as the New York Convention 1958 and the ICSID Convention 1965.
6. K. Muigua., *Making East Africa a Hub for International Commercial Arbitration: A Critical Examination of the State of the Legal and Institutional Framework Governing Arbitration in Kenya*. This is a paper presented at the Kigali International Arbitration Centre Arbitration Workshop for EAC, hosted by the Rwanda Private Sector Federation, held on 24-25 May 2013 At Kigali, Rwanda.
7. K. Muigua *Role of the Court under Arbitration Act 1995: Court Intervention Before, Pending and After Arbitration in Kenya*, Kenya Law Review 2 (2008-2010).
8. J.T. McLaughlin, *Arbitration and Developing Countries*, vol. 13, no. 2 The International Lawyer 211, 212 (1979).

throughout the world.[9] Countries around the world have thus embarked upon promoting themselves as viable seats for international arbitration, along with the promotion of specific arbitration institutions located in them. It is in this recognition of arbitration as one of the most viable approaches to dispute management and resolution that makes arbitration institutions of importance across the continent.

§4.02 ARBITRATION LAWS AND INSTITUTIONS IN THE EAST AFRICAN REGION

This section examines the laws which support domestic and international arbitration and the major arbitration institutions in Kenya (§4.02[A]), Tanzania (§4.02[B]), Uganda (§4.02[C]), Rwanda (§4.02[D]), and Burundi (§4.02[E]). It also briefly examines the arbitration remit of the East African Court (§4.02[F]). It primarily interrogates the role and functioning of these arbitration institutions in each of these countries. All four East African countries have ratified the New York Convention of 1958 and the ICSID Convention of 1965.[10]

[A] Kenya

Kenya's Arbitration Act 1995 (KAA)[11] is based on the UNCITRAL Model Law on International Commercial Arbitration (Model Law), which is designed to assist States in modernizing their arbitration laws. The Model Law is specifically designed for the regulation of international commercial arbitration.[12] One significant difference between the Model Law and KAA is that the KAA covers both domestic and international arbitration.[13] The KAA also defines domestic[14] and international[15] arbitration for ease of reference.

9. William Lawton Kirtley, *Bringing Claims and Enforcing International Arbitration Awards against Sub-Saharan African States and Parties*, 8 The Law and Practice of International Courts and Tribunals 143,143 (2009).
10. For contracting states of the New York Convention, see: http://www.uncitral.org/uncitral/en/uncitral_texts/arbitration/NYConvention_status.html..
11. Arbitration Act, Cap 4 laws of Kenya (No. 11 of 2009), as amended by the Amending Act No. 11 of 2009, L.N. 48/2010. Revised Edition 2012 [2010].
12. UNCITRAL Model Law on International Commercial Arbitration (1985), with amendments as adopted in 2006, United Nations documents A/40/17, annex I and A/61/17, and available at: http://www.uncitral.org/uncitral/en/uncitral_texts/arbitration/1985Model_arbitration.html [accessed 6 Apr. 2016].
13. Section 2 of KAA.
14. Section 3(2). An arbitration is domestic if the arbitration agreement provides expressly or by implication for arbitration in Kenya: and at the time when proceedings are commenced or the arbitration is entered into, (a) where the arbitration is between individuals, the parties are nationals of Kenya or are habitually resident in Kenya; (b) where the arbitration is between bodies corporate, the parties are incorporated in Kenya or their central management and control are exercised in Kenya; (c) where the arbitration is between an individual and a body corporate, (i) the party who is an individual is a national of Kenya or is habitually resident in Kenya; and (ii) the party that is a body corporate is incorporated in Kenya or its central management and control are exercised in Kenya; or (d) the place where a substantial part of the obligations of the commercial relationship is to be performed, or the place with which the subject matter of the dispute is most closely connected, is Kenya.

The KAA generally makes provisions for the conduct of arbitral proceedings and the enforcement of arbitral awards by national courts. The Act's omission on provisions relating to the institutional framework on arbitration is however glaring. It is noteworthy that the KAA does not establish or endorse a sole arbitral institution in the country. Its provisions apply to both ad hoc and institutional arbitrations where Kenya is the seat of arbitration. There are three major arbitration institutions in Kenya: Chartered Institute of Arbitrators, Kenya Branch (§4.02[A][1]), Nairobi Centre for International Arbitration (NCIA) (§4.02[A][2]), and the Centre for Alternative Dispute Resolution (CADR) (§4.02[A][3]).

[1] Chartered Institute of Arbitrators-Kenya Branch

The Chartered institute of Arbitrators, Kenya Branch (CIArb-K) was established in 1984, as one of the branches of the Chartered Institute of Arbitrators, United Kingdom, which itself was founded in 1915 with headquarters in London. CIArb-K is registered under the Societies Act of Kenya.[16] It promotes and facilitates the determination of disputes by arbitration and other forms of alternative dispute resolution (ADR) processes such as: mediation, Conciliation, Neutral Evaluation, Expert Determination and adjudication.[17] CIArb-K currently has over 700 members, evidencing the availability of a wide pool of knowledgeable and experienced arbitrators in Kenya.[18] CIArb-K also facilitates the appointment of arbitrators in its role as appointing authority.

In addition to a dedicated website, CIArb-K has a Secretariat with physical facilities in Kenya for arbitration and other forms of ADR.[19] These facilities include arbitration hearings rooms and other support services.[20] To further support the processes of arbitration and ADR, CIArb-K has published its own Arbitration Rules, 2012.[21] These Rules are binding on arbitrators conducting arbitral proceedings CIArb-K arbitrations.

The Chartered Institute of Arbitrators as is well known is a membership based organization that primarily provides training and education services for dispute

15. Section 3(3). An arbitration is international if: (a) the parties to an arbitration agreement have, at the time of the conclusion of that agreement, their places of business in different states; (b) one of the following places is situated outside the state in which the parties have their places of business: (i) the juridical seat of arbitration is determined by or pursuant to the arbitration agreement; or (ii) any place where a substantial part of the obligations of the commercial relationship is to be performed or the place with which the subject-matter of the dispute is most closely connected; or (c) the parties have expressly agreed that the subject-matter of the arbitration agreement relates to more than one state.
16. Cap 108, Laws of Kenya, Revised Edition 2012 [1998].
17. The Chartered Institute of Arbitrators Kenya Branch Constitution, Clause 2.
18. The Directory of CIArb-K Members is available on its website at: http://www.ciarbkenya.org/membership.html [accessed 8 Jan. 2016].
19. CIArb-K secretariat is located at Kindaruma Lane, Nicholson Drive, Off Ngong Road, Nairobi.
20. Chartered Institute of Arbitrators, Kenya Boardrooms, available at: http://www.ciarbkenya.org/room-hire.html [accessed 20 Mar. 2016].
21. Chartered Institute of Arbitrators Arbitration Rules of December 2012; following the CIArb Headquarters' Model Arbitration Rules and available are at the Institute's offices for a fee.

resolution processes.[22] It is therefore debatable if CIArb-K can be properly described as an arbitration institution in the strict sense. This is more so as CIArb-K was constituted as an organization with one of the objects being to 'generally promote, encourage and facilitate the practice of settlement of disputes by arbitration and alternative means of dispute resolution other than resolution by the courts.'[23] As far as international arbitration practice is concerned in Kenya, CIArb-K has been effective in providing qualified arbitration practitioners to sit as arbitrators in ad hoc arbitrations. However, considering that CIArb-K follows the parent CIArb Headquarters in its mode of operation, it is unlikely that it will develop into an institution offering full institutional arbitration services. As such, it may need to work closely and collaborate with the other institutions in Kenya and the region to support and promote arbitration in Kenya.

[2] Nairobi Centre for International Arbitration

The Nairobi Centre for International Arbitration (NCIA) was set up through the office of the Attorney General of Kenya under the auspices of the Asian-African Consultative Organization (AALCO).[24] This was the result of a Memorandum of Understanding (MoU) concluded between AALCO and the Government of the Republic of Kenya. This MoU was signed on 3 April 2006 during the Forty-Fifth Annual Session of AALCO at its Headquarters in New Delhi to establish an AALCO Regional Centre in Nairobi.[25] The NCIA is therefore the third AALCO Regional Centre[26] in Africa following the Cairo Regional Centre for International Commercial Arbitration, Egypt,[27] and Lagos Regional Centre for International Commercial Arbitration, Lagos, Nigeria.[28]

The NCIA was established under the NCIA Act, 2013.[29] Its functions as set out in section 5 of the NCIA Act include to, 'promote, facilitate and encourage the conduct of international commercial arbitration in accordance with this Act';[30] 'administer domestic and international arbitrations as well as alternative dispute resolution techniques under its auspices';[31] 'ensure that arbitration is reserved as the dispute resolution process of choice';[32] and 'develop rules encompassing conciliation and mediation processes'.[33]

22. See for the Chartered Institute of Arbitrators, http://www.ciarb.org/ [accessed 14 Mar. 2016].
23. The Chartered Institute of Arbitrators Kenya Branch Constitution, Clause 2(i)(a).
24. Asian-African Legal Consultative Organization, *Report on the AALCO's Regional Arbitration Centres*, para. 23, p. 5.
25. Asian-African Legal Consultative Organization, *Report on the AALCO's Regional Arbitration Centres*, AALCO/51/ABUJA/2012/ORG 3, para. 7, p. 2.
26. The other two Centres established under the auspices of the Asian-African Legal Consultative Organisation (AALCO) are the Kuala Lumpur Regional Centre for Arbitration in Kuala Lumpur, Malaysia and Tehran Arbitration Centre in Tehran, Iran.
27. For Cairo Regional Centre, see: http://crcica.org.eg/ [accessed 4 Mar. 2016].
28. For Lagos Regional Centre, see: http://www.rcicalagos.org/ [accessed 4 Mar. 2016].
29. Act No. 26 of 2013, Laws of Kenya.
30. Section 5(a), No. 26 of 2013.
31. *Ibid.*, s. 5(b).
32. *Ibid.*, s. 5(c).
33. *Ibid.*, s. 5(d). Further functions include: to organize international conferences, seminars and training programmes for arbitrators and scholars; to coordinate and facilitate, in collaboration

The NCIA is administered by a Board of Directors with membership drawn from Kenya, Rwanda and Uganda,[34] and a Registrar appointed by the Board of Directors. The Registrar oversees the day to day management of the affairs and staff of the Centre and also acts as secretary to the Board.[35] The NCIA maintains offices[36] in Nairobi and recorded its first reference in 2015.[37] Following other AALCO Regional Centres, the NCIA has its Nairobi Centre for International Arbitration (Arbitration) Rules, 2015.[38] These Rules are based on the UNCITRAL Arbitration Rules. Attached to the NCIA is an Arbitral Court established under section 21 of the NCIA Act. This Arbitral Court has exclusive original and appellate jurisdiction to hear and determine all disputes referred to it in accordance with the NCIA Act or any other written law.[39] A decision of the Court in respect of a matter referred to it is to be final.[40] Rule 33 of the NCIA Arbitration Rules provides that the decisions of the Centre with respect to all matters relating to the arbitration shall be conclusive and binding upon the parties and the Arbitral Tribunal. For clarity on the nature of such matters, recourse is to be to the NCIA Arbitration Rules[41] which provide for a number of instances where the jurisdiction of the court may be invoked. For example, Rule 11(3) of the NCIA Arbitration Rules provides that a party who intends to remove an arbitrator shall, within fifteen days of the formation of the arbitral tribunal or on becoming aware of any circumstances referred to in paragraph (1) and (2),[42] send a written statement of the reasons for requiring the removal, to the Arbitral Court, the Centre, the arbitral tribunal and all other parties. The Arbitral Court is to make its decision on the removal of an arbitrator within fifteen days of receipt of

---

with other lead agencies and non-state actors, the formulation of national policies, laws and plans of action on alternative dispute resolution and facilitate their implementation, enforcement, continuous review, monitoring and evaluation; to maintain proactive co-operation with other regional and international institutions in areas relevant to achieving the Centre's objectives; to in collaboration with other public and private agencies, facilitate, conduct, promote and coordinate research and dissemination of findings on data on arbitration and serve as repository of such data; to provide ad hoc arbitration by facilitating the parties with necessary technical and administrative assistance at the behest of the parties; to provide advice and assistance for the enforcement and translation of arbitral awards; to provide procedural and technical advice to disputants; to provide training and accreditation for mediators and arbitrators; educate the public on arbitration as well as other alternative dispute resolution mechanisms; and, to enter into strategic agreements with other regional and international bodies for purposes of securing technical assistance to enable the Centre achieve its objectives.

34. The names of NCIA Board of Directors, is available at: http://ncia.or.ke/index.php?option=com_content&view=category&layout=blog&id=86&Itemid=1243 [accessed 20 Mar. 2016].
35. For more details see s. 9 NCIA Act.
36. NCIA offices are located at The Cooperative House, Haile Selassie Avenue, Nairobi.
37. Nairobi Centre for International Arbitration, *First Arbitration conducted at the NCIA boardroom*, available at: http://ncia.or.ke/index.php?option=com_phocagallery&view=category&id=1:first-arbitration&Itemid=1263 [accessed 20 Mar. 2016].
38. Legal Notice No. 255, Kenya Gazette Supplement No. 210, 24 Dec. 2015.
39. Section 22(1), No. 26 of 2013.
40. Section 22(2).
41. Nairobi Centre for International Arbitration (Arbitration) Rules, 2015, Legal Notice No. 255, Kenya Gazette Supplement No. 210, 24 Dec. 2015.
42. Rule 11(1): A party may require the removal of an arbitrator if circumstances exist that give rise to justifiable doubts as to the arbitrator's impartiality or independence. (2) A party may remove an arbitrator it has nominated, or in whose appointment it has participated, only for reasons of which the party becomes aware after the appointment has been made.

the written statement, unless the arbitrator resigns from office; or all other parties agree to the removal of the arbitrator.[43]

Rule 6(1) of the NCIA Arbitration Rules provides that where interim payments are required to cover the Centre's administrative costs or the arbitral tribunal's fees or expenses, including the fees or expenses of an expert appointed by the arbitral tribunal, the Centre may, on the approval of the Arbitral Court, make payments out of the deposits held.

The Arbitral Court does not concern itself with interim and conservatory measures as these may only be issued by the arbitral tribunal. Rule 27(1) of the NCIA Arbitration Rules empowers the arbitral tribunal, unless otherwise agreed by the parties in writing, to make various decisions on a provisional basis. These include decisions on security for costs and preservation of property which is the subject matter of the arbitration. It is noteworthy that the same Rule 27(4) preserves the right of parties to apply for such measures before a judicial authority.

Section 10 of the NCIA Act confers on the Registrar (who is also the Chief Executive Officer of the NCIA) with the powers to oversee the business of the Arbitral Court including enforcement of decisions of the Arbitral Court. The Arbitral Court has a President and two Deputy Presidents and the Registrar. The Court is also to have fifteen other members all of whom should be leading international arbitrators. All these fifteen other members of the Court are be appointed competitively by the Board for a period of five years but shall be eligible for re-appointment for one further term of five years.[44]

Though the role of the Arbitral Court is administrative under the NCIA Act and Rules, the nature of its relationship with national courts is not very clear especially during the arbitral hearing. This raises confusion as far as jurisdiction in arbitration matters is concerned. What is clear however is that the Arbitral Court is independent of the Judiciary and has original and exclusive jurisdiction in certain matters as discussed above. It is also noteworthy that the jurisdiction is mainly administrative in nature as opposed to judicial, which is largely vested in the arbitral tribunal. This is perhaps meant to ensure that domestic courts do not interfere with the arbitration process once it starts especially in matters that can either be determined by the arbitral tribunal or the Arbitral Court as per the NCIA Act and the NCIA Arbitration Rules.

[3] Centre for Alternative Dispute Resolution

The Centre for Alternative Dispute Resolution (CADR) is another registered arbitration institution in Kenya that aims to enhance the settlement of disputes through ADR mechanisms.[45] With the recognition of ADR as processes of dispute resolution in

43. Rule 11(6).
44. Section 21(3), No. 26 of 2013. It is expected that the members of the Board will be drawn from both domestic and international arbitration practitioners as this will enhance the scope of the expertise available to the Board.
45. The Centre was registered under the Companies Act Cap 486 of the Laws of Kenya as Company limited by guarantee.

Article 159 of the current Constitution of Kenya, 2010, CADR plans to provide ADR services to enhance such provisions for dispute settlement in Kenya. Its membership is also drawn from the Chartered Institute of Arbitrators, Kenya branch (CIArb-K).[46] Currently, the CADR operates from the premises of the CIArb-K. However, CADR differs from CIArb-K in that it is conceived as an arbitral institution properly so called and not just an association of professionals interested in arbitration and ADR.

There are major benefits for CADR from its association with CIArb-K especially in relation to sourcing qualified arbitrators. In due time it can set up its own facilities from where it can offer arbitration services and also create enough capacity to enable it act as an appointing body and administer the arbitration references. Such capacity development by CADR will leave room for CIArb-K to concentrate on creating awareness of arbitration and other ADR mechanisms, and also offering training and continuous professional development in arbitration to all its affiliated professional bodies. This will leave CADR to concentrate on administering institutional arbitration in Kenya and the region.

[B] Tanzania

The Tanzania Arbitration Act (TAA)[47] was enacted in 1931 as the enabling law for arbitration references where Tanzania is the seat. The TAA has general provisions relating to arbitration by consent[48] as well as provisions on court-annexed arbitration.[49] Further, provisions on arbitration are contained in the Arbitration Rules of 1957,[50] made under the Arbitration Act,[51] so effectively the TAA has a set of arbitration rules annexed to it for use by parties primarily in ad hoc references. It is noteworthy that the arbitration legislation in force (both the TAA and the Rules) pre-dates the UNCITRAL Model Law and has never been changed to take into account its provisions.[52]

The TAA needs to be modernized. For example, it still provides for the appointment of even number tribunals with an umpire.[53] The TAA does not have any provisions on the grounds upon which a party may challenge the appointment of any of the arbitrators. It is also silent on the scope or definition of arbitration but makes reference to international conventions on international arbitration to which Tanzania

46. CIArb-K members become automatic members of CADR.
47. Cap 15, Laws of Tanzania (2002 Revised Edition).
48. *Ibid.*, ss 3-26.
49. Tanzania's Civil Procedure Code (the Code) deals with arbitration where it arises in the course of court proceedings as provided under Schedule 2 of the Code.
50. Published in Government Notice 427 of 1957.
51. Section 20, Ch. 15, Laws of Tanzania.
52. J. Cosmas, *The State Of International Commercial Arbitration in Tanzania: A Comparative Critique And Call For The Reform*, vol. 12 US-China Law Review, 513-529, 521(2015); See also G.L. Cosmas, *Critical Analysis on the Challenges Facing Legal and Institutional Frameworks on Recognition and Enforcement of Foreign Arbitral Awards in Tanzania*, vol. 39 Journal of Law, Policy and Globalization 165-177, 172 (2015); See also C.J. Mashamba, *Alternative Dispute Resolution in Tanzania: Law and Practice* 125 (Mkuki na Nyota Publishers, 2014).
53. First Schedule (s. 4), Clause 2, Cap 337, Laws of Tanzania.

is party.[54] The TAA however, makes express reference to foreign awards in Part IV which applies to foreign awards and not to any award made on an arbitration agreement governed by the law of Tanzania.[55] It generally recognizes foreign awards as binding and enforceable, and may be relied on by way of defence, set-off or otherwise in any legal proceedings.[56] The Act does not make any provisions on institutional arbitration in Tanzania. It also does not endorse a sole arbitral institution in the country. It may, therefore, be implied that the provisions of the TAA apply to both institutional and ad hoc arbitrations where Tanzania is the seat of arbitration. There are two main arbitration institutions in Tanzania: the Tanzania Institute of Arbitrators (TIA) (§4.02[B][1]) and the National Construction Council (NCC) (§4.02[B][1]).

[1] Tanzania Institute of Arbitrators

The Tanzania Institute of Arbitrators (TIA) is a non-governmental organization registered under the Societies Act of Tanzania (Cap 337).[57] The TIA acts as facilitator of arbitration. It assists the parties (in consultation with the parties' arbitrators) to agree ad hoc rules on the procedures which will bind them.[58] The TIA has its own bespoke set of arbitration rules which it uses in conducting both domestic and international arbitration proceedings.[59]

[2] National Construction Council

The National Construction Council (NCC) is a statutory body created under the NCC Act.[60] The NCC is mandated to among others:

> promote and provide strategic leadership for the growth, development and expansion of the construction industry in Tanzania with emphasis on the development of local capacity for socio-economic development and competitiveness in the changing global environment; and facilitate efficient resolution of disputes in the construction industry.[61]

54. Fourth Schedule (ss 28-33), Cap 337, Laws of Tanzania.
55. Section 28(2), Cap 337, Laws of Tanzania.
56. Section 29, Cap 337, Laws of Tanzania.
57. Cap 337, Laws of Tanzania.
58. *'Tanzania'*, Arbitration in Africa, 5 Jun. 2007. Available at: http://www.nortonrosefulbright.com/files/tanzania-25762.pdf [accessed 7 Apr. 2016].
59. Daele, K., et al., *Country Q&A: Tanzania, in Cross-Border Handbooks: Arbitration*, 167 (2010/2011), available at www.practicallaw.com/arbitrationhandbook [accessed 20 Mar. 2016].
60. National Construction Council Act, No. 20 of 1979, Cap 162, Laws of Tanzania, revised ed. 2008, Government Printer, Dar es Salaam.
61. National Construction Council (NCC) Functions, available at: http://www.ncc.or.tz/functions.html [accessed 8 Apr. 2016].

In 2001, the NCC adopted a set of arbitration rules, to enable parties settle their construction disputes under the Rules.[62] The NCC Arbitration Rules (2001 Edition) are available at the NCC offices in Dar es Salaam, Tanzania for a fee. The TCC also maintains a Panel of Arbitrators to facilitate the settlement of such differences and disputes.[63] The arbitration services of the NCC are mainly available to persons in the construction industry although it also offers its services to persons outside the industry.[64]

These two institutions enjoy close collaboration in Tanzania. They jointly organize short professional courses and examination for aspiring arbitrators and jointly compile a list of arbitrators available for appointment.[65] However, for a vibrant institutional framework on arbitration in Tanzania to develop, much more needs to be done to project these two institutions into the international arena and change the perception that they only administer domestic disputes and also are only industry-specific. To begin with, little information can readily be accessed regarding the institutions. These institutions need to disseminate information to the business community in the region and beyond to create awareness of their existence. This may be achieved through setting up resourceful websites with relevant and up to date information, organizing joint promotional activities such as conferences and workshops, amongst others, with other institutions in the region and the continent.

Despite the rigidity of Tanzania's national legal framework on arbitration, it is important for the two institutions to ensure that their arbitration rules reflect international best practices so as to meet the requirements of modern users of international arbitration. These rules need to be flexible enough to allow the parties considerable freedom to agree upon the lawyers to represent them, the procedure to be followed, language of the arbitration, and the size of the tribunal to decide their dispute.

[C] Uganda

Uganda's Arbitration and Conciliation Act[66] was enacted to amend the law relating to domestic arbitration and international commercial arbitration, and provide for the enforcement of foreign arbitral awards.[67] The Act also defines the law relating to conciliation of disputes. Under this Act, national courts may assist parties involved in arbitration with taking evidence,[68] setting aside arbitral awards[69] and recognition and

62. See W. Kapinga et al., *Tanzania, Getting the Deal Through Arbitration* 406-412, 407 (2014), available at: http://www.academia.edu/9872218/Getting_the_Deal_Through_-_Arbitration-_Tanzania_Chapter_2014 [accessed 7 Apr. 2016].
63. See National Construction Council, Settlement of Disputes, available at: http://www.ncc.or.tz/s-dispute.html [accessed on 8 Apr. 2016].
64. See National Construction Council Functions, available at: http://www.ncc.or.tz/functions.html [accessed 8 Apr. 2016].
65. *Ibid.*
66. Arbitration and Conciliation Act, Cap 4, Laws of Uganda, 2000.
67. *Ibid.*, s. 1.
68. *Ibid.*, s. 27.
69. *Ibid.*, s. 34.

enforcement of the arbitral awards.[70] This Act is modelled on the UNCITRAL Model Law.[71] There is one major arbitration institution in Uganda, the Centre for Arbitration and Dispute Resolution (§4.02[C][1]).

[1] Centre for Arbitration and Dispute Resolution

Uganda's Arbitration and Conciliation Act establishes the Centre for Arbitration and Dispute Resolution (CADRE).[72] The Act empowers CADRE to make appropriate rules, administrative procedure and forms for effective performance of arbitration, conciliation or ADR processes; to establish and enforce a code of ethics for arbitrators, conciliators, neutrals and experts; to qualify and accredit arbitrators, conciliators and experts; to provide administrative services and other technical services in aid of arbitration, conciliation and ADR; to facilitate certification, registration and authentication of arbitration awards and conciliation settlements; to provide skills training and promote the use of ADR methods for stakeholders.[73] The Arbitration and Conciliation (Amendment) Act, 2008 provides for the funding of the CADRE by the Ugandan government.[74] While this may help the institution to run smoothly, caution should always be exercised to avoid creating the impression that as a result of the funding, the Centre's activities are not independent of government interference.

CADRE is empowered under the Act to offer both ad hoc and institutional arbitration whether domestic or international. The Act refers to 'administered arbitration' in defining arbitration[75] and allows parties to authorize such institution to take decisions the Act permits them to make.[76] In Uganda, the parties are free to determine the number of arbitrators.[77] However, if the parties fail to determine the number of arbitrators under subsection (1), there shall be one arbitrator.[78]

Redfern and Hunter observed in 1995 that:

> [a]n established and well-organized arbitral institution can do much to ensure the smooth progress of an international arbitration even if the parties themselves- or their legal advisers- have little or no practical experience in the field.[79]

70. *Ibid.*, ss 35 and 36.
71. A.C.K Kakooza, *Arbitration, Conciliation and Mediation in Uganda: A Focus on the Practical Aspects*, (2009) vol. 7 no. 2 Uganda Living Law Journal 268, 272 (December 2009).
72. Arbitration and Conciliation Act of Uganda, 2000, s. 67, Cap 4. The Act was enacted to amend the law relating to domestic arbitration, international commercial arbitration and enforcement of foreign arbitral awards, to define the law relating to conciliation of disputes and to make other provision relating to the foregoing.
73. Section 68, Arbitration and Conciliation Act of Uganda.
74. The Government of Uganda Gazette, No. 33 Volume CI dated 27 Jun. 2008, UPPC, Entebbe, 2008, s. 70A. The preamble to the Amendment Act provides that it is an Act to amend the Arbitration and Conciliation Act, (Cap. 4) in order to provide for funding of the Centre for Arbitration and Dispute Resolution by Government and to provide for other related matters.
75. Section 2, Arbitration and Conciliation Act of Uganda.
76. *Ibid.*, s. 2(2).
77. *Ibid.*, s. 10(1).
78. *Ibid.*, s. 10(2).
79. A. Redfern & M. Hunter, *Law and Practice of International Commercial Arbitration* 155 (2nd ed., London: Sweet & Maxwell, 1991). This view is also quoted in A.A. Asouzu, *Some Fundamental*

CADRE may, therefore, have to do more especially with regard to the qualification and accreditation of arbitrators, to ensure that they can competently administer both domestic and international arbitration. It will also be beneficial for the region for CADRE to closely collaborate with the business community and other arbitral institutions in the region to promote the use of arbitration.

[D] Rwanda

Rwanda's law on arbitration and conciliation in commercial matters is based on the UNCITRAL Model Law (2006 revision).[80] The Act applies to domestic and international commercial arbitration and conciliation.[81] However, the Act does not prejudice the enforcement of any other Rwandan Laws by virtue of which certain disputes may not be submitted to arbitration.[82] Article 12 of the Act expressly provides that the parties to arbitration agreement are free to determine the number of arbitrators which, in any case, shall be an odd number. Failing such determination, the number of arbitrators shall be three. The Arbitrators may be from Rwanda or any other country. Rwanda has one arbitration institution, the Kigali International Arbitration Centre, (§4.02[D][1]).[83]

[1] Kigali International Arbitration Centre

In February 2011 the Rwandan Parliament enacted a law establishing the Kigali International Arbitration Centre (KIAC) as an independent body to administer mediation, adjudication and arbitration.[84] KIAC has a panel of domestic and international arbitrators publicly available on its website.[85] Parties to KIAC arbitration are free to nominate their arbitrators, in accordance with the KIAC Rules.[86] However, when KIAC is called upon to appoint an arbitrator, it does so primarily from its panel of arbitrators. It is noteworthy that prior to the establishment of KIAC, there was no formal organization administering amicable dispute resolution processes in both domestic and international disputes.[87]

KIAC has the potential to promote the development of international arbitration in the region and Africa as a whole. With its international outlook, KIAC can forge

Concerns and Issues about International Arbitration in Africa, vol. 1 African Development Bank Law Development Review 81, 86 (2006).

80. Law No. 005/2008 of 12/02/2008, Official Gazette, Special of 6.03.2008. See also R.F. Oppong, *Legal Aspects of Economic Integration in Africa* 240 (Cambridge University Press, 2011).
81. Article 2.
82. *Ibid.*
83. Bernadette Uwiyceza the former Director General of KIAC examines the Centre in greater detail in Ch. 9.
84. Law Establishing the Kigali International Arbitration Centre, Law No. 51/2010 of 10 Jan. 2010, Laws of Rwanda.
85. Panel of arbitrators is available on KIAC website at: http://kiac.org.rw/spip.php?rubrique25 [accessed 8 Apr. 2016].
86. Kigali International Arbitration Centre Rules, 2012, Arts 12-15, published in the Official gazette No. 22 Bis of 28 May 2012, available at: http://www.kiac.org.rw/IMG/pdf/-3.pdf [accessed 5 Apr. 2016].
87. KIAC, Annual Report July 2012-June 2013, p. 4.

strategic partnerships with the other regional Centres to jointly host conferences, provide trainings, workshops and professional development activities for arbitration practitioners.

[E] Burundi

Although, international arbitration in Burundi is supported by law, there are no comprehensive laws on the same. The Civil Procedure Code of 2005 introduced arbitration in Burundi. However, there is a wider issue of language barrier as far as integration within the EAC is concerned since all their laws are in French only.[88] There is one arbitration centre in Burundi, the Burundi Centre for Arbitration and Mediation (BCAM) (§4.02[E][1]).

[1] Burundi Centre for Arbitration and Mediation

In 2007, the Burundian Government created the Burundi Centre for Arbitration and Mediation (BCAM) to deal with commercial and investment disputes.[89] It is not very evident how busy the BCAM has been.[90] In a 2008 World Bank publication, it was noted that the BCAM, need to project its profile to the international community.[91] To increase its visibility, the Centre may enter into strategic collaboration with the other centres within the region in the area of conferences and other activities of these institutions. BCAM can also organize international and regional conferences, in collaboration with the business community of Burundi to promote the use of arbitration to them. Such collaboration may also include the various government ministries that deal with the international business community in the areas of tourism, investments and trade.

[F] East African Court of Justice

A mention should be made of the role of the East African Court of Justice (the EACJ) which is one of the organs of the EAC established under Article 9 of the Treaty for the Establishment of the EAC.[92] The EAC is a regional intergovernmental organization comprising the Governments of Burundi, Kenya, Rwanda, Tanzania and Uganda for

88. Herbert Smith Freehills Dispute Resolution, *Burundi becomes 150th state party to the New York Convention*, available at: http://hsfnotes.com/arbitration/2014/09/03/burundi-becomes-150th-state-party-to-the-new-york-convention/ [Accessed 8 Apr. 2016].
89. Law No. 1/08 of 17 Mar. 2005, Code on the Organization and Competence of the Judiciary.
90. See *USA International Business Publications, Burundi Mineral & Mining Sector Investment and Business Guide: World Strategic and Business Information Library* 128 (Int'l Business Publications, 2013).
91. See I. Baghdadli et al. (eds), *Breaking the Cycle: A Strategy for Conflict-sensitive Rural Growth in Burundi: Main Report* (World Bank Publications, January 2008).
92. Treaty for the Establishment of the East African Community (EAC Treaty), adopted on 30 Nov. 1999 at Arusha, entered into force on 7 Jul. 2000 (Amended on 14 Dec. 2006 and 20 Aug. 2007).

purposes of East African economic, social, cultural and political integration.[93] In addition to the Court's jurisdiction over the interpretation and application of the EAC Treaty,[94] it has arbitration related jurisdiction. The EAC arbitration jurisdiction covers matters arising from arbitration agreements contained in a contract or agreement concluded by the Community or any of its institutions; and arbitration agreements contained in a commercial contract or agreement which the parties have conferred jurisdiction on the Court to deal with arising disputes.[95]

The EAC Court has formulated the EACJ Arbitration Rules, 2012,[96] made under Article 42 of the EAC Treaty.[97] These Rules apply to very arbitration references pursuant to Article 32 of the EAC Treaty.[98] Where the parties have agreed to submit to arbitration under the Rules, they are deemed to have submitted ipso facto to the Rules in effect on the date of the commencement of the arbitration proceedings, unless they have agreed to submit to the Rules in effect on the date of their arbitration agreement.[99]

Despite the existence of the arbitration rules which have incorporated international best practices on arbitration. It does not however appear that the EAC Court has a vibrant arbitration matters cause list.[100] This may partly be attributed to the fact that the integration process of the East Africa Community is still ongoing. The Member countries have also not submitted any matters to the EACJ jurisdiction on arbitration.

§4.03 CHALLENGES

Having examined the various arbitration institutions that operate in East African countries, this section examines some of the challenges confronting these centres and suggests how the centres can grow their workload, make their services better known and strategically share their regional space.

[A] Effectiveness of Arbitration as a Process

I have noted as it relates to Kenya that in some cases parties will litigate arbitration related disputes all the way to the Supreme Court especially in pursuing setting aside

93. Preamble, EAC Treaty.
94. Article 27, EAC Treaty.
95. Article 32, EAC Treaty.
96. East African Court of Justice Rules of Arbitration, EACJ, Arusha, Tanzania, March 2012. The Rules were made in exercise of the powers conferred on the East African Court of Justice by Art. 42 of the Treaty for the Establishment of the East African Community.
97. Rule 1 provides that unless the parties to arbitration agree otherwise: (a) these Rules shall apply to every arbitration under Art. 32 of the Treaty; (b) the parties to any arbitration may agree in writing to modify or waive the application of these Rules; (c) where any of these Rules is in conflict with any provision of the law applicable to arbitration from which the parties cannot derogate, that provision shall prevail.
98. Rule 1(2)(a), East African Court of Justice Rules of Arbitration.
99. Rule 7(1), East African Court of Justice Rules of Arbitration.
100. H.R. Nsekela, *Overview of the East African Court Of Justice*, a paper presented during the sensitization workshop on the *Role of the EACJ in the EAC Integration*, Imperial Royale Hotel, Kampala, Uganda, 1-2 Nov. 2011. Available at: http://eacj.huriweb.org/wp-content/uploads/2013/09/Overview-of-the-EACJ.pdf [accessed 5 Apr. 2016].

of awards.[101] This situation creates an impression that courts are entertaining litigation at the expense of arbitration, thus, scaring away some potential users of arbitration. The effect of this is that parties who are keen on having their disputes settled faster may avoid jurisdictions where they perceive that they may be dragged before courts for longer than necessary. This has the effect of denying the local arbitration institutions the opportunity to administer such arbitration matters.

[B] Institutional Capacity

I have also observed that there exists a challenge on the capacity of existing arbitration institutions in the region to meet the expectations of modern arbitration users. Much more needs to be done to enhance the capacity of these institutions in terms of the number and quality of available arbitrators, adequate administrative staff and financial support to ensure that they are fully equipped to administer in particular international arbitration references.[102]

It is my opinion that despite the existence in Africa of individuals with the relevant knowledge, skill and experience of international dispute resolution and competent institutions, there has been a general tendency by foreign parties doing business in Africa to appoint non-African arbitrators in their arbitration references.[103] This practice has denied local arbitrators the opportunity to put their skills and expertise in arbitration to use in international disputes. The same also applies to the use of foreign arbitration institutions in preference to local institutions. Some African parties also appoint non-Africans as arbitrators. Indeed, Julian Lew has observed that the near absence of African arbitrators in ICSID arbitration proceedings can in part be explained by the fact that African states predominantly appoint international lawyers to represent their interests.[104]

---

101. Section 35(1) of the Act. See K. Muigua, *Role of the Court under Arbitration Act 1995: Court Intervention Before, Pending and Arbitration in Kenya, supra*, available at: http://www.kenyalaw.org/klr/index.php?id=824 [accessed on 8 Apr. 2016]. See the Arbitration between Kanyotta Holdings Limited and Chevron Kenya Limited (CALTEX) which made its way to the Kenya High Court and Court of Appeal after the award was challenged (2012 eKLR). See *Glencore Grain Ltd v. T.S.S.S Grain Millers Ltd* [2012] eKLR; See also Daily Nation Newspaper, 'Not again! Pattni's new Sh4bn scandal,' of Saturday, 11 May 2013, available at: http://www.nation.co.ke/News/Not-again-Pattnis-new-Sh4bn-scandal/-/1056/1849756/-/14axo7az/-/index.html [accessed 8 Apr. 2016]. The Newspaper partly read 'Controversial businessman Kamlesh Pattni is set to pocket Sh4.2 billion worth of taxpayers' money if the High Court upholds a hefty award issued in his favour by an arbitrator'. It went further to state 'But it is the hefty award against the government authority that is likely to attract public attention given that it is *wananchi* (meaning citizens) and taxpayers who will foot the Sh4.2 billion bill.'
102. Kariuki Muigua, *Making East Africa a Hub for International Commercial Arbitration: A Critical Examination of the State of the Legal and Institutional Framework Governing Arbitration in Kenya*, available at: http://www.kmco.co.ke/attachments/article/114/Making%20East%20Africa%20a%20Hub%20for%20International%20Commercial%20Arbitration.pdf [accessed 8 Apr. 2016].
103. Explanatory note by the UNCITRAL secretariat on the Model Law, United Nations document Al40117, annex I.
104. Julian D.M. Lew et al., *Comparative International Commercial Arbitration*, 237 (Kluwer Law International, 2003).

East African arbitral institutions need ensure that, while parties may choose persons of their choice to appoint as arbitrators, they are also provided with a list of qualified African arbitrators from which they may consider appointment. Arbitration institutions (among others) have databases with arbitrators' qualifications which can be made publicly available for ease of reference by parties seeking to appoint arbitrators. It is important for arbitration institutions to support the visibility of African arbitrators as this will in turn raise their profiles which will lead to increased caseload.

Finally it is important that commercial parties are encouraged to include valid arbitration clauses in their contracts. It has been argued that an arbitration clause should take into consideration the applicable law, state and attitude of the possible seat towards arbitration as well as the effect of its domestic law on arbitration proceedings and outcome so as to ensure that the parties' intentions are not defeated by legal technicalities.[105] This is because it is the arbitration clause that dictates where the proceedings will be held and the applicable law. As such, it is important to have a clear non-ambiguous clause as this will not only save time but will also save resources for the parties by way of minimized challenges before national courts.[106]

[C] Arbitration Users' Concerns

There are various issues of concern to users of arbitration, some of which do not fall within the ambit of arbitration institutions while others do.[107] Users need adequate Information Communication Technology (ICT) infrastructure and other relevant physical infrastructure for the conduct of modern arbitration. Some of these arbitration institutions lack such basic infrastructure. Also some of the centres lack institutional capacity which refers to both physical infrastructure and adequately trained staff to assist parties and arbitrators sitting under their rules. Arbitration institutions in Africa must meet these concerns of users and provide a professional environment for such users.

105. McLaughlin, *Arbitration and Developing Countries*, *supra*, 215.
106. See generally Paul Ngotho, *Pathological Arbitration Clauses in Ad Hoc Arbitrations: Kenya's Experience*, paper presented at the Chartered Institute Of Arbitrators (Kenya Branch) & Centre For Alternative Dispute Resolution (CADR) International Arbitration Conference held at Whitesands Beach Hotel, Mombasa, 7-8 Aug. 2014. Available at: http://www.ngotho.co.ke/PathologicalArbitrationClauses.8.8.14.pdf [accessed 8 Apr. 2016].
107. Examples of issues that fall outside the remit of arbitration institutions include: security of lives and property, insurgency and civil strife, government bureaucracy, support facilities such as airports, hotels, etc. See A.B. Chikwanha, *The Anatomy of Conflicts in the East African Community (EAC): Linking Security with Development*, keynote speech to Development Policy Review Network-African Studies Institute, Leiden University, The Netherlands, Theme for 2007-Development Policy and the Security Agenda for Africa: Reassessing the Relationship, available at: https://www.issafrica.org/uploads/EACANNIE.PDF [accessed 27 Jan. 2016]. See also F. N. Ikome, *Africa's International Borders as Potential Sources of Conflict and Future Threats to Peace and Security*, paper no. 233 Institute for Security Studies (2012).

[D] Suggestions

I have observed elsewhere that government intervention in arbitration can raise fears of bias and the exercise of undue influence.[108] However it is important to note that it is possible for arbitration institutions to receive support from the government while retaining their independence. The governments of East African states can provide seed funding to help the institutions commence their activities. These governments can also (and even more importantly) nominate these institutions in their arbitration agreements. State institutions, such as courts can also play a critical role in supporting the arbitral centres by facilitating the enforcement of international and domestic arbitral awards as well as ensuring that there is minimal court interference in the arbitral process. This will win the confidence of potential arbitration users within and outside the region. Parliament and Courts need to also work in tandem in promoting law reform to ensure that the state arbitration related laws reflect modern trends in arbitration practice.[109] An example of government and arbitration centre collaboration is the case of NCIA and the Kenya National Chamber of Commerce and Industry (KNCCI) in Kenya. KNCCI collaborates with the Government of Kenya in promoting business and foreign investment in the country. Some of these investors enter into partnerships with the government who can promote these institutions as competent to administer their disputes.

Arbitration institutions can also support the training of arbitration practitioners and the teaching of arbitration in Law Schools. A good example is the University of Nairobi, School of Law, which currently offers international commercial arbitration as a course on its Masters of Law Programme. This course is also accredited by CIArb-K so that students who pass this course can apply directly to become Associate members of CIArb-K. This not only boosts the number of persons eligible to pursue a career in arbitration but also helps in creating awareness in the country and the region. It is also a powerful tool for improving the legal capacity and personnel of arbitral institutions, and boosting the development and practice of arbitration generally.

CONCLUSION

The availability of effective and reliable arbitration institutions is an additional factor that encourages investors to enter and carry on business in any jurisdiction. This is because of the confidence in knowing their disputes will be settled expeditiously and in a neutral forum. This will also enhance users' confidence in arbitral institutions in the African continent and directly impact positively on the transformation of arbitration practice in Africa.

---

108. See Kariuki Muigua, *Natural Resources and Conflict Management in East Africa*, paper presented at the 1st NCMG East African ADR Summit held at the Windsor Golf Hotel, Nairobi on 25 and 26 Sep. 2014.
109. Kariuki Muigua, *Promoting International Commercial Arbitration in Africa*, available at: http://www.kmco.co.ke/attachments/article/119/PROMOTING%20INTERNATIONAL%20COMMERCIAL%20ARBITRATION%20IN%20AFRICA.pdf [accessed 5 Apr. 2016].

PART III Arbitration Institutions in Africa

CHAPTER 5

The Experience of LCIA-MIAC

Duncan Bagshaw

INTRODUCTION

This chapter examines the impact of the collaboration between the LCIA and MIAC to answer the question whether, and to what extent, it is necessary or helpful to the success of an Africa-based arbitration institution, for such institution to collaborate with a more established and recognized foreign arbitration institution. Section §5.01 briefly describes the history of Mauritius and its legal system. Section §5.02 engages with the idea of making Mauritius a place for international dispute resolution. Section §5.03 then examines the future prospects of the LCIA-MIAC Centre, followed by a conclusion which gives the author's insights on what steps other African states wishing to become a hub for international arbitration may take.

§5.01 SOME BACKGROUND ON MAURITIUS AND ITS LEGAL SYSTEM

Mauritius is unusual amongst African countries. It is a very small country with a small population of about 1.4 million people.[1] The population is highly ethnically diverse, which is a product of the history of Mauritius. Until the seventeenth Century, Mauritius was completely uninhabited. It was colonized in the eighteenth Century, first by the Dutch and then by the French. In 1810 it became a British colony. During this colonial period many thousands of people were brought to Mauritius to work, first from Africa as slaves, and later from India as indentured labourers. This gives Mauritius its unique culture, with a population which is made up of African, Malagasy, Indian, European

1. See: http://statsmauritius.govmu.org/English/StatsbySubj/Documents/ei1127/population.pdf [accessed 13 Mar. 2016].

and Chinese origins.[2] Whilst this history has been the cause of significant displacement and trauma, it has provided Mauritius with the foundations of its economic development since it achieved independence from the British in 1964. The diverse population of the country has allowed it to maintain strong cultural and diplomatic links with Europe, Africa and Asia. This has been particularly beneficial in recent times to provide sources of business for the development of Mauritius as a place for the incorporation of international businesses and other entities. Many of the users of Mauritius as an international place of business originate in India and Europe. In spite of its diverse population and although it is some 500 kilometres off the coast of Madagascar, Mauritius is in political terms located in the continent of Africa. It is a member of the African Union, the Southern African Development Community, and Common Market for Eastern and Southern Africa. It has played a significant role in recent international political affairs in Africa.[3] For example, Mauritius has been one of the most active participants in the programme to combat piracy in the Indian Ocean.[4]

Despite their diversity of origin, the people of Mauritius share a strong Mauritian identity. This is for several reasons. One reason is that the country has seen a largely stable political environment since it became independent in 1960. All of the population has been able to vote in legislative elections since 1948,[5] and the make-up of the political class has reflected the diversity of the population to an increasing extent since that time, although with a bias towards the wealthier and more educated groups. Language has also had a role to play. In everyday life, Mauritian people speak a form of French known as Mauritian Creole.[6] It is a unique language, based on French but with a different syntax, verb conjugations and vocabulary. It is similar to languages spoken in some other former French colonies such as Haiti. In business, the English and French languages are used, with the English language dominating legal and political matters. This mixture of languages is the result of its particular history. When Mauritius became a British colony in 1810, the handover was made subject to a detailed treaty, called the Treaty of Paris. This guaranteed that the Mauritian people would not immediately have English law forced upon them. Nor would they be obliged to speak English. Instead they were specifically allowed to retain their own language and laws. This Treaty may be said to both reflect, and to have reinforced, the strength of Mauritian identity and, in my opinion, the determination of Mauritian people to shape their own destiny, in spite of the history of the nation as a formerly unpopulated ocean colony.

2. See A. Toussaint, *Histoire de l'île Maurice* (Persée, 1974). See also D. Piat, *L'île Maurice 1598-1810 Sur la route des épices* (Les Editions du Pacifique, 2010).
3. See Mauritius's profile on the Southern African Development Community website, available at: http://www.sadc.int/member-states/mauritius/ [accessed 13 Mar. 2016].
4. Mauritius has hosted trials of individuals accused of piracy and has facilitated work by the UNODC on criminal procedure in piracy cases. For more details see, *UNODC Global Maritime Crime Programme Annual Report 2015* available at: https://www.unodc.org/documents/Piracy/15-07385_AR_ebook_Small.pdf [accessed 13 Mar. 2016].
5. R. Ramtohul, *Engendering Mauritian History: The Hidden Controversies over Female Suffrage*, vol. 17 Afrika Zamani 63-80 (2009) available at: www.codesria.org/IMG/pdf/4-Ramtohul__Zamani_17_2009.pdf?3017/ [accessed 13 Mar. 2016].
6. J. Lee, *Mauritius: Its Creole Language* (3rd ed., Merlin Press, 2008).

As a result of this background, Mauritian law today is a hybrid of French- and English-style laws. Whilst the law remained intact when Mauritius became a British colony, the Courts thereafter operated in an English style, with adversarial proceedings held in front of a Judge who would act as an arms-length tribunal deciding between the parties' cases, rather than as inquisitor in the French style. Parties in Court were, and still are, represented by Barristers who work alongside attorneys (sometimes called *Avoués*). In addition, since the system of property law has developed from the French system, Notaries public also have an important role to play in registrable transactions.

Over the years, much of the new laws enacted by the Mauritian National Assembly have been based on English laws. This has particularly been the case in areas of law which were thought to be important to Mauritius' desire to become an international financial centre and centre of business, such as company law, insolvency law and the law of trusts. The law in the modern era is therefore a mixture of civil-law style Codes, including the *Code Civile* and *Code Penale*, and English-style legislation. Court procedure is similar to English court procedure, although it has changed less in the past fifty years or so than the procedure in the Courts of England and Wales. The parties tend to drive the process at their own pace, through technical written pleadings, motions, disclosure and affidavits. Trials are often lengthy with significant live oral evidence and cross-examination. The law of evidence features prominently in the litigation process.

The structure of the Courts is divided into two principal levels: Magistrates Courts and District Courts hear smaller matters at first instance. The Supreme Court acts as a Court of Appeal from those courts, but it can hear cases at first instance where the amount in dispute is significant or when the case raises an important issue. Appeals from the Supreme Court may be heard by a three-judge bench of Supreme Court Judges.

A significant remnant of Mauritius's past as a British colony is the role of the Judicial Committee of the Privy Council of England and Wales. Mauritius became a Republic in 1990. Although it remains part of the Commonwealth, the United Kingdom monarch is thereafter not the head of state. In spite of this, Her Majesty's Privy Council remains the highest court of Mauritius, by statute.[7] This is a feature of the Mauritian legal system which offers predictability and independence which could make Mauritius an attractive forum for international parties, as discussed below.

§5.02 MAURITIUS AS A PLACE FOR INTERNATIONAL DISPUTE RESOLUTION

This section examines the initiatives taken by the government of Mauritius with clearly defined objectives to promote Mauritius as a centre for international arbitration, taking into consideration the peculiarities of the Mauritian system. To realize this vision, the government of Mauritius revamped their business laws (§5.02[A]), modernized their

7. Constitution of the Republic of Mauritius 1968. See also The Courts Act 1945, ss 70A and 81.

arbitration law (§5.02[B]), modernized their court processes in arbitration related matters (§5.02[C]), and created the LCIA-MIAC Centre (§5.02[D]).

[A] Modernization of Mauritius Business Laws

Until the 1990s, the economy of Mauritius was dominated by three sectors: tourism, agriculture (primarily in the form of growing sugar cane for export) and light manufacturing, particularly clothing.[8] In 1992 the government of Mauritius embarked upon a project to make Mauritius a place of business, in particular a place for offshore (as it was then called) financial services by passing the Mauritius Offshore Business Activities Act 1992. To support this industry, a simple system of taxation was devised and implemented gradually between 1998 and 2006 (culminating in the Finance Act 2006) whereby tax on business profits and personal income was fixed at 15% (which has not changed since) and capital gains tax was abolished. At the same time, a new category of corporation or trust was established which could be set up in Mauritius with a view to doing most of its business in other jurisdictions.[9] Companies (or other legal entities) set up under this system could benefit from a rebate of a large part of the tax they would otherwise pay in Mauritius on the basis that they paid tax overseas.

Mauritius was well placed to provide these services because it has an educated, bilingual population and a stable, predictable economy and legal system with respect to the rule of law. In addition to the low-tax regime, there were also few controls on the movement of funds into and out of Mauritius, and Mauritius had an attractive level of political stability and judicial independence, so that investors would not be unduly afraid of arbitrary deprivation of their assets or business on political grounds.[10] For finality of determination of disputes, the Privy Council is the court of last resort and this also reassures foreign parties that the decision of the Mauritian courts could be appealed to the Privy Council. Mauritius also had, and rapidly expanded, a network of double taxation agreements (DTAs). Such treaties allowed companies from the countries with which Mauritius had such treaties, operating under the Global Business system, to benefit from an agreement that they would not pay domestic tax in their own country, to which they might repatriate their assets or profits, having earned those profits or acquired those assets in Mauritius. The network of DTAs has continued to grow and there are currently at least forty-three such treaties in place.[11]

Mauritius also embarked upon a rapid process of negotiating and signing Bilateral Investment Treaties (BITs) with governments of states in which Mauritian companies (including those incorporated in Mauritius by overseas investors adopting Mauritius as

8. See the World Bank: Overview at: http://www.worldbank.org/en/country/mauritius/overview [accessed 13 Mar. 2016].
9. See the Guide to Global Business issued by the Mauritius Financial Services Commission, which regulate global business companies, amongst others.
10. For discussion on the importance of this, see for example: IDEAS Report, *Political Stability: Crucial for Growth* available at: http://www.lse.ac.uk/IDEAS/publications/reports/pdf/SU004/shepherd.pdf [accessed 13 Mar. 2016].
11. For more details see: http://www.mra.mu/index.php/taxes-duties/double-taxation-agreements [accessed 13 Mar. 2016].

a base) could trade and invest. Those treaties make Mauritius an attractive place to locate a business since they provide additional protections for foreign investors from detrimental treatment in the country of investment. Such treatments include improper expropriation of assets, or unfair discrimination against foreign investors. Mauritius currently has signed at least forty-three BITs.[12]

The offshore system business model, which later became known by the less stigmatized title of 'Global Business', was a success.[13] Foreign investors and wealthy individuals used Mauritius as a place to invest assets, make profits and incorporate companies to hold assets or to trade their businesses. For example, a South African company in the business of distributing foodstuff may incorporate a company in Mauritius which would own, directly or indirectly, the company's operations in West Africa. The system was particularly attractive to investors from India, because of the favourable DTA between Mauritius and India. Such investors would include, for example, a foreign purchaser of a shareholding in an Indian company. The investor may choose to hold its investment in India through a Mauritian special purpose company in order to benefit from the treaty, which would allow profits to be repatriated untaxed from India to Mauritius before being subject to Mauritian tax. Allegations have been made that this relationship was abused by wealthy Indians who sent assets out from India, only to bring them back to India via Mauritius and thereby avoid capital gains and income tax (known as 'round-tripping').[14] The extent of this practice is not known but the government of India has proposed the introduction of new regulations which allow detailed investigations to be made into the true sources of, and ownership of, assets and profits in India, with a view to preventing abuse.[15] In recent times it has encouraged those involved in the Global Business industry in Mauritius to seek to diversify the geographical sources of investment, in order to avoid the risk of losing most of their business in the event of the Indian government renegotiating the DTA.[16] With the Global Business sector growing in importance it was only natural that Mauritius would want to ensure that its legal system was of a standard which would be attractive to international parties. Whilst the availability of the Privy Council was an advantage, the Courts of Mauritius were perceived to be slow[17] and were anecdotally

12. For a list of these BITs see the UNCTAD treaty database at: http://investmentpolicyhub.unctad.org/IIA [accessed 13 Mar. 2016].
13. A change introduced in the Mauritius Financial Services Development Act 2001.
14. See for example: http://articles.economictimes.indiatimes.com/2015-08-09/news/65379646_1_tax-treaty-fsc-mauritius-india-mauritius [accessed 13 Mar. 2016].
15. See for example, Economic Times, *Top FPIs Raise Concerns with Sebi over Mauritius Treaty, GAAR and Participatory Notes*, available at: http://articles.economictimes.indiatimes.com/2015-08-14/news/65524781_1_tax-treaty-mauritius-treaty-capital-gains-tax [accessed 13 Mar. 2016].
16. The Mauritius Finance Minister, Seetanah Lutchmeenaraidoo describes Mauritius thus: 'Singapore is to Southeast Asia what Dubai is to the Middle East, and Mauritius will be vis-a-vis Africa'; while the Deputy Prime Minister and Tourism Minister, Charles Gaetan Xavier-Luc Duval confirmed that: 'Our aim is to contribute towards investment into Africa'. As quoted in Reuters, 'Mauritius eyes Africa as pressure mounts on offshore business', 16 Oct. 2015.
17. See the *OECD Investment Policy Reviews: Mauritius* 92-93 (OECD Publications, 2014).

said to be rather unpredictable at times. Arbitrations were held in Mauritius, particularly to resolve disputes regarding domestic construction projects, but any international dispute would be likely to be resolved through either the London Court of International Arbitration (LCIA) or the ICC in Paris.

The project to make Mauritius a centre for international arbitration is thought to have good prospects of success. Mauritius can be said to be a neutral place, politically African, but removed from mainland Africa, and not part of the main geo-political blocs of North Africa, West Africa, East Africa or Southern Africa, and francophone Africa. Mauritius may be seen as distinct from most other African countries to be neutral between parties from two African states, or parties from one African state and a non-African state. Because its geographical location is between Africa and Asia, it was already clear from around 2005 where many large international arbitration disputes would originate in the future. The fact that all Mauritian professionals are bilingual also means they could communicate in the languages of almost all other African countries, and the two most widely used languages of arbitration, English and French.[18] Mauritius is also considered a safe destination for travel.[19] In addition it has first class hotels and meeting facilities, primarily as a result of its well-developed tourism industry.

These advantages were sufficient to encourage a belief on the part of the government of Mauritius that the country had the potential to become a centre for international arbitration. But that was merely the first step. A belief in the potential of a venue for arbitration is not, on its own, a reason to embark on the long, difficult and expensive process of establishing a new venue from scratch. A perceived favourable arbitration regime may attract investors. The ability to resolve disputes in a reliable and efficient way in the same jurisdiction as investments are domiciled is attractive. If successful the development of an international arbitration centre may become a contribution in itself to the economy, with increased visitors, use of hotels, meeting facilities, lawyers and other services. However there are wider, more profound reasons why the government of Mauritius thought that to develop itself as an arbitral centre would be worthwhile. First, international arbitration has a reputation, which may be deserved, for being an institution dominated by the developed world.[20] Most arbitrators appointed in international matters are from America or Europe, or increasingly from developed Asian countries.[21] Most administered international arbitrations are by

18. With the possible exception of Chinese which is also spoken by a few Mauritians.
19. See for example the UK Government Travel advice at: https://www.gov.uk/foreign-travel-advice/mauritius [accessed 13 Mar. 2016]. See also the USA government travel advice on Mauritius at: http://www.state.gov/misc/1016.htm [accessed 13 Mar. 2016].
20. Christopher R. Drahozal & Richard W. Naimark, *Towards a Science of International arbitration: Collected Empirical Research* 27 (Kluwer Law International, 2005). See also Prime Minister of Mauritius, *Mauritius International Arbitration Conference 2010 Speech*, available at: http://itcoach.intnet.mu/portal/goc/pm/file/miac.pdf [accessed 13 Mar. 2016].
21. *LCIA Statistics: LCIA Registrar's Report 2013* at: http://www.lcia.org/LCIA/reports.aspx [accessed 13 Mar. 2016]. See also to the same effect, ICSID statistics available at: https://icsid.worldbank.org/apps/icsidweb/resources/pages/icsid-caseload-statistics.aspx [accessed 13 Mar. 2016].

institutions in developed countries and hearings are held in developed countries.[22] Most law firms appointed to act in international arbitrations are based in the USA or Europe.[23] Therefore establishing attractive, credible centres for arbitration in the developing world provides a platform from which this Americano-Eurocentric dominance of the field can be gradually eroded. A centre of excellence in Africa can offer opportunities for African arbitrators and lawyers to play a more important role in arbitration resolving international disputes involving African parties, and arising out of African projects.[24] The Mauritian arbitration community and the government of Mauritius believed Mauritius was well placed to provide such a centre and consciously set about putting structures in place to achieve this through the modernization of its laws and courts, and the creation of the LCIA-MIAC Arbitration centre.

[B] The International Arbitration Law of Mauritius

It is not an exaggeration to say that the legislation governing arbitration in Mauritius is amongst the most advanced, supportive and favourable in the world. Mauritius acceded to the New York Convention in 2002, but its arbitration law at that time was contained in the *Code de Procedure Civile*, which was similar to the law of France before it was substantially reformed in 2001.[25] The *Code de Procedure Civile* continues to govern domestic arbitration although there have recently been calls to reform the law on that subject.[26] In order to make Mauritius an attractive place for international parties to hold arbitration, it was clear that a new legislation was required. The new law was drafted by a team of arbitration specialists from the Office of the Attorney General of Mauritius with contribution from some leading arbitration lawyers from London.[27] The new legislation titled, International Arbitration Act (IAA) was modelled on the UNCITRAL Model Law (2006 revision) with various additions and some variations. These variations were made to improve upon the Model Law and make Mauritius even more attractive as a seat of international arbitration. Since the arbitration law of any jurisdiction is an important part of what makes it an attractive seat, some important features of the IAA are examined below.

The IAA applies to international arbitrations, which means arbitrations where the parties have their place of business in different states, or where the place of performance of the contract is different from the place where the parties have their place of business, or where the seat of arbitration is in a state different from that in which the

22. See for example the findings of Queen Mary University of London, *International arbitration survey on Choices in International Arbitration 2010*, and their *2013 Survey on Corporate Choices in International Arbitration*, available at http://www.arbitration.qmul.ac.uk/research/index.html [accessed 13 Mar. 2016].
23. *Ibid.*
24. See the speech given by Salim Moollan at the closing ceremony of the 2nd ICCA Congress, Miami, 2014: ICCA Congress Series, Miami 2014, Kluwer Law International.
25. *Oxenham v. France Maritime Agency Ltee (FMA)* 2016 SCJ 10; see also, J. Peeroo et A. Guilmain, *Pour une réforme du droit mauricien de l'arbitrage international en matière de reconnaissance et d'exécution des sentences*, vol. 3 The New Bar Chronicle (Mauritius) (9-14 Nov. 2011).
26. *Ibid.*
27. These lawyers included Salim Moollan QC, Toby Landau QC, and Mr Ricky Diwan.

parties have their place of business.[28] The IAA also applies if the parties expressly agree that it should apply to their arbitration. This latter provision allows parties in any arbitration to opt-in to the legislation, which means that any arbitration seated in Mauritius, including an entirely domestic Mauritian arbitration, may be governed by the IAA if the parties so choose.

The IAA includes similar provisions on the powers and duties of the arbitral tribunal to those found in the UNCITRAL Model Law. It also provides the same limited grounds for setting aside arbitral awards as those in the UNCITRAL Model Law. However the court which has the power to set aside an award (and indeed to make any decision in a matter governed by the IAA) is a three-judge panel of Supreme Court judges. This skips one entire stage (that of a single Supreme Court judge) of the usual Mauritian court process, shortening any court proceedings. It also ensures that in any matter before the Court under the IAA, the decision will be made by three judges rather than one. This is helpful both on the grounds that 'three heads are better than one', and because the case thereby receives the combined understanding and knowledge of three judges rather than risking being heard by a single judge who has a limited knowledge of arbitration law. The direct resort to the three-judge bench also reduces delay and the opportunities for parties to abuse the court process. The three judges must be drawn from a special panel of six Supreme Court judges, called 'Designated Judges', who are appointed by the Chief Justice to hear all cases under the IAA. These judges are given special training in arbitration law. Having a small pool of judges also increases the rate at which the Designated Judges gain experience of the subject, since cases will come before each Designated Judge more often than if cases were shared between all of the Supreme Court judges.

The IAA includes detailed provisions on interim measures. Arbitral tribunals in arbitrations seated in Mauritius have the power to make a range of orders for interim reliefs.[29] The Supreme Court will enforce such orders unless one of a limited range of grounds can be shown. The grounds include the same grounds for refusing to enforce a final award which are set out in section 39 of the IAA; plus where a party shows that the applicant has not complied with any requirement of security imposed by the arbitral tribunal; or where the interim measure has been set aside by the arbitral tribunal or an appropriate court.[30] The Supreme Court itself has the same power to make orders for interim relief as it has in relation to any proceedings in the Supreme Court, however its powers are restricted so as to limit its ability to act to urgent cases where the arbitral tribunal cannot for the time being act effectively, or where the tribunal agrees to the Court intervening.[31]

Perhaps the most innovative feature of the IAA is the procedure by which challenges to arbitrators are resolved, and by which other matters regarding the arbitral tribunal are resolved in the absence of a designated institution. Under the IAA, where a party wishes to challenge an arbitrator, the party is required to first apply to the

28. Section 1 IAA.
29. Section 21, IAA.
30. Section 22(4) (a), IAA.
31. Section 26, IAA.

tribunal and, if the arbitrator does not withdraw, then to apply to any arbitration institution designated in the arbitration agreement.[32] Where institutional rules are chosen, this is likely to be the institution administering the arbitration. If unsatisfied with the decision of any appointed institution, or if no institution is designated, the party may then bring its challenge before the Secretary General of the Permanent Court of Arbitration (PCA).[33]

The Secretary-General of the PCA will make a decision on the challenge after receiving written submissions and issue the decision in writing.[34] There is no appeal from that decision and the parties must continue the arbitration with that decision gives effect to, either by the challenged arbitrator continuing, or replaced, as the case may be. The Supreme Court retains all its powers upon challenges to the award at the end of the proceedings or after a decision on jurisdiction if that decision is made separately earlier in the proceedings.[35] This means that an award may be challenged on grounds which are the same as those on which the challenge to the arbitrator was made before the PCA. The Court would not be bound by the decision of the PCA in that situation and would consider the challenge to the award afresh.[36]

The IAA clearly provides that parties may be represented in arbitration proceedings seated in Mauritius by any person they choose, which may or may not be a person legally qualified in Mauritius or anywhere else.[37] The IAA also provides that hearings in arbitration proceedings seated in Mauritius may take place anywhere, or by electronic communications, but the award will be deemed to have been made in Mauritius.[38]

[C] Modernization of the Court Structure

A special regime for determining and awarding costs in cases before the Supreme Court under the IAA has been put in place.[39] In non-arbitration cases, costs are usually awarded in favour of the successful party on a fixed scale, regardless of the actual costs incurred. In large and complex cases, this can leave the successful party substantially out of pocket, since the amounts which may be awarded under the fixed scale will fall well short of the costs of, say, instructing a Senior Attorney and Senior Counsel to act in a case which goes to trial. In cases under the IAA, the Supreme Court will generally award costs to the successful party against the unsuccessful party (although it has a

32. Section 14, IAA.
33. Based in The Hague, but with an office in Mauritius to facilitate the performance of its role there, the PCA is an international, intergovernmental body which is the default appointing authority under the UNCITRAL Arbitration Rules; and the PCA has long experience of making such decisions.
34. For the role of the PCA as appointing authority see, http://www.pca-cpa.org/showpage9a4c.html?pag_id=1492 [accessed 13 Mar. 2016].
35. Section 20, IAA.
36. See para. 73 of the Travaux Préparatoires to the IAA, published in the Updated Handbook to the International Arbitration Act 2008 (Government of Mauritius, 2014).
37. Section 31, IAA.
38. Sections 10 and 36(5), IAA.
39. The International Arbitration Claims Rules 2013, Part 5.

discretion to make other orders as appropriate) and will determine the amount of those costs by making an assessment of the amount of costs actually incurred, and awarding such part of those costs as the Court finds are reasonable.[40] Claims to the recognition and enforcement of international arbitration awards in Mauritius must be brought before the Supreme Court, which will sit as a three-judge panel.[41] The Claimant's application will be made without notice in the first instance and, assuming that the application complies with the essential requirements, an interim order will be made which will become enforceable in the event that the Defendant does not apply to set it aside within three months of receipt of the award. The ground for refusing enforcement of the arbitral award is the same as those set in Article V of the New York Convention.[42]

The Supreme Court of Mauritius considered the law on enforcement of arbitral awards in detail in the case of Cruz City 1 Mauritius Holdings.[43] In this case an application was made by Cruz City 1 Mauritius Holdings to enforce an arbitral award made in London for a sum of over USD 350 million, arising out of a dispute regarding a property development project in India. The defendants sought to resist enforcement of the award on various grounds, all of which were rejected by the Court. In particular, the Court made it clear that where enforcement is resisted on the grounds that enforcement of the award would breach public policy, the public policy in question must be a specific, demonstrated principle of the international public policy of Mauritius. The Court also rejected an argument that the system of enforcement of international arbitration awards in Mauritius is inconsistent with the Constitution. Overall, the decision is a strong indication of the positive attitude of the Supreme Court of Mauritius to the enforcement of arbitral awards. The case presented various opportunities for the Court to decline enforcement of the award, if it had so minded, but the Court's careful examination of the grounds relied upon to resist the enforcement and its reliance on the purpose and spirit of the IAA in reaching its decision evidence its pro-arbitration stance.

[D] Establishing the LCIA-MIAC Arbitration Centre

The fourth limb of the vision of the government of Mauritius in making Mauritius a destination for international arbitration was to establish an arbitral institution at around the same time that it passed the 2008 IAA. It was obvious that, to have a chance of becoming recognized as a credible venue for international arbitration, within a short time, Mauritius needed an administrative institution which would provide services at the level of the major arbitration institutions of the world. Such institution would also need to be irreproachably independent and fee from any political or other improper influence. In order to achieve this, without having to wait many years to build such a reputation organically, it was decided by the Government of Mauritius to seek the

40. *Ibid.*
41. The Convention on the Recognition and Enforcement of Foreign Arbitral Awards Act 2001. See also ss 2 and 42, IAA.
42. Section 39, IAA.
43. *Cruz City 1 Mauritius Holdings v. Unitech and Others* [2014] SCJ 100.

support of the LCIA to partner with the new arbitration institution. There were precedents for this, as the LCIA had previously supported the establishment of new arbitration centres in Dubai[44] and India.[45]

It has always been important for the arbitration centre established in Mauritius to be a Mauritian centre (and hence an African centre) and not a branch of the LCIA. This had to be balanced against the need for the centre to be truly international and protected against any actual, perceived or improper influence. The structure of LCIA and Mauritius International Arbitration Centre (MIAC) was designed with the need for this balance in mind. So the LCIA-MIAC is a company incorporated under the Companies Act of Mauritius as Mauritius International Arbitration Centre Limited (MIAC Ltd). The constitution of MIAC Ltd provides that its governance shall be in accordance with an agreement made between the Government of Mauritius, MIAC Ltd and the LCIA. The agreement provides a detailed scheme for the operation and management of MIAC Ltd. The key aspects of the structure are that MIAC Ltd is managed by a board of five directors. Two directors are appointed by the LCIA, two by the Government of Mauritius and the fifth, the Chairman of the Board, is appointed unanimously by the other four directors. The secretariat is headed by the Registrar assisted by Deputy Registrars if appointed. The Registrar and any deputies are appointed by the Board. Where there is any disagreement amongst the Board, the LCIA has the casting vote over the choice of Registrar. The remainder of the secretariat staff are appointed by the Board on the recommendation of the Registrar.

The Arbitration Rules of LCIA-MIAC are similar to those of the 1998 LCIA Arbitration Rules. They have not yet been updated to be consistent with the current 2014 LCIA Rules, though they already incorporated some of the amendments to the LCIA Rules which were introduced in 2014. These include: the additional duty on arbitrators to seek the 'expeditious' resolution of cases, in addition to their duty to resolve cases fairly and efficiently;[46] and a provision that deems the law governing the arbitration agreement to be the law of the seat, unless the parties have expressly agreed to another law.[47]

Where the structures of LCIA-MIAC and the LCIA intersect most closely is in their use of the LCIA Court. The LCIA Court is a body of independent arbitrators, separate from the LCIA itself, and is governed by its own separate constitution.[48] The LCIA Court is made up of thirty-five arbitrators, no more than five of whom may be British citizens. Its role under the LCIA Rules and the LCIA-MIAC Rules is essentially the same.

LCIA-MIAC charges fees for its services in a similar way to those charged by the LCIA. Work done by the secretariat is charged at hourly rates depending on the

44. LCIA-DIFC was established as an arbitral institution at the heart of the Dubai International Financial Centre. For more details see, www.lcia-difc.org [accessed 13 Mar. 2016].
45. LCIA India was established in 2009 as a direct subsidiary of the LCIA and closed in 2016.
46. Articles 5.3, 14.3 and 14.4, LCIA-MIAC Arbitration Rules.
47. Article 16.3, LCIA-MIAC Arbitration Rules. This provision is designed to preclude protracted arguments over which law governs the arbitration agreement, such as happened in *Sulamerica CIA Nacional De Seguros SA and Others v. Enesa Engenharia SA and Others* [2012] EWHC 42 (Comm) and on appeal [2012] EWCA Civ 638.
48. For the constitution of the LCIA Court see: www.lcia.org [accessed 13 Mar. 2016].

seniority of the staff-member doing the work.[49] At the start of the arbitration a fixed registration fee must be paid.[50] A small overhead of 5% of the arbitrators' fees is also charged in addition to the hourly administrative costs, to cover overheads. The fees payable to LCIA-MIAC are substantially less than those charged by the LCIA.[51] LCIA-MIAC can distinguish itself from the LCIA in one important further respect. Whilst LCIA-MIAC has access to the database of arbitrators held by the LCIA from which the LCIA identifies potential candidates for appointment, LCIA-MIAC also has the opportunity to develop and draw upon a pool of both African arbitrators and those based elsewhere. Thus at the very least, there is an opportunity for the LCIA-MIAC Secretariat to become familiar with arbitrators who may not be as well known to the London secretariat.

LCIA-MIAC has had a slow start in that, to date, only one fully administered case is known to have been handled. However that was not unexpected. It has always been known by the Government of Mauritius that the project will take time to get up to speed and that the arbitration centre itself will not be busy with a heavy caseload for some years.[52] LCIA-MIAC is targeting international disputes, such that it cannot rely on an immediate flow of domestic disputes to provide a source of business in the short term. This strategy has both advantages and disadvantages. On the positive side, the strategy preserves the clarity of LCIA-MIAC mission and the idea that it will focus on international arbitration and dedicate its resources to that field. Such focus is also consistent with the overall nature of the Mauritius international arbitration project. In a jurisdiction where legislation has been passed specifically to cover international arbitration, it is logical for an arbitral institution to have a similar focus and specialism. The drawback of the strategy is that, with this focus, LCIA-MIAC cannot expect significant numbers of domestic cases to be referred to it for administration. Its marketing strategy has been to promote itself as a specialist international arbitration institution. Furthermore, the rates and regime of charging for administrative services in relation to arbitration will probably not be attractive to parties to domestic disputes. Such parties are more familiar with ad hoc arbitration without administrative fees to pay in addition to those of the arbitral tribunal. However LCIA-MIAC has organized hearings in Mauritius of arbitration cases not otherwise administered by it.[53]

49. LCIA-MIAC Schedule of Fees is available at: www.lcia-miac.org [accessed 13 Mar. 2016].
50. This fixed fee is currently MUR 50,000.
51. Currently the fees charged by the LCIA-MIAC secretariat are around 55% of those charged by the LCIA. For example the hourly rate payable for Counsel at the LCIA is GBP 225 while for the equivalent rate for LCIA-MIAC is MUR 4,000 (approximately, GBP 80).
52. As Professor Jan Paulsson reminded the government officials present at the MIAC 2010 conference that establishing a new arbitral seat and centre, 'takes patient agriculture...the harvest is perhaps 15 years in the future'. *MIAC 2010 Book* (Government of Mauritius, 2010).
53. Though LCIA-MIAC has had limited business, it has been recognized in a report published in 2014 by the African Development Bank on Arbitration Venues in Africa available at: http://www.afdb.org/fileadmin/uploads/afdb/Documents/Procurement/Project-related-Procurement/Assessment_Report_of_arbitration_centres_in_C%C3%B4te_d%E2%80%99Ivoire__Egypt_and_Mauritius.pdf [accessed 13 Mar. 2016]. LCIA-MIAC also received the GAR 2015 award for up-and-coming regional arbitration centre.

§5.03 LCIA-MIAC AND ITS FUTURE PROSPECTS

As described above, LCIA-MIAC has been carefully designed and structured to operate at the standards of major established arbitration institutions, whilst maintaining its own identity and independence from any improper influence. However there are certain challenges which face LCIA-MIAC which should be acknowledged. Some should be taken more seriously than others. Counter-intuitively, one of Mauritius's lesser obstacles lies in its own beauty. As a tropical island, with turquoise seas, white beaches and mangoes hanging in the trees, Mauritius may be said to lack the obvious characteristics of an arbitration venue, which tend to be established in large cities which are also financial centres. There may even be a fear on the part of lawyers that by choosing Mauritius as a venue, they have selected a less 'serious' venue than if they had chosen somewhere with less obvious aesthetic charms. The truth is that all cities which are major arbitration venues have features which attract parties other than their arbitration infrastructure. It is not unreasonable to suggest that parties and their lawyers take advantage of the cuisine if arbitrating in Paris, or shopping if arbitrating in New York.

There are two parts to addressing this issue: First, those considering arbitrating in Mauritius should understand that it is not a desert island. It is ranked by the World Bank *Doing Business Report* 2016 as the best country in Africa to do business partly because the infrastructure for business is sophisticated and reliable.[54] Most of the major international banks and the 'big four' accountancy firms have major offices in Mauritius. The hotels which also serve the tourism industry provide extensive high quality spaces for hearings and other services. The Government of Mauritius has announced an intention to establish a dedicated first class hearing centre which should open in 2016.[55] With the hearing centre in place, Mauritius will the physical infrastructure required for major international hearings.

More difficult to address for Mauritius may be the feeling of potential users of the centre that it falls between two categories of arbitration venue: on the one hand as a major, international, non-African centre, on the other as one of those centres which have been or may be established in the major cities of the African continent; Lagos, Johannesburg, Cairo, Nairobi.[56] Whilst those centres have their own challenges they do offer venues in major economies which are home to substantial infrastructure development, resources extraction and exploitation and large populations with the potential to produce major projects which can lead to large disputes. Mauritius is an African venue, and LCIA-MIAC is an African centre. In addition to being an obvious solution where the dispute calls for an African venue but one party is cautious about arbitrating in the other major African cities mentioned above, a real opportunity lies for

54. See the *World Bank Doing Business Report 2016* available at: http://www.doingbusiness.org/~/media/GIAWB/Doing%20Business/Documents/Annual-Reports/English/DB16-Full-Report.pdf [accessed 13 Mar. 2016].
55. This was part of the speech of the Solicitor-General at the Mauritius International Arbitration conference 2014.
56. Kigali also deserves a mention here for its arbitration centre, although it is not a major city in itself.

Mauritius in the need for African centres which can be chosen which are not necessarily the source of the major contracts and projects. This can be seen in the success of cities like Geneva or Stockholm as arbitration venues.

Mauritius can also benefit from its increasing use as a place of incorporation of companies and other structures by international investors. Where a party has already chosen Mauritius as a place to establish companies and to invest funds, there is an increased likelihood that they will be minded to choose it as a place of arbitration. The legal infrastructure in Mauritius is undeniably favourable and, with increased familiarity on the part of those using Mauritius as a place of business, they are also likely to feel more comfortable in agreeing to arbitrate there.

The final challenge for Mauritius which justifies specific mention is that, whilst it is geographically located closer to Asia and sub-Sahara Africa than most European cities, it is not yet as accessible as it can be. Its latitude means that the journey from anywhere around the Equator is fairly long. Mauritius currently has direct flights to London, Paris, Frankfurt, Nairobi, Johannesburg, Dubai, New Delhi, Kuala Lumpur, Singapore, Hong Kong, Shanghai and Perth.[57] However many of these destinations are not served by daily flights, making journeys inflexible. It would seem sensible for Mauritius to also have direct flights to at least major West African cities.

Finally the recent closure of the LCIA India arbitration centre,[58] another project by the LCIA to establish an LCIA-style centre in an emerging centre for arbitration, is a troubling development for other new centres. Mauritius will probably note this news with concern. However, the two environments of India and Mauritius are very different and the decision of the LCIA to withdraw from India does not necessarily indicate that Mauritius will suffer the same fate.

CONCLUSION

In reflecting on the question set out at the beginning of this chapter, on whether MIAC collaboration with LCIA is an indispensable factor in LCIA-MIAC story (which other African centres can follow), it is clear from the discussion above that the partnership gave greater credibility to the MIAC brand but it took more than getting the LCIA on board. For other African countries wishing to make their countries destinations for international arbitration references, there must be a modernization of their arbitration laws; clearly defined government policy to support arbitration and make the state attractive to arbitration; review of the court structure with possible provision of specialist arbitration trained judges; and provision of support services. To paraphrase the current Registrar of LCIA-MIAC,[59] in living memory, Singapore was little more than a fishing village. Mauritius is already a busy centre of business for Africa. It has the ingredients for the making of a credible venue for arbitration. It has a long way to go to prove that it can combine these ingredients into a successful cake.

57. These routes are serviced by several airlines including Air Mauritius.
58. http://www.lcia-india.org/ [accessed 13 Mar. 2016].
59. Ndanga Kamau, speaking at the ICCA 2016 Congress Roadshow, Lagos, Nigeria in November 2015.

CHAPTER 6

The Lagos Court of Arbitration Centre

Megha Joshi & Tolu Obamuroh

INTRODUCTION

Arbitral institutions play a major role in facilitating the use and practice of arbitration in resolving commercial and investment disputes. This chapter discusses the mission and the structure of the Lagos Court of Arbitration (LCA) and the role of the Lagos State Government (LASG) in its establishment. It examines the nature of this relationship from the experience of the LCA.

Principle 7 of the Chartered Institute of Arbitrator's London Centenary Principles in International Arbitration[1] states:

> Functional facilities for the provision of services to International Arbitration proceedings including transcription services, hearing rooms, document handling and management services, and translation services.

This Principle 7 refers to the availability of arbitration institutions to administer arbitral references. The LCA provides such services in Lagos as one of the infrastructure instituted by the LASG to promote the use and practice of arbitration and Alternative Dispute Resolution (ADR).[2] This chapter examines the goal of the LASG to make Lagos a favourable seat for arbitration (§6.01); the LCA and the services it provides (§6.02); and the mission of the LCA contribution to the development of arbitration in Africa (§6.03).

1. The CIArb Principles are described as identifying principles that are necessary for an effective, efficient and safe seat for the conduct of arbitration. These Principles are available at: https://www.ciarb.org/docs/default-source/centenarydocs/london/the-principles.pdf?sfvrsn = 4 [last accessed 26 Apr. 2016].
2. This chapter focuses on the administration of arbitration by the LCA. However the LCA also administers various alternative dispute resolution mechanisms such as mediation. For more details see [LCA website] [last accessed 26 Apr. 2016].

§6.01 LAGOS AS A SEAT OF ARBITRATION

This section briefly describes the place of Lagos in Nigeria (§6.01[A]) and the legal environment of Lagos State for arbitration (§6.01[B])

[A] Lagos State

As the most populous state in Nigeria,[3] Lagos was the political capital of Nigeria from Nigerian independence in 1960 to December 1991 when Abuja became the capital of Nigeria.[4] However, Lagos state remains the financial, commercial and industrial nerve centre of Nigeria with more than 2,000 manufacturing companies and 250 financial institutions. Lagos state accounts for 60% of the industrial investment and 90% of the foreign trade in Nigeria, and 65% of the nation's commercial activities.[5] Lagos state therefore contributes more than 30% to the Nigerian gross domestic product. The state continues to be a national and regional headquarters for major multinational corporations.[6] In addition, Lagos is home to the Apapa Port, one of the largest ports in Africa and logistical hub of Nigeria.[7]

These lead to a high volume of economic activities and commercial transactions that occur in Lagos, which also makes the occurrence of disputes inevitable. Thus, having an efficient dispute resolution system is an important requirement for sustaining the pace of commercial relations and activities to continue stimulating economic growth. It is acknowledged that potential investors feel less inclined to invest in an economy with poor contract enforcement and dispute resolution mechanisms.[8]

Commercial parties litigate their disputes before Nigerian courts. However, the courts are overwhelmed by an inefficient judicial system, which leads to congested dockets and delays and restricts access to justice.[9] These inadequacies of the judicial system cause great losses of resources and time to the parties. Arbitration and other ADR mechanisms fill this gap created by the legal system. According to the authors of Commercial Arbitration Law and Practice in Nigeria, arbitration is an effective means of resolving commercial disputes because it is a process of presenting a dispute to an arbitrator for adjudication as well as being the most commonly used alternative to

---

3. Nigeria is a federation of thirty-six states and a federal capital territory with an estimated population of 175 million. Lagos state (one of the thirty-six states) is home to about 18 million of these people.
4. Lagos State Investor Handbook, *A Guide to Business and Investment in Lagos State*, 2012.
5. Lagos State Investment Potentials available at: www.lagosstate.gov.ng/pagelinks.php?p = 10 [last accessed 29 Apr. 2016].
6. Examples include ExxonMobil, Chevron, Deloitte, and General Electric Deloitte Touche Tohmatsu Limited, and General Electric.
7. http://www.lagosstate.gov.ng/about-lagos/ [last accessed on 18 May 2016].
8. http://www.oecd.org/investment/toolkit/policyareas/investmentpolicy/contractenforcementanddisputeresolution.htm [last accessed on 18 May 2016].
9. P. Anyebe, *Towards Fast Tracking Justice Delivery in Civil Proceedings in Nigeria*, available at http://www.nials-nigeria.org/journals/Peter%20Anyebe-%20Towards%20Fast%20Tracking.pdf [last accessed on 18 May 2016].

litigation.[10] In support of this view, the Queen Mary 2015 International Arbitration Survey, found that arbitration is the preferred mode for resolving international commercial disputes, with about 90% of respondents indicating their preference for international arbitration, either as a stand-alone method (56%) or together with other forms of ADR (34%).[11] Several reasons have been suggested to explain this popularity of arbitration with disputants. These include neutrality, confidentiality of process and use of subject matter expert adjudicators, party autonomy, and finality of decisions.[12]

[B] Positive Legal Environment for Arbitration in Lagos

Recognizing the centrality of arbitration and ADR to its economic growth and investment drive, the LASG embarked on legal and judicial reform not just to make Lagos an attractive investment destination and the dispute resolution hub of sub-Saharan Africa but also as a means of decongesting the overcrowded court dockets.[13] The LASG enacted the Lagos Multi-Door Court House Law 2007 and the Citizens' Mediation Centre Law 2007, which established the Lagos Multi-Door Courthouse (LMDC)[14] and the Citizens Mediation Centre (CMC)[15] respectively. In addition to these initiatives, the State amended the High Court of Lagos State Civil Procedure Rules to incorporate access to ADR processes into the civil procedure rules as well as to provide judicial support for the operation of ADR. These various initiatives all largely perform public interest function of decongesting the courts and providing speedy access to justice. There was a gap in these provisions: a modern fully equipped institution which will provide dispute administration services for high value disputes. It was in this context that the then Governor of Lagos State, Babatunde Raji Fashola, through the State Attorney General, Olasupo Shasore, set up the Lagos State Arbitration Reform Committee (LSARC) to make recommendation to the government on how to make Lagos State an attractive seat and to develop and deepen the practice of arbitration and ADR.[16] The Committee's Terms of Reference include:[17]

- Reviewing the current Arbitration and Conciliation Act as contained in the Laws of Lagos State and propose a new Arbitration Law for Lagos State to be passed in the shortest possible time.

---

10. C.A. Candide-Johnson & O. Shasore, *Commercial Arbitration Law and Practice in Nigeria* 27 (LexisNexis, 2012).
11. Improvements and Innovations in International Arbitration (QMUL and White & Case LLP) available at: http://www.arbitration.qmul.ac.uk/research/2015/ [last accessed 29 Apr. 2016].
12. G. Born, *International Commercial Arbitration: Law and Practice* 9-15 (Kluwer Law Int'l, 2012).
13. Lagos State Arbitration Reform Committee Report, February 2008, p. 11.
14. The LMDC is a court annexed ADR institution and for details see: [last accessed on 18 May 2016].
15. The CMC is a free service available for the resolution of low value disputes and for details see: http://cmc.com.ng/about%20us.html [last accessed on 18 May 2016].
16. ICF Project Paper, *LCA Project*, 4.
17. *Ibid.*; Commercial Arbitration Law and International Practice in Nigeria, p. 241.

- Reviewing the proposed Uniform State Arbitration and Conciliation Bill with a view to adopting into the new Arbitration Law such of its provisions as are suitable and relevant to the socio-economic circumstances in Lagos State.
- Considering the viability of a LCA.
- Considering any issues which are reasonably incidental to the above terms of reference and any additional terms which the committee may deem necessary to promulgate an Arbitration Law that is of contemporary international standard and position Lagos as a hub for arbitration in and beyond the West African sub-region.

The LSARC was influenced by the work of the National Committee set up by the Federal Government to review the law of arbitration in the States of Nigeria.[18] The National Committee produced the State Arbitration Bill. The LSARC after several deliberations proposed the enactment of the Lagos State Arbitration Law 2009 and the LCA Law 2009 establishing the LCA. The 1988 Arbitration and Conciliation Act (ACA) is a federal statute, which applies to domestic and international arbitration in Nigeria.[19] The ACA, which is based on the 1985 UNCITRAL Model Law, is long overdue for a review.[20] The Lagos Arbitration Law 2009 (LAL) is a modern law which is supportive of arbitration, for example, it provides for a sole arbitrator in default situations,[21] consolidation and concurrent arbitral proceedings,[22] award of interest,[23] security for

18. The National Committee on the Reform and Harmonization of Arbitration and ADR Laws in Nigeria.
19. Cap A 18, Laws of the Federation of Nigeria 2010. There is an ongoing debate as to whether in view of the 'list' system which Nigeria operates under the Constitution of the Federal Republic of Nigeria 1999 (as amended) ('the Constitution'), the Federal Government has the legislative competence to enact an arbitration law that applies throughout the federation and trumps States law. Under the list system, there is a division of power between the tiers of government (with the Federal Government having exclusive subject matter competence on matters contained in the Exclusive, shared competence between Federal and State Governments on the Concurrent List – with Federal law prevailing in the event of conflict with States law, and the Residual List. The Residual List is not really a list under the Constitution, but matters not covered by both the Exclusive and Concurrent Lists are deemed to be a residual matter on which States have exclusive competence to legislate). Arbitration is not listed under both Exclusive and Concurrent Lists of the Constitution. The Federal Government is a government of enumerated powers and powers not specifically granted to it by the Constitution belong to States. Reference to Item 68 Exclusive Legislative List, Part 1, Second Schedule of the Constitution which gives exclusive competence to the Federal Government regarding 'any matter incidental or supplementary to any matter mentioned elsewhere in this list' offers no useful help, as contracts on which arbitration is based is not listed. Applying the 'Pith and Substance' doctrine does not advance the argument in favour of the Federal Government as arbitration is based on contract and under the Nigerian law, States have exclusive competence except in respect of contract involving the Federal Government or any of its agencies.

    As important as the debate is, it will only matter in default situations where the parties fail to specify the applicable laws and procedures. Party autonomy and freedom of contract allow parties to specify in their agreement that either both laws and any other will govern their arbitration.
20. The UNCITRAL Model Law for International Commercial Arbitration 1985 was revised in 2006.
21. Section 7(3) of LAL.
22. Section 40 of LAL.
23. Section 46 of LAL.

costs[24] and the arbitrator's exercise of a lien over the award until his or her fees are paid.[25]

§6.02 THE LAGOS COURT OF ARBITRATION

This section discusses the structure of the LCA (§6.02[A]); its funding (§6.02[B]); the services it provides (§6.02[C]); and its arbitration training initiatives (§6.02[D]).

[A] The Structure of the LCA

The objectives and functions of the LCA as contained in its enabling law, the LCA Law 2009, include:

- Providing extensive world-class case management and administrative services which will not be confined to the conduct of arbitration and ADR under its own rules and procedures.
- Promoting resolution of disputes in the territory of Lagos State by arbitration and other ADR mechanisms.
- Maintaining a Panel of Neutrals consisting of arbitrators, mediators and other experts with special skills and experience in specialized areas and who are willing to be members of tribunals or panels constituted by the Court of Arbitration in respect of any dispute referred to it.
- Helping practitioners to be effective as counsel and arbitrators in arbitration proceedings and as mediators in mediation sessions through training.
- Limiting the frequency of court intervention through judicial engagement and education;
- Policy advocacy through engagement with the various organs of government, especially the legislature and the judiciary.
- Institutionalizing the practice of ADR in Nigeria and the African continent.
- Acting as appointing authority and fund-holder for deposits filed in respect of the costs in otherwise ad hoc proceedings.
- Assuming such other functions necessary to effectively carry out its main functions of resolving disputes by other mechanisms apart from litigation.[26]

The LCA is private sector driven, independent of regulation, direction, control, participation or intervention by any arm of the government of Lagos State.[27] This independence of the LCA is guaranteed by the structure of the institution and the conditions of the take-off grant provided by the LASG which was aimed at making the institution self-reliant. The administrative structure of the LCA is modelled after the

24. Section 53 of LAL.
25. Section 49(2) of LAL.
26. *Supra.*
27. Section 1(2), LCA Law 2009.

three-tier structure of the London Court of International Arbitration (LCIA) comprising of a Board of Directors, a Secretariat and the LCA members.

The LCA Board of Directors is made up of fifteen reputable persons with expertise and experience in arbitration and ADR. Under the LCA Law, the first members of the Board of directors of the LCA were appointed by the then Governor of Lagos State on the recommendation of the State's Attorney General.[28] Subsequently, all the members of the Board of directors have been appointed by the members of the LCA at a General Meeting.[29] The President of the Court is appointed for a term of two years for a maximum consecutive period of four years; while other members of the Board are appointed for a maximum term of five years.[30] The Board closely monitors the administrative functions of the LCA and sets conditions for membership of the LCA. The Board also makes regulations towards the achievement of the goals and objectives of the LCA.[31]

The LCA Secretariat is led by an Executive Secretary who is responsible for the day-to-day management of the organization and reports directly to the Board of the LCA. The Executive Secretary is the main point of contact between the members of the LCA and the general administration of the LCA.[32] The Secretariat is responsible for the administration of all disputes referred to the LCA. The Executive Secretary is assisted by the Associate General Counsel and two other counsels.

The LCA also has registered members who pay an annual subscription fee. The registered members make up the General Meeting of the LCA. Under the LCA Law 2009, membership of the LCA is open to any person of good standing that has bona fide interest in arbitration or ADR. Membership is also open to persons who have satisfied conditions set by the Board. Such conditions include the payment of an annual subscription fee.[33]

The vision for the LCA is that it would become an institution for the users of its services and be governed by such users. To achieve this vision, the LCA possesses a panel of experienced and impartial neutrals of professionals from different sectors of the economy.

[B] Funding of the LCA

Funding is significant issue for any arbitration institution. This is because funding has a direct impact on the type and quality of the activities of the institution. In addition, the source of the funding for an institution may raise concerns about its independence from its funders. This concern is aggravated in cases of State sponsored institutions like the LCA. In the opinion of the authors, what is most important is not whether an institution receives support from the government but whether such support gives the

28. C.A. Candide-Johnson& O. Shasore, *supra*, 212.
29. Section 4, LCA Law 2009.
30. *Ibid.*
31. Sections 2 and 11 LCA Law 2009.
32. Section 6 LCA Law 2009.
33. Section 2 LCA Law 2009.

government some degree of control over the operations of the institution and its dispute management functions. In addition the LCA received funding through a grant from the Investment Climate Facility for Africa Fund.[34]

As part of its support for the LCA, the LASG provided a start off grant, land and built the premises in which the LCA is headquartered.[35] The LCA permanent headquarters is known as the International Centre for Arbitration and ADR (ICAA) in a Lagos suburb. To the knowledge of the authors, the ICAA is the first purpose-built ADR centre in Africa. The ICAA has over twenty hearing rooms of various sizes, each with three adjoining break-out rooms for recesses. Each hearing or meeting room is equipped with modern furniture and the latest audio and visual equipment. Finally, the ICAA was designed to accommodate the offices of other professional ADR organizations, and currently accommodates the offices of the Chartered Institute of Arbitrators Nigerian Branch, Chartered Arbitrators Nigeria, Maritime Arbitrators Association of Nigeria, and the Lagos Chamber of Commerce International Arbitration Centre (LACIAC) in addition to the LCA.

[C] Services Provided by the LCA

The LCA has its own set of arbitration rules, the LCA Arbitration Rules 2013.[36] The LCA Arbitration Rules are an adaptation of the Rules of Arbitration of the LCIA and the UNCITRAL Rules of Arbitration. The Rules are used for both domestic and international commercial disputes. The LCA Arbitration Rules contain an important provision for the appointment of a Special Measures Arbitrator in cases where parties need urgent and, or special measures prior to the constitution of an Arbitral Tribunal. Under the LCA Arbitration Rules, parties can determine the basis for the computation of the arbitrator's fees using either the time or value scales. Under the time scale the rate of fees payable to the arbitrator is USD 300 per hour or USD 2500 per day. Similar to the LCA administrative fee schedule, the value scale is based on a percentage formula, for example, where the dispute is up to USD 50,000, the minimum arbitrator fee payable is USD 2,700 up to a maximum of 16.2180% of the amount of the dispute. However, where the dispute in question is less than USD 5 Million, the administrative fee for arbitration under the LCA Arbitration Rules is limited to NGN 200,000.

One of the key attractions of arbitration is the role of party autonomy which gives parties the freedom to choose their decision maker and the procedure that would govern the arbitration. Party autonomy gives contracting parties the power to fashion their own remedial process within the limits of the law and public policy. It is not unusual for parties, through their arbitration agreement to designate an institution to

34. The ICF is a supranational organization based in Tanzania which works to improve the investment climate in Africa by supporting initiatives by governments, private companies and development partners aimed at removing barriers to doing business in Africa. For more details, see: http://www.icfafrica.org/ [last accessed 2 May 2016].
35. The LASG gave the cash sum of NGN 160,000,000 to the LCA as a start-off grant.
36. The text of the LCA Arbitration Rules 2013 and Mediation Guidelines 2011 are available at: http://lca.org.ng/arbitration/#guidelines [last accessed on 18 May 2016].

appoint an arbitrator on their behalf. LCA provides this service of appointing arbitrators under its Rules as the institution or in supporting of ad hoc references as appointing authority.

To perform this service, the LCA maintains a panel of neutrals composed of individuals whose identity, qualification, specialty and experience have been scrutinized by the institution prior to such enlistment. All the Neutrals must be members of the LCA, and they must also be approved for listing by the LCA Neutrals Selection Committee.[37] The LCA acts as the appointing authority if stipulated in a contract upon request by the parties. If parties are choosing the neutrals themselves, they may select from the LCA's list of neutrals or can be short-listed and recommended based on the experience(s) and expertise of the neutrals. The LCA may recommend individuals outside its panel of neutrals, especially when the nature of a dispute requires certain expertise and experience, not available from the LCA Panel of Neutrals. There are due diligence measures in place before the appointment of any arbitrators is confirmed, such as ensuring that there are no conflicts of interest. The LCA currently has over forty neutrals on its Panel.

The LCA administers a Small Claims Scheme for the resolution of claims involving amounts in disputes not exceeding NGN 5 million.[38] The Scheme is only available where both parties agree to settle their dispute under the Scheme either before or after the dispute arises. The Scheme is designed as a summary procedure. The nature of the process and the small value disputes under the Scheme create an opportunity for young arbitration practitioners to gain experience and apply their arbitral skills and subject matter expertise.

As the LCA is a relatively new institution, there have been few instances of cases where the LCA has been nominated in the dispute resolution clause. However there have been many more cases where parties have agreed to the LCA administering their disputes and managing the dispute resolution process, or to act as the appointing authority.[39] Many more multi-national and Nigerian companies (mainly in the oil and gas sector) have adopted the LCA's arbitration clause in their contracts.[40] As the Nigerian economy continues to grow and organizations enter into contractual relationships, there will be an increase in the demand for arbitration (and other ADR) services which the LCA has positioned itself as the arbitration institution of choice in Nigeria.[41] Two examples are the Lagos Home Ownership Mortgage Scheme (Lagos HOMS)

37. This can be found on the LCA website www.lca.org.ng [last accessed 2 May 2016]. The neutrals vetting process ensures only qualified, specialist and skilled arbitrators and experts are listed on the Panel, and the LCA ensures the neutral appointment/selection process is completely transparent.
38. At the current exchange rate, this amounts to the equivalent of USD 30,000.
39. M. Joshi, *The Role of Arbitration Institutions in the Development of Arbitration in Africa*, paper delivered at the conference on the Role of Arbitration Institutions in the Development of Arbitration in Africa, African Union Commission, Addis Ababa, 23 Jul. 2015.
40. *Ibid.*
41. The LCA dispute resolution services are top-notch and cost effective. All of the fees and the schedule are agreed at the beginning of the process and the LCA can address any issue quickly, as well as intervene when parties cannot agree or enforce penalties when instructions are not adhered to. Under the 'ADR Audit' Scheme, the LCA Secretariat work with corporate organizations, to review their existing caseloads and to recommend suitable ADR mechanisms (usually

contracts, and under the Eko Atlantic City Project,[42] both of which include the arbitration clause of the LCA.

[D] LCA Arbitration Training Initiatives

Arbitration (and ADR) processes require special skills, which can be acquired through focused training on arbitral skills, its law, rules and practices. One of the key requirements for developing a 'safe seat' as stated in the Chartered Institute of Arbitrators London Centenary Principle is:

> an implemented commitment to the education of counsel, arbitrators, the judiciary, experts, users and students of the character and autonomy of International Arbitration and to the further development of learning in the field of arbitration.

The LCA therefore provides different types of arbitration training programmes in the performance of one of its core mandates which is to promote arbitration (and ADR) in Nigeria. The LCA Training School offers a practical approach to learning premised on relevant theoretical foundations. Both approaches are necessary in order to develop skilled arbitration practitioners with proficient advocacy skills. In addition to providing substantive knowledge of arbitration (and ADR), the training includes a mock arbitration hearing (modelled after the Willem C. Vis International Commercial Arbitration Moot). Successful participants in this training have the opportunity to improve their skills through various LCA schemes such as the Small Claims Scheme mentioned above.

§6.03 LCA CONTRIBUTION TO THE DEVELOPMENT OF ARBITRATION IN AFRICA

Since the LCA began operations in 2012, it has built strong relationships with various international and regional multilateral business groups and organizations, whose members support its work and vision, and have undertaken to use the dispute resolution services offered at the LCA and ICAA. In this regard the LCA maintains partnerships with the: Investment Climate Facility for Africa; Nigeria Bar Association; International Council for Commercial Arbitration; Lagos State Judiciary; FCT High Court, LACIAC; International Senior Lawyers Project; LCIA-MIAC, JAMS, ICC; among other institutions and law firms. The focus of these partnerships is to promote the use, as well as deepen the practice of arbitration (and ADR) in Nigeria.[43]

---

mediation) for resolving them. In addition, the LCA also advises and help individuals and organizations to review their disputes resolution clauses/agreements

42. The Eko Atlantic City Project is presently the largest infrastructural development project in Africa. For more information, see http://www.ekoatlantic.com/ [last accessed on 18 May 2016].
43. An example is when in November 2015 the LCA collaborated with the Young Members Group of the International Council for Commercial Arbitration (ICCA) to hold a one day training workshop on topics such as 'How to get into arbitration' and 'the role of the local counsel in international arbitration', in Lagos.

The LCA organizes and actively participates in events, roundtables, conferences, publications, appearances on the radio and television to create and promote awareness of the mechanisms of arbitration and ADR.[44] In addition, the LCA particularly engages with members of the Nigerian judiciary to promote the knowledge and understanding of arbitration to the participating judges. It also engages with the private sector, and lobbies the government to support laws and initiatives for the promotion of arbitration and ADR.[45] These promotional activities have led to a greater appreciation of the need to resolve disputes via means separate to litigation, general commercial awareness of Lagos and the wider knowledge of the LCA as an arbitration institution. As a knowledge-driven centre, the LCA regularly hosts ADR awareness and sensitization events such as the 'ADR Speaker Series' and the 'Industry Specific Roundtable Series'. These events provide space for knowledge sharing on the practice and use of arbitration and ADR. These are in addition to other ADR outreaches to some Universities and the Nigerian Law School.[46] Furthermore, the LCA Library and Resource Centre is currently being equipped to provide access to both physical and online research materials on arbitration and ADR.[47]

In 2014, the LCA and LACIAC signed a Memorandum of Understanding (MoU) in line with the Arbitration in Lagos Project. The goal for this MoU is to promote Lagos as the centre of choice for the resolution of Africa related disputes through the process of arbitration. Both institutions are working together in engaging the legislature and judiciary to lobby for constitutional and legislative reform and the expeditious enforcement of arbitration awards in Nigeria.[48]

CONCLUSION

The LCA, though established under the visionary leadership of the LASG, remains an independent, vibrant and modern arbitration institution with clear vision of fulfilling its overarching mandate of promoting the use and practice of arbitration (and ADR) in Nigeria. The LCA continues to provide qualitative arbitration and ADR services and to

44. An example is the hosting by the LCA on 29 Oct. 2015 of the Second Annual International Law Association (Nigerian Branch) event where the suitability of Nigeria as a seat for international arbitration was examined. Attendants at this event included members of the Nigerian judiciary and arbitration practitioners.
45. An example is a conference hosted by the LCA titled, West Africa Regional Alternative Dispute Resolution Conference which held at Eko Hotel Convention centre, Lagos on 5 Nov. 2013. This conference brought together legal experts, entrepreneurs, investors and the government to discuss ADR processes.
46. In January 2016, the LCA collaborated with the University of Lagos ADR Society to provide ADR training to students of the Faculty of Law, University of Lagos. Also, in February 2016, the LCA collaborated with students of the Liberation Chambers, Faculty of Law, Obafemi Awolowo University, Ife for a two-day ADR training seminar.
47. The library will provide access textbooks, journal, and periodicals on ADR, including online resources hosted by Kluwer Arbitration, Westlaw and LexisNexis, among others.
48. As part of the LCA commitment to the development of arbitration in Africa, it will host the second SOAS University of London Arbitration in Africa conference titled 'Rethinking the Role of Courts and Judges in Supporting Arbitration in Africa' in its Centre from 22-24 Jun. 2016.

engage, through training and policy advocacy, critical stakeholders of the Nigerian Bar Association, Judiciary, business leaders and policy makers, to promote understanding of the law and practice of arbitration. Finally, the LCA will continue to collaborate with other arbitration services providers in and outside Nigeria, and to share experience towards the transformation of the arbitration in Africa.

CHAPTER 7
The Ghana Arbitration Centre

Emmanuel Amofa

INTRODUCTION

National laws on arbitration govern or regulate arbitral procedure in every country. The laws set the parameters within which arbitral tribunals exercise their mandate in a state which is the seat of the arbitration proceedings. While arbitration rules spell out the mode of commencement of arbitration, the procedure for appointment of arbitrators, the fees to be paid by parties and other procedural matters, national laws provide the backbone to arbitration proceedings where there is a vacuum created by the arbitration rules of an institution or where the arbitral tribunal requires the coercive powers of national courts to ensure compliance with its orders and rulings. This chapter will examine the critical linkage between the Alternative Dispute Resolution (ADR) Act 2010, (Act 798)[1] which is the national law governing arbitration in Ghana and the Rules and Procedures of the Ghana Arbitration Centre (GAC).[2] *Redfern and Hunter on International Arbitration* captured the critical role of national systems of law in international arbitration succinctly as follows:

> An understanding of the interplay between the private arbitral process and the different national systems of law that may impinge upon that process is fundamental to a proper understanding of international arbitration. This interplay may take place at almost any phase of the arbitral process. It may be necessary at the outset of an arbitration for the claimant to ask the relevant national (or local) court to enforce an agreement to arbitrate, which the adverse party is seeking to circumvent by commencing legal proceedings, or it may be necessary to ask the

1. Act 798 is available at: http://www.wipo.int/edocs/lexdocs/laws/en/gh/gh036en.pdf [accessed 29 Mar. 2016].
2. See website of the GAC www.arbitrationcentregh.com [accessed 29 Mar. 2016].

relevant court to appoint the arbitral tribunal (if this cannot be done under the arbitration agreement or under the relevant rules of arbitration).[3]

Arbitration rules by themselves in whatever form cannot operate independently from the national laws. For a mutual and coherent system of arbitration practice, national laws must complement arbitration rules of institutions. This chapter will examine how Act 798 supports parties who have adopted the Rules of the GAC in resolving their disputes in five sections. Section §7.01 gives a brief history of arbitration legislations in Ghana; §7.02 examines some salient features of Act 798; §7.03 examines the linkages between Act 798 and the GAC Rules; §7.04 examines the similarities between Act 798 and the GAC Rules; §7.05 examines the differences; and a conclusion.

§7.01 BRIEF HISTORY OF ARBITRATION LEGISLATION IN GHANA

For a comprehensive and thorough assessment of the connection between Act 798 and the Rules of GAC Rules, a brief historical synopsis of the law in existence before the enactment of Act 798 and the evolution of the GAC will be instructive. The Arbitration Act, 1961 (Act 38) was the legislation which governed arbitration in Ghana prior to the 2010 ADR Act. Act 38 was modelled after the 1950 English Arbitration Act.[4] Act 38 was defective in many respects as it did not engender and encourage the use of international arbitration. It was difficult for parties to choose Ghana as the seat of their arbitration since Act 38 failed to address important issues such as identifying matters which are arbitrable. Some notable features of Act 38 included the definition of arbitration, stay of proceedings and reference to court and the incorporation of the New York Convention on the Enforcement of Arbitral Awards, 1958 (which Ghana ratified on 8 July 1968) as a schedule.

Beyond these provisions, Act 38 did not reflect much of the provisions of the UNCITRAL Model Law on International Commercial Arbitration 1985[5] (Model Law) or acceptable international principles of arbitration such as party autonomy, the doctrine separability and the competence of an arbitration tribunal to determine its own competence. Indeed, Kwadwo Sarkodie observed that:

> The 1961 Act pre-dated many important developments in commercial arbitration – not least, Ghana's accession to the United Nations Convention on the Recognition and Enforcement of Foreign Arbitration Awards 1958 (the 'New York Convention') and the publication of the UNCITRAL Model Law on International Commercial Arbitration 1985 (the 'UNCITRAL Model Law'). Accordingly, by the turn of the millennium Ghanaian arbitration law was outdated in many respects, and in need of revision and updating if it was to reflect and serve modern commercial needs, including those of the construction industry.[6]

---

3. N. Blackaby et al., *Redfern and Hunter on International Arbitration* 58 (6th ed., Kluwer Law International/OUP 2015).
4. The 1950 Act was replaced by the English Arbitration Act 1975. It was also subsequently repealed by the English Arbitration Act 1996.
5. Amended in 2006.
6. See Kwadwo Sarkodie, *Arbitration in Ghana – The Alternative Dispute Resolution Act 2010* (Mayer Brown Practices 2011) at: https://m.mayerbrown.com [accessed 29 Mar. 2016].

It became imperative for Ghana to repeal Act 38 to bring the law on arbitration in line with modern trends of resolving commercial, construction, investment and other disputes through arbitration. It was noted that a modern law on arbitration will be one of the ingredients for attracting foreign direct investment in Ghana so following a series of stakeholder meetings, it was agreed that Act 38 should be repealed.

While the process of repealing Act 38 was set in motion, a group of senior members of the Ghanaian legal Profession mooted the idea of establishing an institution which will provide a forum for the settlement of commercial, investment, construction and mining disputes among other specialized areas of law through arbitration and other ADR mechanisms. This idea culminated in the incorporation and establishment of the GAC in 1996. Thus both Act 798 and the GAC were conceived at the same period. However, the GAC is a private initiative and it is registered as a company limited by guarantee with the following objects:

- To provide a forum for the resolution of disputes through arbitration and other ADR mechanisms.
- To promote the resolution of disputes by arbitration and ADR and the study of the laws, rules, practices and procedures relating thereto.
- To promote opportunities for educating the public through the reading of papers, delivering of lectures and the holding of seminars on the subjects of arbitration and ADR.
- To affiliate and or co-operate with any other centre, societies or organizations which have similar objectives.
- To provide accreditation for members of the Centre to act as arbitrators or mediators or conciliators in resolving domestic and international disputes.

Upon its incorporation, the GAC adopted its own Arbitration Rules and procedures for administering arbitration. The Rules of the GAC are streamlined with simplified procedures.

On 31 May 2010 Ghana enacted the ADR Act 2010 (Act 798) which repealed Act 38, and it is currently the primary legislation on the law of arbitration in Ghana. Among other objectives the Memorandum accompanying the Bill to Parliament stated that the purpose of replacing the Arbitration Act, 1961 (Act 38) was:

> to bring the law governing arbitration into harmony with International Conventions, rules and practices in arbitration, provide the legal and institutional framework that will facilitate and encourage the settlement of disputes through alternative dispute resolution procedures.[7]

§7.02 SALIENT FEATURES OF ACT 798

This section examines key features of Act 798 and is divided into five subsections which will consider the scope of Act 798 (§7.02[A]), the separability doctrine

7. The Alternative Dispute Resolution Bill.

(§7.02[B]), the courts power to stay proceedings §7.02[C]), party autonomy §7.02[D]), and the enforcement of domestic and foreign awards §7.02[E]).

[A] Scope of Application

Certain national laws or indeed international conventions make express provisions for matters that may be determined by arbitration.[8] To that extent where the subject matter of arbitration is not arbitrable at the seat of arbitration or the place of enforcement of an award, the award obtained in that regard may be set aside.[9] Under section 1 of Act 798 the following matters are excluded from the purview of the Act and are not arbitrable:

(a) the national or public interest;
(b) the environment;
(c) the enforcement and the interpretation of the Constitution; or
(d) any other matter that by law cannot be settled by an ADR method.

The scope of application of section 1 of the Act 798 has been the subject of critique by several commentators.[10] While it is agreed that matters involving the interpretation and enforcement of the Constitution, which is the fundamental law of the country is the sole prerogative of the Supreme Court of Ghana,[11] there is a genuine doubt as to why matters involving the environment ought not to be arbitrable.

8. See for example, Arbitration Act 1996 (Ch. 7:15; No. 6 of 1996) of Zimbabwe; s. 35 of the Nigeria Arbitration and Conciliation Act. See also Art. 1 of the Model Law and Art. V(2) of the Convention on the Recognition and Enforcement of Foreign Arbitral Awards 1958 (New York) Convention.
9. See for example, Art. 34(2)(b)(i) of the Model Law and Arts II(1) and V(2)(a) of the New York Convention.
10. For a thorough critique of s. 1 of Act 798; see Mante, Joe & Ndekugri, Issaka, *Arbitrability in the Context of Ghana's. New Arbitration Law* vol. 15, no. 2 Int. ALR 31-41 (2012); Nene A.O. Amegatcher, *Ghana's ADR Act, A Progressive or Retrogressive Piece of Legislation* available at: http://www.ghanabar.org/a-daniel-come-to-judgment/ [accessed 29 Mar. 2016]. See also Kwadwo Sarkodie, *supra*.
11. See Art. 130(1)(a) of the Constitution of the Republic of Ghana (1992). See also the case of *Attorney General v. Balkan Energy Ghana Ltd & Others* [2012] 2 SCGLR 998 where the Ghana Supreme Court interpreted a Power Purchase Agreement (PPA) between the Government of Ghana and Balkan Energy Ghana Ltd was an international business or economic transaction within the meaning of Art. 181(5) of the 1992 Constitution of Ghana and therefore required prior Parliamentary approval. The background to this case was that following a dispute between the defendants and the Government of Ghana regarding the PPA, the defendants initiated arbitration proceedings against the Government of Ghana under the auspices of the Permanent Court of Arbitration. The Government of Ghana raised the point that the PPA needed parliamentary approval under Art. 181(5) of the 1992 Constitution, but that approval had not been sought and therefore rendered the PPA invalid as having been executed in breach of the Constitution. The Government of Ghana had argued before the arbitral tribunal that non-compliance with the constitutional provision made the PPA invalid, including its arbitration clause, and consequently the arbitral tribunal had no jurisdiction over the dispute. The Government of Ghana subsequently sought an interpretation from the Supreme Court to the question as to whether the PPA was an international business transaction which required prior Parliamentary approval before execution.

What is even more disturbing is the fact that Act 798 does not provide an explanation of what constitutes matters of 'environment' which makes it a source of potential disagreement. The exclusion of matters of national or public interest from arbitration suffers from the same malaise of obscurity. In the interpretation provision of the Act, there is no definition of what is a matter of, 'national' or 'public interest'. Edward Torgbor holds the view that:

> But the application of the Act in terms of section 1 to 'matters' other than those relating to 'the national or public interest', 'the environment' and 'any other matter that by law cannot be settled by an alternative dispute resolution method' lacks sufficient definitiveness. This is because 'matters', 'any other matter' and the concepts of 'national or public interest' and 'environment' are nebulous.[12]

Will the Government of Ghana be justified in refusing to appear before an arbitral body or institution on the ground that the subject matter of the dispute is a matter of public interest? For example, a loan facility, which was procured from an international finance company to be used for the construction of the country's railway network? Will a dispute between an employer and contractor working on, for example, an afforestation project be arbitrable under Act 798 in the event of a dispute particularly as the project has a semblance of protecting the environment? These are only hypothetical issues but they demonstrate the impact of the vagueness and uncertainty of the scope of the arbitrability provision under Act 798 and are a potential source of conflict. It is therefore possible that a successful party with an arbitral award, where the subject matter is on the environment, may have practical difficulties in enforcing such an award in Ghana because of this arbitrability question.

[B] Separability Doctrine

Apart from the scope of the subject matter of arbitration, the Act upholds the independence of an arbitration agreement in section 3, which is rooted in the concept of separability. The effect is that an arbitration agreement which forms or is intended to form part of another agreement shall not be regarded as invalid, non-existent or ineffective because that other agreement is invalid or did not come into existence or has become ineffective. In the case of *Attorney General v. Balkan Energy Ghana Ltd & Others* the Supreme Court had to determine the question of whether the arbitration contained in clause 22.2 of the Power Purchase Agreement (PPA) entered into between the Government of Ghana and Balkan Energy (Ghana) Ltd constitutes an international business transaction within the meaning of Article 181(5) of the Ghana Constitution. The Supreme Court held that the arbitration agreement does not constitute an international business or economic transaction within the meaning of Article 181(5) of the Ghana Constitution. The court further held that:

12. Edward Torgbor, *Ghana Outdoors: The New Alternative Dispute Resolution Act 2010 (Act 798): A Brief Appraisal* vol. 77 no. 2 Arbitration 211, 219 (2011).

> An international commercial arbitration draws its life from the transaction whose dispute resolution it deals with. We therefore have difficulty in conceiving of it as a transaction separate and independent from the transaction that has generated the dispute it is required to resolve.[13]

The Supreme Court did not make reference to section 3 of Act 798, and it is not clear whether the Supreme Court was disaffirming the doctrine of separability introduced into Act 798. The court missed the opportunity of firmly endorsing this doctrine of severability of arbitration agreement, which is commonly accepted in arbitration, whether domestic or international.[14]

[C] Stay of Proceedings

Act 798 recognizes the autonomy and inviolability of the arbitration agreement. In this regard, section 6 of the Act empowers a party to apply to the court to stay proceedings in a matter commenced by the other party in court in defiance of an arbitration agreement.[15] A similar provision was contained in section 8 of the repealed Arbitration Act which was an issue in the case of *State Insurance Corporation, Takoradi v. Badu.*[16] The defendant in that case filed an application for stay of proceedings together with the defence which involved an insurance contract containing an arbitration clause. The Plaintiff objected to the application on the ground that the applicant had not demonstrated a willingness to submit their differences to arbitration and that by filing the defence the applicant had taken a step in the action and had thereby waived whatever rights they may have under the arbitration clause. The Court held that the plaintiff's objection could not be sustained because he himself had not alleged that he tried to invoke the arbitration clause but the defendants were unwilling to go to arbitration. It further held that since the defendants filed their motion for stay at the same time as their defence in which the objection was raised they have not taken such a step in the action as will preclude them from pursuing their objection.

In addition, where in an action before a court, the court is of the view that the action can be resolved through arbitration, the court with the consent of the parties may refer the matter to arbitration although there is no arbitration agreement.[17] This

13. *Attorney General v. Balkan Energy Ghana Ltd & Others* [2012] 2 SCGLR 998, 1037.
14. See Thaddeus Sory, *The International Arbitration Review* Ch. 20, 1-12 (6th ed., June 2015) on further discussion on the Balkan Energy case and its effect on separability provided under s. 3 of Act 798.
15. Compare this with analogous provisions in Art. 8 of the Model Law and ss 4 and 5 of the Nigeria Arbitration and Conciliation Act, 1999 (Cap A 18 LFN 2004). By the provisions contained in the Model Law and Cap A 18 LFN 2004, the party applying to stay proceedings must do so before submitting his substance or statement of defence to the action. By s. 5(1) of the Arbitration and Conciliation Act of Uganda Cap 4, a party intending to stay proceedings in court and refer the matter to arbitration, shall do so after the filing of his statement of defence. There is no such provision in s. 6 of Act 798 regarding the step to be taken by the party in the proceedings in court before applying to stay proceedings. See also O.O. Olatawura, *Stay of Proceedings in Nigerian Law of Arbitration: Analysis of its Functions, Applications and Problems,* vol. 28 no. 4 Arbitration International 689-720 (2012) on evaluation of ss 4 and 5 of Cap A 18 LFN 2004.
16. [1965] GLR 105.
17. Section 7(1) of Act 798.

novel provision is a departure from the conventional process of staying proceedings in court upon the application of a party where there is a subsisting arbitration agreement prior to the events leading to a dispute.[18] It will seem that this provision of the court 'procuring' the consent of the parties although not couched in mandatory terms is adequate to petrify parties into accepting the reference by the court may be against the parties' desire. It is in this context that Emilia Onyema evaluates the strong influence of the court on the parties in seeking their consent to refer the matter to arbitration. She observes as follows:

> Practically, it is difficult to see how a party can withhold its consent under section 7 nudge by the court. It is suggested that in the light of the power (subtle as it is) wielded by a High Court judge over parties in a matter before it, it may not be practicable for a party to withhold its consent to such suggestion by the court. This clearly begs the question on the genuineness of the consent from the parties which may be more forced than voluntary. It therefore appears that the legislator was more interested in the formality of obtaining a written consent than evidence of a genuine intention of the parties to arbitrate their dispute. This may not necessarily lead to a just means of decongesting the court docket. It is important that the court enables the parties actualize a genuine intention to arbitrate and not 'force' a written consent to arbitrate their dispute.[19]

From the tenor of section 7(1) Act 798 it is plausible that the rationale for granting the court the power to obtain the consent of the parties to refer their dispute to arbitration is to promote and enhance the use of arbitration to resolve disputes than litigation, which is at the heart of the Act. While that is a laudable objective it should not be pursued to the extent of affecting the voluntariness of parties to resort to arbitration to resolve their dispute.

An innovative provision introduced in Act 798 is where a court before which an action is pending is enjoined on its own volition or suo motu to stay proceedings and refer the parties to arbitration if the said action before the court is the subject of an arbitration agreement.[20] Where in some other laws[21] the onus of applying for stay of proceedings in court and referring parties to arbitration is placed on the parties, section 7(5) vests that responsibility in the court just like the preceding section 7(1). The purpose of such a provision is intended to promote the use of arbitration with a view to decongesting the court of cases. It should be observed however that as parties have the freedom to enter into a contract under the well-known principle of pacta sunt servanda, the parties are similarly free to revoke their arbitration agreement. Where the parties agree to resolve their dispute in court other than by arbitration, the parties have impliedly revoked their arbitration agreement and the court should not compel them to resolve the dispute through arbitration.

18. See Art. 8 of Model Law, ss 4 and 5 of Cap A18 LFN 2004 and s. 6 of Act 798.
19. See Emilia Onyema, *The New Ghana ADR Act 2010: A Critical Overview* vol. 28 no. 1 Arbitration International 101-124, 113-114 (2012).
20. Section 7(5) of Act 798.
21. See for example, s. 6(1) of Act 798, Art. 8 of Model Law, ss 4 and 5 of Cap A18 LFN 2004 and Arbitration and Conciliation Act of Uganda Cap 4.

Kwami Tetteh has observed that the mandatory 'shall' in the provision suggests that 'the judgment of the court in any action that escapes the attention of the court for reference to arbitration may be attacked on appeal for non-compliance with the provision.'[22] After evaluating the provision, he noted succinctly as follows:

> The underlying considerations that have informed the courts' reluctance to stay such proceedings suo motu may be explained: firstly, arbitration is contractual – it is based on the expressed will of the parties in an arbitration agreement. The parties are free to discharge or suspend the operation of the arbitration agreement concluded between them; it is not within the province of the judge to interfere by mandatory reference to arbitration. The courts must encourage and facilitate out-of-court resolution of actions but they do not have the power to compel the parties to do so. A statute that seeks to confer such coercive power on a court would, in all practicality, bar the right of access to the court of any person who is party to an arbitration agreement.[23]

It would seem that the observation that section 7(5) of Act 798 is mandatory and therefore non-compliance would be the subject of attack on appeal was given strong credence in the recent decision of the Supreme Court in the consolidated appeals of *Westchester Resources Ltd v. Ashanti Goldfields Co. Ltd*; *Africore (Ghana) Ltd v. Ashanti Goldfields Co. Ltd*.[24] In these appeals the Supreme Court was called upon to determine whether a court had jurisdiction to try a case and rule on its merits when it had earlier referred the matter to arbitration. The relevant facts are that the respondents sued the appellant in the High Court for damages for breaches of a mining exploration agreement. Pursuant to an arbitration clause in the said agreement and upon application by the respondents, the court stayed the action and referred the claims therein to arbitration. Having constituted the arbitral tribunal after series of misunderstanding, the parties were also not ad idem as to the procedural rules to govern the arbitration. In these circumstances and subsequent to correspondence between the parties, the matter went back to the trial court for determination at the respondents' instance. In the course of the proceedings the consolidated suits were struck out and never relisted before their final determination by the trial court in favour of the respondents.

The Supreme Court held that there was nothing in the Arbitration Act[25] which warrants the resumption of jurisdiction over this case by the court in the circumstances that transpired after the case had been referred by the court to arbitration. The Supreme Court held that:

> ...the trial in the court below of these consolidated cases despite their prior reference to arbitration under the Arbitration Act, 1961, (Act 38) is a nullity for lack of jurisdiction.

22. See S. Kwami Tetteh, *Civil Procedure: A Practical Approach*, 1125 (2011).
23. *Ibid.*, 1126. See also the Supreme Court cases of *Rockson v. Ghana Football Association* [2010] SCGLR 443 and *Republic v. High Court, Accra, ex parte Asakum Engineering and Construction Ltd*. [1993-94] GLR 643, where the Court held that parties can voluntarily agree to resort to alternative dispute resolution (ADR) mechanisms such as arbitration or mediation. Where parties adopt the ADR mechanism to resolve their dispute it does not entirely oust their right to the law courts.
24. Unreported: Consolidated Civil Appeal No. J4/63/2013, 11 Nov. 2015.
25. This is the repealed Arbitration Act of 1961 (Act 38).

Admittedly, the court did not make reference to section 7(5) of Act 798 in arriving at its decision but the reasoning and import of the decision in *Westchester* is in accord with the purpose of section 7(5). So parties to an arbitration agreement would have to resolve their dispute by arbitration and not litigation even if they subsequently consider the option of litigation as their preferred choice.

[D] Party Autonomy

Under Act 798, party autonomy remains the guiding principle and a strong pillar underpinning it. Party autonomy as a significant concept in arbitration is where parties are given the freedom to decide on matters relating to their arbitration dispute. The autonomy includes determining the number of arbitrators,[26] deciding the place of arbitration,[27] liberty to agree on the procedure for appointing an arbitrator[28] deciding on the language to be used in the arbitral proceedings,[29] freedom to agree on the form of the award[30] and similar other provisions contained in Act 798.[31] In addition to the express provision on party autonomy the use of the expressions 'unless otherwise agreed by the parties' and 'with the consent of the parties' reinforces the fact that parties have certain leverage in taking decisions in the arbitration proceedings. It is for this reason that parties would not be encumbered in the application of Act 798 in resolving their dispute.

[E] Enforcement of Foreign Awards

The Act incorporates the Convention on the Recognition and Enforcement of Foreign Arbitral Awards 1958 (New York Convention) as a schedule.[32] The Act sets out in great detail the procedure for the enforcement of foreign awards which also principally includes the provisions of the New York Convention.[33] The enforcement of foreign awards provision in Act 798 is a marked improvement from the repealed statute.[34] At the time of acceding to the New York Convention, Ghana made a reciprocity reservation so that a foreign award from a Contracting State is enforceable only to the extent that it is a reciprocating State declared by the President by legislative instrument; or that by a State which is not a party to the New York Convention but has been declared by legislative instrument by the President on the basis of reciprocity. Pursuant to section 36(2) of the repealed Arbitration Act, Ghana enacted the Arbitration (Foreign

26. Section 13(1) of Act 798.
27. Section 11(1) of Act 798.
28. Section 14(1) of Act 798.
29. Section 32(1) of Act 798.
30. Section 49(1) of Act 798.
31. See other provisions on party autonomy by Edward Torgbor *supra*, at p. 213. See also Kwadwo Sarkodie *supra* on the role of party autonomy in Act 798.
32. First Schedule of Act 798.
33. Section 59 of Act 798.
34. Section 36 of Arbitration Act, 1961 (Act 38).

Awards) Instrument, 1963 (LI 261) which listed the countries declared to be 'reciprocating States' under the New York Convention.[35]

Two interesting observations must be noted: first, the New York Convention was incorporated as a schedule to Act 38 in 1961 before Ghana acceded to the New York Convention in 1968;[36] second, at the time of accession, Ghana did not make any reciprocity reservation;[37] yet in 1963 it enacted LI 261 recognizing reciprocating States in accordance with Article I(3) of the New York Convention. Clearly, prior to the repeal of Act 38 it should be possible for an award from a Convention State, not included in the list under LI 261 to be enforced in Ghana based on the fact that Ghana did not make any reciprocity reservation.

Whatever doubts that may exist, it is arguable that under Act 798, the countries from where foreign awards may be recognized and enforced in Ghana have been expanded to include awards from: (i) those countries with a reciprocity arrangement with Ghana; (ii) New York Convention awards; and (iii) awards under an international convention ratified by the Parliament of Ghana.[38] Finally, by reason of the fact that Ghana did not make any reciprocity reservation at the time of accession, it should be noted that Act 798 has impliedly repealed LI 261 which no longer has effect.

§7.03 LINKAGE BETWEEN ACT 798 AND THE GAC ARBITRATION RULES

This section examines some of the linkages between the provisions of Act 798 and the Arbitration Rules of GAC; and evaluates how Act 798 complements the operations of the GAC in seven subsections.

[A] Recognition of Arbitration Institutions

Without doubt, Act 798 introduced very important principles of international arbitration which bring Ghanaian law on arbitration in conformity with international best practices and standards. Even more pertinent is the connection that the Act establishes with dispute resolution institutions in Ghana. This connection will assist arbitration institutions to thrive under the established legal regime. In addition, for the first time in the legislative history of Ghana, the Act recognizes persons or institutions as key stakeholders in the resolution of disputes by arbitration. Hitherto, existing legislation was silent on the involvement of arbitration institutions in the arbitral process.

35. The countries are: Austria, Bulgaria, Byelorussian Soviet Socialist Republic, Cambodia, Central African Republic, Ceylon, Czechoslovakia, Ecuador, Federal Republic of Germany, Finland, France, Greece, Hungary, India, Israel, Japan, Madagascar, Morocco, Norway, Poland Romania, Syria, Thailand, Ukrainian Soviet Socialist Republic, Union of Soviet Socialist Republics and United Arab Republic. It should be noted that the names of some of the countries have changed.
36. http://www.newyorkconvention.org/list + of + contracting + states [accessed 29 Mar. 2016].
37. http://www.uncitral.org/uncitral/en/uncitral_texts/arbitration/NYConvention_status.html [accessed 29 Mar. 2016].
38. See on enforcement of awards under Act 798, Emilia Onyema, *The New Ghana ADR Act 2010: A Critical Overview* vol. 28, no. 1 Arbitration International 101-124, 115 (2012).

Act 798 expressly permits parties to an arbitration agreement to refer the dispute to a person or institution for resolution. Section 5 of the Act provides:

> 5(1) A party to a dispute in respect of which there is an agreement, may subject to the terms of the agreement, refer the dispute to
> (a) any person or institution for arbitration; or
> (b) the Alternative Dispute Resolution Centre established under part IV to facilitate the arbitration.
>
> 5(2) Where reference is made to a person or institution other than the Centre, the *procedure and rules* shall be as the parties and arbitrators determine. (Emphasis added)

Although the ability of parties to use arbitration institutions in the absence of a clear legislative provision is not in doubt,[39] section 5, however, is an express commitment by the Ghanaian legislator to expand the frontiers of dispute resolution. This is because the Act offers parties to arbitration different options of who to refer their disputes for resolution. These are, 'any person or institution or the Alternative Dispute Resolution Centre'. In addition to these categories, the Act further confers upon an 'appointing authority' (which is defined to mean any person or authority including the Alternative Dispute Resolution Centre (ADRC)) the power to take any action in relation to arbitration proceedings.[40] The combined effect of section 5 and the definition of 'appointing authority' in section 135 is that parties have the option of using the GAC or any institution beside the ADR Centre envisaged under Act 798 to provide a forum for the resolution of disputes through arbitration and other ADR mechanisms.

Furthermore, by virtue of the same section 5 of Act 798, parties involved in ad hoc arbitration proceedings may agree to use the services of the GAC to appoint arbitrators or to administer the arbitration.[41] The parties are invested with such options because Act 798 allows them to make their own arrangements to appoint arbitrators by the concept of party autonomy. For instance in the years 2014 and 2015 ad hoc arbitrations formed a large part of the caseload of the GAC.[42] In all these cases, the parties did not only empower the GAC to appoint arbitrators, but also, to administer their arbitrations and under the Rules of the GAC.[43]

39. There is no such equivalent of s. 5 in the Model Law, ss 4 and 5 of Cap A18 LFN 2004 and Arbitration and Conciliation Act of Uganda Cap 4.
40. Section 135 of Act 798.
41. A typical arbitration agreement normally filed with the GAC is in the following terms:

> Any dispute or differences arising out of or in connection with this Agreement including any matter regarding its existence, validity, termination or interpretation shall be referred to and finally resolved by arbitration under the Arbitration Act, 1961 (Act 38) of Ghana or any statutory re-enactment or modification thereof for the time being in force. The language of the arbitration shall be English. The arbitral tribunal shall comprise a sole arbitrator who shall be appointed (in the absence of agreement) between parties, by the Courts of Ghana. The place of arbitration shall be Accra, Ghana. Any award of the sole arbitrator shall be enforced without delay.

42. Eighteen cases were recorded during the period.
43. The administrative services the GAC provides includes: maintenance of a file of all written communications in the arbitration, facilitating communication, providing meeting and hearing rooms, stenographic, transcript and clerical assistance.

[B] Stay of Proceedings and Referral

One critical linkage between Act 798 and the GAC is the opportunity a party is offered to refer a dispute to arbitration where a court stays judicial proceeding commenced in disregard of an arbitration agreement. Section 6(1) of the Act provides:

> Where there is an arbitration agreement and a party commences an action in a court, the other party may upon entering appearance and on notice to the party who commenced the action in court, apply to the court to refer the action or a part of the action to which the arbitration agreement relates, to arbitration.

The courts have exercised their power under section 6(1) to refer parties to arbitration.[44] Where the arbitration agreement refers to the GAC as the forum for resolving the dispute, the courts have given effect to the arbitration agreement by referring the parties to the GAC. In the case of *Anglogold Ashanti (Ghana) Ltd v. Mining & Building Contractor*,[45] the parties' agreement included an arbitration clause in the following terms:

> Any dispute arising out of or in connection with this agreement other than dispute relating to claim, including any question regarding its existence, validity or termination, shall be referred to and finally resolved through arbitration under the auspices of the Ghana Arbitration Centre and adopting the Rules of Arbitration under the United Nations Commission on International Trade Law (UNICITRAL Rules) which UNICITRAL Rule are deemed to be incorporated by reference into this clause.

The Plaintiff instituted action in the High Court to which the Defendant entered conditional appearance and brought an application under section 6(1) of Act 798 for stay proceedings and referral to the GAC in accordance with the arbitration agreement between the parties. The High Court dismissed the Defendant's application for stay of proceedings on the ground that though the parties inserted into the agreement an arbitration clause, which under normal circumstances will bind the parties, they have also exempted virtually everything. This decision was reversed on appeal by the Court of Appeal which held that the arbitration clause:

> enjoins the parties to appear first and foremost before an arbitral forum to iron out their differences and untie any naughty knot that is in difference between them. … Once there is an arbitration clause, the same should be respected by both parties.[46]

44. See the cases of State Insurance Corporation, *Takoradi v. Badu supra*; *Khoury v. Khoury* [1962] 1 GLR 98, where the Supreme Court held that both questions of law and of fact can be determined by an arbitrator and therefore stayed proceedings. *BCM Ghana Ltd v. Ashanti Goldfields Ltd* [2005-2006] SCGLR 602.
45. Civil Appeal No. H1/201/2015 dated 17 Dec. 2015 (unreported).
46. The Court of Appeal also used the opportunity to reconfirm the conditions required to satisfy before a court will grant a stay which it had set out in the earlier case of *George Kodua v. Interbeton B.V.* Suit No. H1/53/2004 dated 26 Nov. 2004 Court of Appeal (unreported). These include: evidence of a valid arbitration agreement, applicant must be a party to the agreement and not have taken any step in the proceedings, and service of the process on respondent.

Where a party applies to the court to stay proceedings and refer the dispute to arbitration, the GAC has invariably been the parties' first choice institution. This is in part because it is the only formal institution providing services on arbitration in Ghana; and the ADRC envisaged under Act 798 has not been established.

A collaborative provision in the GAC Rules is Article 47(a) which does not deem it a waiver of the right to arbitration for a party to commence litigation over disputes covered by arbitration under the GAC. Article 47(a) provides:

> No judicial proceedings by a party relating to the subject matter of the arbitration shall be deemed a waiver of the party's right to arbitrate.

Therefore where parties have adopted the Rules of the Centre in their arbitration agreement, it appears that Article 47(a) does not foreclose their right to resolve their dispute by arbitration notwithstanding that one party commences judicial proceedings. The use of phrase 'judicial proceedings' in Article 47(a) is imprecise and it is not clear whether it includes interim applications made to the court for preservation of assets, for instance, before commencement of the arbitration.

It should be observed however, that Article 47(a) is subject to the mandatory laws of Ghana if the seat of arbitration is in Ghana. The Courts have determined the stage a party is deemed to have waived their right to arbitration. In the case of *Skanska Jensen International v. Klimatechnik Engineering Ltd*,[47] the Supreme Court held that a party with full knowledge of the arbitration agreement will be deemed to have waived his right to apply for a stay of proceedings if he files pleadings in the litigation, including a statement of defence and counterclaim.

In a subsequent decision of the Supreme Court regarding the time for applying for stay of proceedings and referring a matter to arbitration, the Court held that the objection to the court's jurisdiction must be raised promptly. The Court stated as follows:

> It must however, be pointed out that in any pending case whether the arbitration agreement is domestic or non-domestic, the filing of the action and taking steps in the action does not oust the jurisdiction of the High Court to hear the action. It is the duty of the party who wants the action to be referred to arbitration to timeously raise the objection by the proper procedure provided by law. It is also the duty of the plaintiff who wants to proceed with the case to convince the court why the arbitration clause should be disregarded to enable the court to hear the case.[48]

As noted earlier,[49] stay of proceedings under Act 798 is not limited to only cases where there exists an arbitration agreement which a party defies by resorting to litigation. The court on its own motion and with the consent of the parties may refer a matter before the court to arbitration. This will be where in the view of the court, the dispute can appropriately be resolved through arbitration. Under section 7(5) of Act 798 it is mandatory for a court to refer a dispute to arbitration if the court realizes that

47. *Skanska Jensen International v. Klimatechnik Engineering Ltd* [2003-2004] SCGLR 698.
48. See *Republic v. High Court, Tema; Ex Parte MY Shipping PVT Limited (Dee Jones Petroleum & Gas Limited & MVMY Arctic Interested Parties)* [2011] 1 SCGLR 237.
49. Section 7(1) of Act 798.

the action before it is covered by an arbitration agreement. Under both sections 7(1) and 7(5) of Act 798, courts have jurisdiction to refer the parties to an institution or person as the parties may agree. In 2015 the courts referred eight cases to the GAC under these sections of the Act. Such referral is covered under Article 9 of the Rules of GAC provides as follows:

> Parties to any existing dispute may commence arbitration under these Rules by filing at the headquarters of the Centre, two copies of the written agreement to arbitration under these Rules (Submission), signed by the Parties.

Under this provision, the order of reference by the court with the consent of the parties to resolve the dispute by arbitration is considered for all practical purposes as an agreement to resolve present disputes that is to say a submission agreement of the parties. Depending on the terms of the court order,[50] the GAC constitutes an arbitral tribunal to determine the dispute. Clearly the provisions on stay of proceedings in Act 798 have strengthened the connection between the Rules of the GAC and the Act. Where the seat of arbitration is Ghana, a party has the power to challenge the breach of the arbitration agreement by the other party and in addition request the court to refer the parties to arbitration under the auspices of the GAC or any other institution or person as the case may be.

[C] Powers Exercisable by the Arbitral Tribunal

The arbitral tribunal may need to exercise various powers during the arbitration and the Act and GAC Rules provide complimentary powers. Article 33 of the Rules of the Centre empowers the arbitral tribunal to inspect or investigate property or a site as part of its evidence gathering duty. This power of inspection or investigation will enable the arbitrator to visit the *locus* or call for the delivery of equipment for inspection for purposes of making a determination of an issue in the dispute. It offers a practical tool to the arbitrator to have a first-hand evaluation of the matters in controversy in resolving the dispute. Section 31(8)(a) of Act 798 also grants arbitrators the same powers. The procedure for giving effect to section 31 is in pari materia with Article 33 of GAC Rules which has been applied by the GAC in four arbitration matters administered by the GAC. It is apparent from these provisions that where the GAC's Rules are adopted in a matter where the seat of arbitration is Ghana, parties will have recourse to the mandatory procedural rules of Ghana so far as the powers of the arbitrator are concerned as it relates to the inspection or investigation of the subject matter of arbitration.[51]

Section 31(9) of Act 798 gives an arbitrator the authority to subpoena a witness or at a party's request subpoena a witness to testify at the proceedings. The GAC Rules

50. A typical order of the court is in the following terms: 'Application for stay of proceedings granted. The parties are to contact the Ghana Arbitration Centre for help in setting up the arbitration in this case. Case adjourned to abide the outcome of the arbitration'.
51. See Edward Torgbor, *Opening up International Arbitration in Africa*, 215-216; and Emilia Onyema, *The New Ghana ADR Act 2010: A Critical Overview*, 106-107 for further discussion on the powers of the arbitrator under Act 798.

in Article 31(b) empower an arbitrator, when authorized by law, to subpoena a witness or order document production. It should be observed from the above provision that the power given to the arbitrator under the Rules of the Centre must be authorized by the procedural law of the seat of arbitration. This is particularly important since an arbitrator does not possess the coercive power of the state to compel the attendance of witnesses at an arbitration proceeding.[52] It is plain from the reading of section 31(9) of Act 798 that an arbitrator applying the Rules of the Centre would derive the necessary support under the Act to compel the attendance of an involuntary witness. On occasions where an arbitral tribunal has not obtained the cooperation of a witness, the GAC has employed the services of the judiciary to compel witnesses to attend arbitration hearings. In one case, the arbitral tribunal directed a party to apply to the High Court for a writ of *subpoena* to be served on an individual to testify at the arbitral hearing. Upon the grant of the application, the writ of subpoena was served by bailiffs of the court and the witnesses attended.

Article 34 of the Rules of the Centre gives an arbitrator the power to make orders for the preservation of property, which is the subject matter of arbitration proceedings. These powers are necessary to ensure that the status quo is maintained so that a party is not unfairly prejudiced at the end of the arbitration proceedings where the subject matter may have been dissipated. Although such powers are given to the arbitrator, it is possible that a recalcitrant party may refuse to comply with an order issued by an arbitrator in arbitration proceedings. Where the seat of the arbitration proceedings or hearing is in Ghana, Act 798 provides the required support and assistance for the enforcement of such orders. The Act has elaborate provisions in which a party may seek the assistance of the High Court to enforce orders issued by the arbitrator.

It is not uncommon for an arbitral tribunal to be confronted with an application to grant one form of interim relief or another pending the final determination of the dispute. The GAC Rules empower an arbitrator to issue orders for purposes of protecting property which is the subject matter of the dispute.[53] The Act also grants an arbitrator the power to make orders of interim relief to protect or preserve property at the request of a party. The powers of the High Court to support arbitral proceedings are detailed under the Act. In more specific terms, the High Court has power in relation to arbitral proceedings to grant interim injunction necessary to facilitate the arbitration hearings. It would be useful to set out the full powers of the High Court to support arbitral proceedings as provided in section 39 of the Act as follows:

> (1) Unless otherwise agreed by the parties, the High Court has power in relation to an arbitral proceedings to make an order:
> (a) for the taking of evidence of witnesses;
> (b) for the preservation of evidence;

52. Under s. 27 of the Arbitration and Conciliation Act of Uganda Cap 4, at the request of an arbitral tribunal or a party, a court may give the necessary assistance in taking evidence in accordance with its rules of taking evidence.
53. See Emilia Onyema, *International Arbitration in the West African States*, in Boseman Lise (gen ed.) *Arbitration in Africa: A Practitioner's Guide*, 120-122 (Kluwer Law International 2013) on analyses of the powers of the arbitrator under the GAC Rules.

(c) in respect of the determination of any question or issue affecting any property right which is the subject of the proceedings or in respect of which any question in the proceedings arise:
    (i) for the inspection, photography, preservation, custody or detention of property; or
    (ii) for the taking of samples from or the observation of an experiment conducted upon, a property; and for that purpose authorizing any person to enter any premises in the possession or control of a party to the arbitration;
(d) for the sale of any goods the subject of the proceedings;
(e) for the granting of an interim injunction or the appointment of a receiver.

(2) Where the case is one of urgency, the Court may on the application of a party to the arbitral proceedings, make orders as it considers necessary for the purpose of preserving evidence or assets.[54]

It is apparent from the above provisions that although interim reliefs under the GAC Rules are limited to inspection or investigation and the safeguarding of property, parties who have adopted the Rules of the Centre with the seat of arbitration in Ghana have greater opportunity under Act 798 to invoke the support of the High Court for various interim reliefs. Finally, in arbitration proceedings under the auspices of the Rules of the GAC, a party seeking to preserve evidence which is crucial in the resolution of the dispute may, by application seek the support of the High Court for an order to the preserve the particular piece of evidence despite the absence of an express provision in the Rules of the Centre in that regard.

[D] Administering Oaths

The general rule in Ghana is that in both civil and criminal proceedings the evidence of any witness should be sworn. The Evidence Act, 1975 (NRCD 323) provides:

> Subject to any enactment or rule of law to the contrary, every witness before testifying shall take an oath or affirmation that he will testify truthfully, and any statement made by a witness without such oath or affirmation shall not be considered as evidence.[55]

Oath taking in civil trials is a requirement under the laws of Ghana, and this is also reflected in Article 27 of the Rules of the GAC which provides:

> The Arbitrator has discretion to require witnesses to testify under oath administered by any duly qualified person or if required by law or demanded by either party, shall do so.

54. See Art. 17 of the Model Law on elaborate provisions on interim measures to be provided by the court.
55. Section 61 of National Redemption Council Decree.

The discretionary power of an arbitrator to require witnesses to testify on oath or the demand by parties for oath to be administered under the Rules of the Centre is confirmed under section 31(10) of Act 798 which provides:

> The arbitrator may direct a party or a witness to give evidence on oath or affirmation and may for that purpose administer the oath or affirmation.

Where it is a requirement under the rules of a particular arbitral institution such as the Rules of the GAC or where parties in arbitration demand that witnesses must take an oath, an arbitrator may invoke the provisions of section 31(10) of Act 798 to administer such oath under the laws of Ghana.

[E] Finality of Arbitral Award and Enforcement

Another area of fundamental linkage between the Rules of the Centre and Act 798 is the finality and binding nature of arbitral awards as well as its enforceability. One critical feature that distinguishes arbitration from other ADR processes (such as mediation and conciliation) is the finality and binding character of arbitral awards. Perhaps it is the finality of awards that makes arbitration more attractive and acceptable when compared with other ADR processes. Apart from the award being final it is almost invariably binding on the parties and so to be complied with unless it is set aside by a competent court.

By parties agreeing to use arbitration to resolve their dispute, there is an implied consent of the parties to comply with an award issued pursuant to the arbitration proceedings. In a recent case the Supreme Court of Ghana affirmed the finality and binding principle of an arbitral award.[56] The Court held:

> [T]he finality rule must be made to bite. In so far as the award is not tainted, and the procedural and natural justice rules had been observed, the parties should be prepared to accept the decision of an arbitral tribunal even if they have reason to believe a court or some other tribunal would have adjudged matters differently. ...Thus in the absence of any clear evidence of impropriety on the part of the arbitrators or umpire, if our courts would routinely review and overturn, on the law and the merits, awards which were given within jurisdiction and were not improperly procured, and in respect of which the procedural or natural justice rules were never breached, the speed and above all, the finality of the arbitral process would be greatly undermined and jeopardised. The courts have a duty to support and give validity to arbitral awards properly procured. Although the courts have the right to set aside an arbitral award, that power is exercised with circumspection.

56. See *Klimatechnik Engineering Limited v. Skanska Jensen International* [2005-2006] SCGLR 913. The decision in this case was based on the repealed Arbitration Act of Ghana. It is contended that the decision is still sound law with equal applicability to Act 798 to the extent that of giving effect to the finality principle. See also the Nigeria Supreme Court case of *Ras Pal Gazi Construction Company v. Federal Capital Development Authority* [2001] 5 SC (pt II) 16. The decision in this case shares similar sentiments to the *Klimatechnik* on the finality of an arbitral award.

In spite of this decision by the Supreme Court, it is common that losing parties fail to comply with the award. What happens if a party fails to comply with the terms of the award issued by or under the auspices of the Rules of the Centre? Article 42 of the Centre's Rules recognizes an award that is in writing and signed as final and binding on the parties and must be executed by the winner in the manner required by law. This means that there ought to be a favourable legal regime that will enable a successful party to reap the fruits of his victory from the arbitral award. The question that comes to mind immediately is how the mandatory laws of the country ensure the enforcement of arbitral awards should a losing party fail to comply with the award. A careful reading of Article 42 reveals that a party must invoke the applicable procedural law to enforce such an award.

Where a party seeks to enforce an arbitral award in Ghana, Act 798 provides an effective framework for enforcing awards. In the first place, like the Rules of the Centre, Act 798 endorses the principle of finality and the binding nature of an arbitral award under section 52.[57] Once an award is delivered it is prima facie final and binding on the parties unless it is set aside. Section 58 of Act 798 sets out the circumstances under which an award may be set aside. The grounds articulated under section 58 draws inspiration from the Model Law[58] and the New York Convention.[59] Unless a party seeking to set aside an arbitral award is able to prove any of these grounds, the award crystallizes and matures for enforcement. The second matter of extreme importance is the procedure to adopt for the enforcement of an arbitral award. Section 57 of Act 798 gives a clear indication as to how the arbitral award is to be enforced. It provides that:

> An award made by an arbitrator pursuant to an arbitration agreement may by leave of the High Court be enforced in the same manner as a judgment or order of the Court to the same effect.
>
> Where leave is so given, judgment may be entered in terms of the award.

Under the laws of Ghana, a successful party in arbitration is not left without a remedy to proceed against a recalcitrant party who decides to disregard the orders of an arbitral award. Arbitral awards obtained under the Rules of the GAC have been successfully enforced in Ghana. It is apparent from section 57 that the procedure or method of the application for leave is not provided. The successful party is only enjoined by the provision to seek leave to enforce. However, in practice, the successful party seeking to apply for leave to enforce the award serves a notice of his intention to apply for leave to the losing party. Once the leave is granted by the court, the successful party applies any of the known methods of execution of a judgment to enforce the award.

The harmony between the GAC Rules and Act 798 should encourage parties to use the Rules of the Centre in the settlement of their disputes. It also serves as an

57. Compare Art. 35 of the Model Law, s. 31(1) of the Nigeria Arbitration and Conciliation Act and s. 35 of the Arbitration and Conciliation Act of Uganda Cap 4 which use only the word 'binding'. The effect of arbitral award is final under these statutes.
58. Article 34(2)(a) and (b) of the Model Law.
59. Article V(1) and (2) of the New York Convention.

attraction for parties to use arbitration to resolve disputes emanating from their contracts.

[F] Representation by Counsel

Another important issue for examination is the representation of parties by counsel of their choice in arbitration. This is a matter which is sometimes taken for granted by both parties and counsel. It should be noted that the right of a party to counsel of his choice is an inalienable right which should not be compromised simply because the chosen counsel is not a registered member of the legal profession in the place of arbitration. In Ghana under the Legal Profession Act[60] as amended, a person is entitled to practice as a lawyer if that person has been issued with a valid solicitor's licence. A lawyer may practice as a barrister or solicitor or both and shall be an officer of the court.[61] By the terms of Act 32, a person not registered as a lawyer in Ghana cannot appear in the courts of Ghana on behalf of parties. However, Act 32 does not debar persons without a solicitor's licence from appearing before arbitral tribunals. To interpret 'counsel' in section 42(1) of Act 798 in such manner as to limits it to lawyers with valid solicitor's licence in Ghana will be restrictive of the right of parties to appoint a person of their choice to represent them at the arbitration. The use of the phrase 'and other person' in section 42(1) of Act 798 widens the category of persons who can represent a party at arbitration proceedings.

Besides, insisting that a counsel cannot represent her client in arbitration proceedings at the place of arbitration because he is not a member of the legal profession in that country, will defeat the flexibility associated with arbitration as transcending state boundaries. Such challenges will not arise where parties adopt the GAC Rules and importantly, if the parties choose Ghana as the seat of their arbitration. Article 22 of the GAC Rules provides:

> Any party may be represented by counsel. A party intending to be so represented shall notify the other party and the Centre of the name and the address of Counsel at least three days prior to the date set for hearing at which counsel is first to appear.

It is important to note that this is a contractual provision which will be subject to the mandatory laws on rights of audience or licences to practice law or render legal service in any jurisdiction. It is also noted that section 42(1) of Act 798 refers to representation by counsel without any qualification as to the counsel's nationality or need for registration to practice law in Ghana. Whatever doubt that may be entertained regarding representation of a party at arbitration hearings has been laid to rest under Act 798. Section 42(1) provides:

60. Act 32 of 1960.
61. See ss 2 and 8 of Act 32.

> Unless otherwise agreed by the parties, a party may be represented by counsel or any other person chosen by the party.[62]

As observed the Act makes it possible for counsel from any other jurisdiction to represent a party in arbitration proceedings in Ghana and that person need not be a Ghanaian or registered to practice law in Ghana. The Act recognizes the autonomy of parties to engage counsel or any other person of their choice to represent them in arbitration. The GAC has hosted arbitrations conducted under the rules of some arbitral institutions such as the International Chamber of Commerce (ICC); and ad hoc references under the UNCITRAL Arbitration Rules, with foreign lawyers representing the parties without any challenges.

[G] Immunity from Liability

There is the view that arbitrators, like judges of state courts, should enjoy immunity from liability arising out of their duties as adjudicators. In Ghana, the immunity granted to judges from acts or omissions or commissions while discharging their functions is guaranteed under the Constitution.[63] Article 127(3) of the Constitution provides:

> A Justice of a Superior Court, or any person exercising judicial power, shall not be liable to any action or suit for any act or omission by him in the exercise of the judicial power.

Judicial power in Ghana is vested in the judiciary by Article 126 of the Constitution of Ghana. The Judiciary consist of the superior courts of judicature (includes the Supreme Court, Court of Appeal, and the High Court), and the lowers courts or tribunal as established by Parliament. Arbitration as a private mechanism for dispute resolution does not fall within this list. Thus in Ghana, arbitrators are not conferred with immunity under the Constitution.

However, in view of the role played by arbitrators in the resolution of disputes, it is arguable that they should be granted some immunity for the effective discharge of their functions. Section 54 of Act 798 provides arbitrators with some protection from liability for any act or omission in connection with the arbitration. It provides:

(1) Except for the consequences of deliberate wrongdoing neither an appointing authority nor an arbitrator is liable for any act or omission in connection with an arbitration.

(3) An appointing authority or the arbitrator is not a necessary party in a judicial proceedings relating to an arbitration.

62. There is no such equivalent provision in the Model Law, the Nigeria Arbitration and Conciliation Act and the Arbitration and Conciliation Act of Uganda, Cap 4.
63. 1992 Constitution of Republic of Ghana.

Therefore, in Ghana, arbitrators enjoy partial immunity. They shall only be held liable for deliberate wrongdoing in the course of discharging their functions. The implication of this provision is that a party to arbitration proceedings cannot join an arbitrator in any judicial proceedings arising from the arbitration where such proceeding does not directly arise from the arbitrator's wrongdoing. *Redfern and Hunter on International Arbitration* identifies other reasons why arbitrators should enjoy immunity. They hold the view that:

> it helps to endure the finality of arbitral awards by preventing an unsuccessful party from suing the arbitrator; fewer skilled persons would be prepared to act as arbitrators if they were to run the risk of incurring substantial liability; arbitrators have no interest in the outcome of the dispute and should not be compelled to become parties to it; and it ensures the protection of the public, in those cases in which truly judicial functions are exercised (presumably by unburdening the courts of many disputes).[64]

It is principally for reasons such as these that Article 47 of the Rules of the GAC exclude the Centre or an arbitrator from becoming a party in judicial proceedings relating to the arbitration.

Notwithstanding section 54(1) and (3) of Act 798 and Article 47 of the Rules of the GAC, it must be pointed out that Act 798 does not preclude the High Court from revoking the authority of an arbitrator under certain circumstances, listed under section 18(2). The circumstances under which an arbitrator's power may be revoked as stipulated in section 18 are confined to the termination of the powers of the arbitrator prior to, or during the course of the arbitration proceedings. Once a dispute has been determined, it is apparent from section 54 that there cannot be a revocation of the appointment of an arbitrator. However, the actions complained of may become a ground for setting aside the award.

The force of sections 23(1) and 42(1) of Act 798 gives partial immunity to arbitrators to the extent that there is no conduct deliberately committed by the arbitrator to undermine the arbitral process. These provisions, in addition to Article 47 of the Rules of the GAC guarantee an individual's ability to assume the position of an arbitrator without the fear of being subjected to judicial proceedings for acts genuinely discharged as an arbitrator without bad faith.

§7.04 SIMILARITIES BETWEEN ACT 798 AND THE GAC RULES

So far the discussion has concentrated on trying to establish the synergy between the Rules of the GAC and the law governing the practice of arbitration in Ghana. Of special interest is the protection and support that the GAC and the arbitrators appointed under its Rules enjoy in Ghana. This feature of complementarity apart, there are striking similarities in some of the provisions of Act 798 and the Rules of the GAC. Although some provisions are not *in pari materia*, the philosophical underpinnings of the provisions in Act 798 and the Rules of the GAC are the same. Some of these provisions

64. *Redfern & Hunter on International Arbitration, supra*, at p. 324.

are examined below to further demonstrate the linkage between the Rules of the GAC and Act 798.

[A] Arbitrator to Decide Her Jurisdiction

It is now accepted in arbitration laws and rules that arbitrators have the jurisdiction to determine their own competence over the arbitration. This concept of competence-competence is internationally accepted and finds expression in many institutional arbitral rules.[65] Article 54 of the GAC Rules makes the same provisions. In essence Article 54 reinforces the concept of separability of the arbitration agreement which empowers an arbitrator to rule or determine the existence or validity of an arbitration agreement. Second, the provision also invests an arbitrator with the power to rule on her competence as regards her jurisdiction to determine the matter. This principle of competence-competence is also enacted in section 24 of Act 798.

In the case of *Attorney General v. Balkan Energy Ghana Ltd & Others*,[66] the Supreme Court failed to give effect to section 24 of Act 798 when it held that the Power Purchase Agreement (PPA) was an international business transaction within the meaning of the Constitution of Ghana which required parliamentary approval. Since that approval was not sought, the arbitral tribunal constituted by the parties to determine their dispute lacked jurisdiction to hear the matter. It is regrettable that the Court's decision did not take into account section 24 of Act 798 which empowered the arbitral tribunal to determine the existence or validity of the PPA which relates to the arbitration agreement. The Supreme Court thereby usurped the powers of the arbitral tribunal to rule on its jurisdiction.

An arbitral panel constituted under the Rules of the GAC, has power both under the Rules of the GAC and the law of the seat of arbitration, if in Ghana, to rule on its jurisdiction in respect of the existence, scope or validity of the arbitration agreement or matters affecting the authenticity of the arbitration agreement. Apart from the substance of what constitutes competence-competence, both the GAC Rules and Act 798, give an indication of when the matter can be raised. Under Article 54(c) of the Rules of the GAC, the matter of jurisdiction can be raised at the very 'first opportunity or time of filing an Answering Statement to the Demand or filing a reply to the Counterclaim that gives rise to the objection'. Section 25(1) and (3) of Act 798 also allow a party to object to the arbitrator's jurisdiction before taking the first step in the proceedings or immediately after the matter complained of arises in the course of the arbitral proceedings.

It appears that the period of raising the objection to the jurisdiction of an arbitrator by a party is therefore the same under Act 798 and the GAC Rules. The Rules of the GAC however, provide some specificity as to the exact time for raising the

65. See for examples: Art. 23 of UNCITRAL Rules as revised in 2010; Art. 6(9) of ICC Arbitration Rules (2012); Art. 23 of LCIA Arbitration Rules, 2014.
66. [2012] 2 SCGLR 998.

objection. This should be done before filing an Answer to a Demand or Claim or a Reply to a Counterclaim. Although a party is granted the right to object to the jurisdiction of an arbitrator or the (in)arbitrability of a claim under the Rules of the GAC and Act 798, it seems, however, that the rationale for this provision is that any objection to the jurisdiction of the arbitral tribunal must be done timeously and at the very beginning of the proceedings.

The timeliness of an objection to the jurisdiction of the arbitral tribunal will enable the arbitrator to determine the objection either as a preliminary matter in an interim award or as part of the final award. For all practical purposes, an arbitral tribunal under the Rules of the Centre, and with its seat in Ghana, is well placed to determine a matter affecting its jurisdiction. Under section 26(1) of Act 798, a party who is dissatisfied with the ruling of an arbitrator on the objection to her jurisdiction can apply to the appointing authority, if there is one, or to the High Court for the determination of the arbitrator's jurisdiction. An appeal from a decision of the High Court, or judicial review in the case of an appointing authority, does not lie except with the leave of the court.[67] Such leave to appeal shall only be granted if the matter involves a point of law, fundamental to the case, or deserves special consideration by the Court of Appeal.[68]

Although the parties have the liberty to decide whether an application to the appointing authority or the Court should constitute a stay of the arbitral proceedings, the opportunity given to the parties to use the appellate procedure in the judicial system to determine the jurisdiction of the arbitrator is likely to engender delay in the determination of the matter and undermine the expeditious resolution of the dispute. The determination by the High Court or judicial review by an appointing authority, should finally determine the matter without a further right of appeal as contained in Act 798.[69]

---

67. Section 26(5) of Act 798.
68. Section 26(6) of Act 798. See also Emilia Onyema, *The New Ghana ADR Act 2010: A Critical Overview* vol. 28, no. 1 Arbitration International 105-106 (2012) on a critique of the jurisdiction of the arbitrator under Act 798.
69. On this score the provisions contained in Art. 16(3) of the Model Law and s. 16 of the Arbitration and Conciliation Act of Uganda Cap 4 are instructive. The latter provides that: 'Where the arbitral tribunal rules as a preliminary question that it has jurisdiction, any party aggrieved by the ruling may apply to the court, within thirty days after having received notice of that ruling, to decide the matter. The decision of the court shall be final and shall not be subject to appeal.'

    It is perhaps for the reason to uphold the competence-competence principle that Art. 23(5) of the LCIA Rules provide that by agreeing to the LCIA Rules parties agree not to apply to a state court to review the decision of a tribunal on matters affecting the competence of the tribunal. Article 23(5) provides that:

    > By agreeing to arbitration under the Arbitration Agreement, after the formation of the Arbitral Tribunal the parties shall be treated as having agreed not to apply to any state court or other legal authority for any relief regarding the Arbitral Tribunal's jurisdiction or authority, except (i) with the prior agreement in writing of all parties to the arbitration, or (ii) the prior authorisation of the Arbitral Tribunal, or (iii) following the latter's award on the objection to its jurisdiction or authority.

[B] Settlement before Conclusion of Arbitration Proceedings

It is not uncommon that in the course of arbitration proceedings, parties may settle their dispute without going through a full adjudication on the merits. Article 44 of the GAC Rules gives recognition to such settlement. Settlement by the parties before conclusion is also given statutory backing in section 47 of Act 798, and the terms of settlement may also be recorded as an arbitral award. The award on agreed terms shall contain, in substance, the terms of an arbitral award provided for under section 49 of the Act.

The key issue here is that an arbitral award which is derived from parties' settlement during the GAC arbitration shall be recognized as final and binding in terms of the award and thus enforceable. Some parties applying the Rules of the GAC have taken the benefit of this provision and settled their dispute prior to the conclusion of the arbitration proceedings. In two separate cases filed with the GAC, after the close of pleadings the tribunal engaged the parties with a view to resolving the dispute. A settlement was reached and the tribunal terminated the arbitration proceedings and the settlement was recorded as an award of the arbitral tribunal.

The form and content of such award must comply with the requirements provided in section 49 of Act 798 discussed above. Similarly, by Article 42(a) of the Rules of the GAC, an arbitral award whether obtained prior to the conclusion of arbitration proceedings or at the completion of an arbitration shall be in writing and be signed by the arbitrator. Act 798 states that a signed copy of an award shall be delivered to each party.[70] The Rules of the GAC however, contain a more elaborate provision on the mode of delivery of an award to parties. Article 45(a) states that:

> Parties shall accept as legal delivery of the Award the placing of the Award or a true copy thereof in the mail by the Centre, addressed to such party at its last known address or to its attorney, or personal service of the Award, to the filing of the Award in any manner which may be prescribed by law.

[C] Other Provisions

Article 19 GAC Rules require a prospective arbitrator to disclose to the GAC and the parties any circumstances likely to affect his impartiality including any bias or any financial or personal interest she may have in the result of the arbitration, or any past or present relationship with the parties or their counsel.[71] The same provision of disclosure by an arbitrator prior to confirmation of their appointment is contained in section 12(5) of Act 798. Undoubtedly such provisions ensure the integrity of the arbitral process.[72] In practice, under the GAC Rules, a person nominated as arbitrator

70. Section 49(5) of Act 798.
71. Article 19 of the Rules of the GAC.
72. See for example ss 12(4) and 15(1) on the matters that ought to be taken into consideration before appointing an arbitrator. See also Emilia Onyema, *International Arbitration in the West African States*, in Boseman Lise (gen ed.) *Arbitration in Africa: A Practitioner's Guide*, 120-122.

shall, before confirmation, disclose in writing, any circumstances they think are likely to raise reasonable doubts on their independence or impartiality.

Another similarity between Act 798 and the Rules of the GAC is the power given to an arbitrator to re-open a hearing.[73] An arbitrator may on application by a party or for appropriate reason in the view of the arbitrator, re-open the hearing before an award is made.[74] The hearing will not be re-opened where it will delay the making of an award within the time agreed by the parties. According to Redfern and Hunter, the rationale of re-opening a hearing may be to give the parties an opportunity to produce all relevant evidence in support of their case before an award is delivered. The authors note:

> First, fresh evidence may come to light after hearing, but before the arbitral tribunal has issued its award. In these circumstances, the arbitral has discretion to reopen the proceedings at the request of the party wishing to present the new evidence. Clearly, it should refuse to do so where the fresh evidence is not needed for deliberations, or if the new material appears to be a spurious attempt to delay the proceedings.[75]

In the event that no time limit is stipulated in the arbitration agreement or the parties had not agreed on the time of making an award, the arbitrator shall make an award within thirty days of the closing of the re-opened hearing.[76]

Under the Rules of the GAC an arbitrator may grant any remedy or relief which the arbitrator deems just and equitable and within the scope of the agreement of the parties, including but not limited to, specific performance of a contract.[77] Section 50 of Act 798 has a similar a provision which makes it possible for a party to enforce for instance a relief for specific performance or any other equitable relief.[78]

The Rules of the GAC and Act 798 both provide a mechanism for expeditious resolution of disputes depending on the amount involved in the claim and counter-claim, as the case may be.[79] Where the expedited rules are invoked, the respective procedures stipulate that notices to parties from the GAC or arbitrator shall be by telephone or other electronic communication.[80] Pursuant to the purpose of expeditious settlement of disputes, hearings under the expedited procedures shall be completed in a day[81] and an award shall be made within five days and seven days respectively. These expedited procedures under the Rules of the GAC have not yet been invoked to determine the practicality of the timelines stipulated under the procedures.

---

73. There is no such equivalent provision in the Model Law and the Nigeria Arbitration and Conciliation Act and the Arbitration and Conciliation Act of Uganda, Cap 4.
74. Article 36(a) of the Rules of the GAC and s. 46 of Act 798.
75. See *Redfern and Hunter on International Arbitration, supra* 412.
76. Section 46(3) of Act 798 and Art. 36(c) of the Rules of the GAC.
77. Article 43 of the Rules of the GAC.
78. Edward Torgbor, *supra* 217, observes that the power to order specific performance is another special power by an arbitration statute, being absent, for example, from the Model Law and most African arbitral jurisdiction.
79. Article 7(e) and 55 of the Rules of the GAC and s. 60 of Act 798.
80. Article 55 *supra* and Rule 1 of Third Schedule of Act 798.
81. Article 58 of the Rules of the GAC and Rule 3(3) of Third Schedule of Act 798.

§7.05 DIVERGENT PROVISIONS

In spite of the many striking similarities between Act 798 and the GAC Rules, there are few noticeable divergent provisions which must be mentioned. While the Rules of the GAC provide that in the absence of agreement between the parties on the number of arbitrators, the dispute shall be heard and determined by a sole arbitrator,[82] section 13 of Act 798 provides for a default of three arbitrators.[83]

In the event that there is the need to fill a vacancy for the position of an arbitrator by reason of death, resignation, revocation or disqualification, the Rules of the GAC provide that the vacancy shall be filled in accordance with the procedure for appointment of arbitrators under the Rules. However, if the vacancy is in respect of a neutral arbitrator as opposed to party-appointed arbitrators, the two remaining arbitrators shall continue to act as arbitrators unless the parties agree to the contrary.[84] Act 798 on the other hand allows the parties to agree on how the vacancy is to be filled and whether the proceedings before the previous arbitrator should be adopted. In the absence of agreement between the parties, the appointing authority is given the mandate to appoint a new arbitrator who shall determine whether to adopt the previous proceedings if the parties are unable to reach an agreement.[85]

There is also a difference in approach to the organization, management or prehearing conference. The management or prehearing conference is a key part of the arbitral process which determines how the arbitration proceedings will be conducted.[86] While Act 798 allocates the responsibility of convening a management conference to the arbitrator, Article 10 of the GAC Rules gives the GAC the discretion, at the request of a party, to schedule a prehearing conference. Emilia Onyema notes that matters to be considered at the prehearing stage are within the province of the arbitrator and therefore finds it inappropriate that the GAC is invested with that power. In her view, 'It is advisable that parties in international references expressly opt out of this article'.[87]

Another difference between the GAC Rules and Act 798 is in the area of judicial intervention in the arbitral process. While the GAC Rules allow for limited court assistance[88] in supporting arbitration proceedings, some mandatory provisions of Act 798 allocate powers to the court to intervene in the arbitral process.[89] For example, section 40 of the Act grants a party to arbitral proceedings the right to apply to the Court

82. Article 17 of the Rules of the GAC.
83. Section 13(2) of Act 798.
84. Article 20 of the Rules of the GAC.
85. Section 21 of Act 798.
86. Such meeting deals with matters such as, agreeing issues for resolution, date, times and place of meetings, estimated duration of hearing, applicable law, rules of evidence, etc. See s. 29(1) of Act 798. There is no such equivalent provision of management conference in the arbitration legislation of Nigeria, Uganda, Kenya, Zimbabwe and the Model Law.
87. See also Emilia Onyema, *International Arbitration in the West African States*, in Boseman, L. (gen ed.), *Arbitration in Africa: a Practitioner's Guide*, 123 (Kluwer Law International 2013).
88. See for instance Arts 42(b) and 47(a).
89. See for instance s. 16 (challenge of appointment of arbitrator), s. 18 (revocation of arbitrator's authority), s. 26 (determination on objection to jurisdiction), s. 28 (party not notified of arbitral proceedings) s. 40 (determination of preliminary points of law) and s. 56 (determination of arbitrator's fees).

to determine any question of law that arises in the course of the arbitration proceedings. This provision offers courts the opportunity to disturb the arbitration proceedings on account of determining a point of law. Arbitral tribunals are constituted to determine not only factual disputes but also matters of law between the parties unless the parties have expressly excluded that authority from the purview of the arbitrators.

Indeed, the Supreme Court held that a court will order a stay of proceedings even if the matter in dispute involved both questions of fact and of law.[90] Even more worrying is the fact that a decision of the court on a question of law shall be treated as a judgment of the Court with the possibility of an appeal upon leave being granted. This puts the matter squarely within the judicial ambit so it becomes subject to the vicissitudes of the court's dilatory processes. This section 40 of the Act is a mandatory provision so that GAC arbitral references with seat in Ghana will be subject to it except expressly excluded by the parties.

It must be noted that excessive judicial intervention may discourage parties from choosing Ghana as a seat for their arbitration. Act 798 has been criticized for its excessive judicial intervention in arbitral proceedings.[91] Edward Torgbor has noted that:

> Excessive judicial presence in arbitration, with an ever-present High Court and an over shadowing Court of Appeal, can inhibit arbitration from maturing in a complete and free-standing procedure for conducting arbitral proceedings fully and finally.[92]

It must be conceded that Act 798 provides several opportunities for judicial intervention beyond the limits permitted under the UNCITRAL Model Law and the arbitration laws of other states.[93] These interventions may be moderated to optimize judicial intervention. On this score, Edward Torgbor concludes as follows:

> But judicial intervention can be minimized somewhat by effective arbitration rules and sound practices that make such intervention unnecessary or of the very last resort.[94]

CONCLUSION

It has been argued that Act 798 provides the requisite legal infrastructure for arbitration to flourish in Ghana by giving opportunities to private institutions such as the GAC to promote the use of arbitration as an efficient mechanism for resolving disputes. Apart from certain mandatory provisions in the Act, which have been noted would apply to arbitration proceedings with seat in Ghana, parties are otherwise at liberty to opt out or

90. See for example *Khoury v. Khoury* [1962] 1 GLR 98.
91. See Edward Torgbor, *Ghana Outdoors: The New Alternative Dispute Resolution, supra*; and Nene A.O. Amegatcher Daniel Come Judgment, *supra*.
92. Edward Torgbor, *supra*, at p. 219.
93. See Art. 5 of the Model Law, s. 34 of Nigeria Arbitration and Conciliation Act, and s. 10 of Kenyan Arbitration Act which provide in explicit terms restriction on court intervention in arbitral proceedings except as provided in the law.
94. Edward Torgbor *supra*, at p. 219.

adopt their own rules of procedure to govern their arbitration. Beyond that, and as evidenced by the several provisions of the GAC Rules and Act 798 examined, it is apparent that there exists a harmony between the GAC Rules and Act 798 that makes arbitration under GAC Rules in Ghana attractive to disputants.

To a large extent, the sustenance of the complementarity between the national arbitration law and the rules of a resident arbitration institution will also be affected by the approach adopted by national courts towards the administration of disputes by arbitration institutions and arbitral tribunals. It is pertinent that national courts do not unnecessarily intervene in the arbitral process with a view to delimiting the powers of the arbitral tribunal or truncating the arbitral process. It is important for Ghanaian courts to interpret the provisions of Act 798 more liberally to reflect international best practices, which was the rationale underpinning the repeal of the old arbitration law, Arbitration Act, 1961 (Act 38) to bring it in conformity with international conventions, rules and practices as envisioned in the Memorandum accompanying the Bill to Parliament before it was enacted. A receptive approach by national courts to arbitration processes should strengthen the inextricable bond between the Rules of the GAC and Act 798 which ultimately, projects Ghana as an arbitration friendly jurisdiction.

CHAPTER 8

Arbitration Centres in French-Speaking African Countries

Jean Alain Penda

INTRODUCTION

The economic growth in sub-Sahara African countries has led to an increase in the demand for both domestic and international arbitration, which in turn has resulted in an increase in the number of arbitration institutions operating in the continent to administer such disputes. There is evidence to suggest that non-African arbitral institutions administer the majority of these arbitration disputes connected to Africa, and these disputes are decided by non-African arbitrators. This chapter will examine these issues with a particular focus on French-speaking African countries.[1] Fifteen out of the twenty-one francophone sub-Sahara African countries are Member States of OHADA.[2] This chapter will briefly describe OHADA and its arbitration regime (§8.01); examine some arbitration institutions operating under the OHADA regime (§8.02); and discuss the challenges these institutions grapple with by virtue of their being located within the OHADA region (§8.03).

1. The word 'Francophone' refers to French as a cultural background, regardless of any ethnic or geographical background. In Africa, this legacy came from the French and Belgian empires explaining why in Sub-Saharan Africa: at least, eighteen countries inherited their legal systems from the Roman law and civil law as opposed to the British Common Law. Cameroon is, however, an exception due to its bilingual and bijural nature.
2. Francophone sub-Sahara African countries are: Benin, Burkina Faso, Burundi, Cameroon, the Central African Republic, Comoros, the Democratic Republic of Congo, Djibouti, Guinea, Chad, Côte d'Ivoire, Gabon, Madagascar, Mali, Mauritania, Niger, the Republic of Congo, Senegal, Somalia, Togo and Rwanda. The following countries are not OHADA members: Burundi, Djibouti, Madagascar, Mauritania, Somalia, and Rwanda.

§8.01 THE OHADA LEGAL SYSTEM AND ITS ARBITRATION REGIME

This section will examine the OHADA legal system (§8.01[A]) and its arbitration regime (§8.01[B])

[A] The OHADA Legal System

OHADA is the acronym for the 'Organisation for the Harmonisation in Africa of Business Law'.[3] The organization was established under the OHADA Treaty in 1993[4] with fourteen founding Member States though its membership has now expanded to seventeen African countries.[5] The vast majority of these states are French-speaking,[6] though Article 42 of the 2008 revised OHADA Treaty makes French, English, Spanish and Portuguese the official languages of the organization. The OHADA legal system came about as a result of the desire of its Member States to improve the business climate in the region. OHADA aims to harmonize business laws by implementing uniform laws,[7] as a means to ensure not only legal and judicial security but also a predictable legal environment in each of its Member States. Such predictability, it is believed, is useful for the resolution of business disputes. The OHADA initiative is therefore unique, due to the mutual reinforcement of the structures and laws of its Member States, all for the purpose of stimulating the business environment.[8] The OHADA Treaty noted in its preamble the preference of its Founding Fathers for arbitration as the dispute resolution mechanism of choice for resolving business disputes. The Preamble states:

> Desiring to promote arbitration as an instrument to settle contractual disputes.

Thus, in 1999 the OHADA Uniform Arbitration Act (UAA) came into force and became directly applicable in all OHADA Member States.[9] The UAA was one of the earliest uniform acts adopted by OHADA clearly because of its perceived importance by

3. Referred to in French as 'L'Organisation pour l'Harmonisation en Afrique du Droit des Affaires'.
4. The OHADA Treaty was signed on 17 Oct. 1993 in Mauritius and entered into force on 18 Sep. 1995. The Treaty was subsequently revised on 17 Oct. 2008 in Quebec, Canada.
5. Benin, Burkina-Faso, Cameroon, Central African Republic, Chad, Republic of Congo, Comoros, Equatorial Guinea, Gabon, Guinea, Guinea-Bissau, Mali, Niger, Senegal, Togo, and Democratic Republic of Congo (joined the OHADA Treaty in 2012, making it the seventeenth OHADA State Party).
6. Non-Francophone countries include Equatorial Guinea (predominately Spanish-speaking), and Guinea-Bissau (Portuguese).
7. Nine Uniform Acts have already been adopted and enforced in the OHADA Member States. These Uniform Acts include Uniform Acts on General Business Law, Commercial Companies and Economic Interest Groups, Secured Transactions, Bankruptcy, Debt Collection Procedures, Accounting, Arbitration, Transportation of Goods by Road and Cooperatives.
8. These structures are the institutional bodies that constitute the Organization (the Council of Ministers, the Permanent Secretary, the Common Court of Justice and Arbitration and the Regional Professional School of Magistrates) and statutory instruments known as 'Uniform Acts'. This is the mechanism put in place to ensure the efficacy of the OHADA system.
9. The UAA was adopted on 11 Mar. 1999 and entered into force on 11 Jun. 1999. OHADA Uniform Acts in force automatically apply in that state when a it joins, which is why the UAA applies in all current seventeen OHADA Member States.

the Member States. The OHADA arbitration regime is modern primarily because the quality of the arbitration law of a state is one of the most important factors affecting its choice as seat of arbitration. It is intended to reassure foreign investors that, in the event of a dispute, arbitration will be held in the region and governed by its laws, which embody internationally recognized principles. These innovations have had a significant influence on the advancement of alternative dispute resolution (ADR) in the OHADA region and more widely on the African continent. These advancements aim not only to increase arbitration references on the continent but also to create an opportunity for arbitrators of African origin to fully participate in the system and to encourage and promote the use of arbitration in the continent.

[B] The OHADA Arbitration Regime

The OHADA arbitration regime offers a choice between two systems for arbitration cases. Under the first system, arbitration can be administered under the arbitration rules of the Common Court of Justice and Arbitration (CCJA).[10] The CCJA is both an arbitration institution with its own set of arbitration rules that administers arbitration proceedings, and a judicial court. The CCJA has final jurisdiction over all OHADA uniform acts. In addition, the CCJA has original jurisdiction to enforce or annul arbitral awards and support arbitral proceedings under its rules.[11] This is the OHADA institutional arbitration body, with jurisdiction over contractual disputes when the parties are domiciled in an OHADA Member State or when the contract is to be executed in the OHADA territory.[12]

Under the second system, arbitration is administered under the UAA. The UAA governs both domestic and international ad hoc arbitration proceedings[13] when the seat of the arbitration is in one of the Member States.[14] The UAA applies to natural persons, legal entities, states and state entities or public bodies.[15] Its rules are optional as parties are free to choose whether to apply them or not.[16] Hence, the UAA may be chosen by the parties as the applicable procedural law without having a seat of arbitration in an OHADA Member State.

Accordingly, when deciding which rules and institutions govern arbitration cases under the OHADA regime, the following three options are to be considered: (i) The rules of the UAA will govern the arbitration proceedings if the arbitration clause refers

10. Other Institutions of the Organisation for the Harmonisation in Africa of Business Law include; the Conference of Heads of State and of Government; the Council of Ministers; the Permanent Secretariat; the Regional Professional School of Magistrates.
11. The CCJA reviews all awards before they are rendered, although the Court may only amend the form of an award and not its substance, as is the case under the ICC Rules.
12. Article 22 OHADA Treaty *and* Art. 2.1 of the CCJA Arbitration Rules.
13. Article 2 UAA; see Gaston Kenfack Douajni, *L'internationalité de l'arbitrage OHADA*, vol. 13 no. 3-4, European Journal of Law Reform 397 (2011).
14. Article 21 UAA.
15. Article 2 UAA.
16. Although optional, rules related to requirements of formalism, the number and impartiality of the arbitrators, and the drafting of awards remain compulsory.

to the UAA. Thus, there will be no institutional framework.[17] (ii) If the arbitration clause refers to the rules of an arbitration institution within an OHADA Member State, other than those of the CCJA. (iii) The CCJA as an arbitral institution and its rules will govern the proceedings if the arbitration clause refers to arbitration under the OHADA Treaty or the CCJA Arbitration Rules.[18]

Therefore, OHADA has developed a unique and sophisticated arbitration system, through its regional arbitration institution, the CCJA, which is also an alternative to other arbitration institutions in the region, as well as a viable alternative to local courts. It is this latter type of OHADA arbitration institution that is primarily considered in this chapter.

[1] The Legal Framework

This section will examine the OHADA Treaty, the UAA, and the CCJA Arbitration Rules as the three main instruments governing arbitration in the OHADA region. The OHADA Treaty is the key instrument in the arbitration regime, providing the source and power of its arbitration law. For instance, it is the OHADA Treaty that gives power and authority to the CCJA to ensure the uniform interpretation and application of the Treaty, the Regulations to further the Treaty's implementation and the Uniform Acts including the UAA.[19] Furthermore, the OHADA Treaty makes provisions on CCJA Arbitration,[20] including provisions concerning the duties of arbitrators, including their appointment, replacement and challenges to their suitability.[21]

The UAA is the governing law for arbitration in OHADA Member States. Its provisions set out arbitration rules applicable to any arbitration, whether ad hoc or institutional, other than CCJA arbitration, where the seat of arbitration is located in an OHADA Member State. The UAA applies to both domestic and international arbitration[22] and by application of Article 10 of the OHADA Treaty supersedes any previously existing national law which conflicts with its provisions.[23]

The OHADA arbitral laws are similar to international arbitral norms. The latter are the preferred choice of arbitration users at the time of choosing a place of arbitration. These norms are also reflected in, for example, the UNCITRAL Model Law on International Commercial Arbitration (Model Law), which has influenced the

17. Except where the institution allows parties to choose a different set of rules and still administer the reference.
18. The CCJA Arbitration Rules were adopted on 11 Mar. 1999 and entered into force on 10 Apr. 1999.
19. Article 14 OHADA Treaty.
20. CCJA arbitration is examined in greater detail under Ch. 2 above.
21. Title IV (Arts 21-26) OHADA Treaty.
22. See Gaston Kenfack Douajni, *L'internationalité de l'arbitrage OHADA*, vol. 13 no. 3-4 European Journal of Law Reform 397 (2011).
23. CCJA decision 001/2001/EP, 30 Apr. 2001. This decision was obtained by the Minister of Justice of Côte d'Ivoire though the letter n°137/MJ/CAB-3/KK/MB on 11 Oct. 2000 requesting an advisory opinion of the CCJA; Pierre Meyer, Professeur de Droit à l'Université de Ouagadougou (Burkina Faso), « *Droit de l'arbitrage* », p. 10, doc. ERSUMA, October 2009.

provisions of the UAA.[24] It is generally accepted that the Model Law seeks to harmonize arbitration regimes on a worldwide scale.[25] Another example is the Convention on the Recognition and Enforcement of Foreign Arbitral Awards (New York Convention).[26] The New York Convention has gained worldwide recognition and acceptance. On the African continent, thirty-three out of her fifty-four countries have acceded to the New York Convention. Ten out of the fifteen French-speaking OHADA Member States have acceded to the Convention.[27] The New York Convention is considered the foundational instrument for international arbitration.[28] The Convention requires courts of contracting states to give effect to private agreements to arbitrate and to recognize and enforce or set aside arbitration awards made in other contracting states. Therefore in OHADA Member States, arbitral awards can be enforced under the New York Convention or the provisions of the UAA.[29] Given the scope and the geographical reach of the OHADA arbitral laws, it will be interesting to interrogate how these instruments interplay.

[2] *The Interplay between the UAA and CCJA Arbitration*

Arbitration under the UAA and CCJA operate as two distinct systems and therefore operate two different sets of rules. Hence, rules laid down in the UAA and the CCJA Arbitration Rules differ on important issues such as grounds for challenge[30] and enforcement of arbitral awards.[31] Despite the fact that both arbitral instruments exclude the right to ordinary appeal of the arbitral award before the national courts of Member States.

24. The UNCITRAL Model Law on International Commercial Arbitration was adopted by the United Nations Commission on International Trade Law on 21 Jun. 1985. In 2006 the model law was amended to include more detailed provisions on interim measures. Unlike the Model Law, the UAA allows the arbitral tribunal to order the interim enforcement of the award, Art. 28 UAA.
25. None of the OHADA Member States have adopted the Model Law. In sub-Sahara Africa, six countries have so far adopted the Model Law.
26. The New York Convention was adopted on 10 Jun. 1958 and entered into force on 7 Jun. 1959. The Convention has 156 state parties with thirty-six signatory African countries (out of fifty-four African countries) See: http://www.uncitral.org/uncitral/en/uncitral_texts/arbitration/NYConvention_status.html.
27. The following OHADA francophone countries have acceded to the New York Convention: Benin, Burkina Faso, Cameroon, the Central African Republic, Côte d'Ivoire, Gabon, Guinea, Mali, Niger, and Senegal.
28. see Luca G. Castellani, *International Trade Law Reform in Africa*, vol. 13 no. 3-4 European Journal of Law Reform 480 (2011); Thomas E Carbonneau, *Arbitration in a Nutshell* 287 (2nd ed., West 2009).
29. Article 34 UAA.
30. Under the CCJA Arbitration Rules, an award can be challenge by action for nullity (Art. 30), revision Art. 29, and tierce-opposition. Article 47; Art. 26 UAA lists the grounds for the challenge of an arbitral award (absence, nullity or expiration of arbitration agreement; irregularity of constitution; violation of the arbitrators' mission; violation of the contradictory principle; violation of the international public policy; insufficiency or absence of motivation).
31. Article 30 UAA provides for the two-tier procedure for the enforcement of arbitral awards; Arts 30-31 CCJA Arbitration Rules have provided for the recognition of the arbitral awards and the enforcement by a competent national judge.

Under the UAA, parties may seek annulment of the arbitral award on limited grounds before the national courts of the seat of arbitration.[32] The national court judgment in the setting-aside proceeding is subject to ultimate appeal before the CCJA (as the supranational court of OHADA). However proceedings under CCJA Arbitration Rules are subject to more limited grounds for setting-aside,[33] which proceeding is directly taken before the CCJA itself.[34] It must be immediately noted that there is no right of appeal to any other court from the decision of the CCJA.[35]

On the mechanisms for the enforcement of awards, the UAA provides that the award may be submitted to a national court for the grant of exequatur[36] and it may be refused only if it is established that the award is contrary to the international public policy of the Member States.[37] Where a national court refuses to enforce an arbitral award, the decision will be finally determined by the CCJA.[38] Whereas for arbitral awards made under the CCJA Arbitration Rules, enforcement orders are issued by the President of the CCJA,[39] and such awards may only be refused on limited grounds, also before the CCJA. More importantly, when an enforcement order is granted by the CCJA, the arbitral award becomes enforceable in all OHADA Member States.[40] This is a practical advantage of arbitration under the CCJA Rules over arbitration under the UAA.

Although parties are required to be vigilant and careful when choosing a seat of arbitration and the arbitral rules to govern their disputes in the region, the OHADA set of rules and institutions have been acknowledged as modern, effective and appealing enough to increase the number of arbitration references in the region.[41]

§8.02 ARBITRATION INSTITUTIONS OPERATING WITHIN THE OHADA REGION

Arbitration institutions operating within the OHADA region can be categorized into two types: the CCJA as a regional arbitration institution and all other arbitration institutions located in various OHADA Member States. The CCJA arbitration centre is the leading institution, set up under the OHADA Treaty.[42] Unlike any other institutional

32. Article 26 UAA.
33. Article 30(6) of the CCJA Arbitration Rules.
34. The Abidjan (Côte d'Ivoire) Court of Appeal Decision n° 741 of 2 Jul. 2004, the Court of Appeal refers to Art. 25 of the OHADA Treaty which provides that the CCJA is the only court to have jurisdiction regarding recognition of awards rendered under its rules.
35. Article 30(1) and 30(2) CCJA Arbitration Rules.
36. Articles. 30 and 31 UAA.
37. Article 3(4) UAA.
38. Article 32 UAA.
39. Article 30 CCJA Arbitration Rules.
40. Article 31 CCJA Arbitration Rules.
41. Louis Degos and Dara Akchoti, *The Democratic Republic of the Congo Joins OHADA and its Arbitration Mechanisms* (K&L Gates Publication), available at: http://www.klgates.com/arbitration-world-09-19-2012/ [accessed 18 Apr. 2016].
42. The CCJA is located in Abidjan, Côte d'Ivoire.

arbitration[43] with its own set of rules.[44] As the OHADA supranational court, arbitral awards made under the CCJA Rules have potentially important and far-reaching consequences as domestic court judgments across the Members States.[45] Furthermore, as the supranational and apex court in which the OHADA judicial security has vested its powers, the CCJA ensures, through judgments and advisory opinions, the uniform application and interpretation of all the Uniform Acts.[46]

The Member States arbitration institutions are governed by arbitration rules laid down in the UAA.[47] Table 2 in the appendix contains a list of arbitration institutions in OHADA Member States.[48] These are private institutions established in various forms. Most, if not all of them, are created as non-profit organizations and incorporated as associations.[49] The majority operate under the umbrella of the local chamber of commerce and industry or are simply attached to such chamber.[50] These arbitration institutions offer different services. Although the UAA makes no distinction between domestic and international arbitration,[51] some institutions administer disputes that are domestic or regional,[52] others offer services that have only domestic[53] or both domestic and international reach.[54]

Most of these arbitration institutions provide additional value added services to their local arbitration community. This includes the dissemination of information on ADR, through production of books, forms, institutional information, among others.[55]

43. The International Chamber of Commerce (France), the American Arbitration Association (United States), the London Court of International Arbitration (United Kingdom), and the International Centre for Settlement of Investment Disputes (World Bank).
44. The OHADA Treaty and the CCJA Arbitration Rules.
45. See Claire Moore Dickerson, *The Common Court of Justice and Arbitration: Exogenous Forces Contributing to its Influence,* vol. 79, 63 no. 1 Law and Contemporary Problems 63 (2016); See also Art. 10 OHADA Treaty.
46. Claire Dickerson, *supra,* at p. 63; See also Art. 10 OHADA Treaty.
47. Article 1 UAA similar to Art. 1(2) UNCITRAL Model Law.
48. The contact information of some arbitration institutions in the region is not readily available.
49. This is the case of the following institutions; Groupement Inter-Patronal du Cameroun in Douala (Cameroon); Centre Africain pour le Droit et le Developpement headquarter in Yaoundé (Cameroon) with branches in other OHADA Member States; (Congo Arbitration Centre) in the Democratic Republic of Congo.
50. This is the case for the following institutions: the Centre for Arbitration, Mediation and Conciliation (CAMeC) in Benin, (CAMC-O) in Burkina Faso, (CAMC-CA) in the Central African Republic, (CAMC-GA) in Gabon, (CECAM) in Mali, and (CAMC) in Senegal, the National Centre for Arbitration, Conciliation and Mediation (CENACOM) in the DRC, the Centre for Mediation and Arbitration (CEMACO) in Congo, (CMAN) in Niger, and the Court of Arbitration, Mediation and Conciliation of Togo (CATO).
51. *Supra* note 23.
52. GICAM Arbitration Centre in Douala, Cameroon, for example.
53. The Centre for Arbitration, Mediation and Conciliation (CAMeC) in Benin, (CAMC-O) in Burkina Faso, (CAMC-CA) in the Central African Republic, (CAMC-GA) in Gabon, (CECAM) in Mali, (CAMC) in Senegal, the National Centre for Arbitration, Conciliation and Mediation (CENACOM) in the Democratic Republic of Congo, the Centre for Mediation and Arbitration (CEMACO) in Congo, (CMAN) in Niger, CATO and the Arbitration Centre of Guinée (CAG) in Guinée.
54. Côte d'Ivoire Arbitration Court (CACI), the CPAM Arbitration Centre in Cameroon.
55. These are generally available on their websites, for example:(http://www.courarbitrage.ci/) for CACI in Côte d'Ivoire; CAMC-O in Burkina Faso at: http://www.camco.bf/; CECAM in Mali at: http://www.cecam-mali.com/?cecam=home; and CAC in Democratic Republic of Congo at: http://cac-rdc.net/index.php [all accessed 18 Apr. 2016].

These institutions also organize workshops and training seminars on arbitration, along with awareness campaigns. However the frequency of such events may be subject to question especially with the growth of interest in arbitration within the region. For example, Marie-Andree Ngwe has noted the interesting outreach service GICAM offers to businesses to raise awareness of arbitration including arbitrator training facilities and provisions.[56] She further noted that though the GICAM Arbitration Centre is attracting more arbitration users and references, more need to be done regarding communication and training in order to attract those African businesses choosing non-African arbitrators and seats of arbitration outside the continent.[57] Despite these efforts it must be noted that the GICAM caseload is lower than that of institutions outside the region and to some extent outside the continent.[58]

Another effective and proactive institution striving to implement a different culture for arbitrators and arbitration institutions is the African Centre for Law and Development (CADEV).[59] Its department for arbitration and mediation in 2011 set up the Centre for Permanent Arbitration and Mediation (CPAM).[60] As a non-profit organization, CADEV operates through various projects, including but not limited to COJA (African Congress of Business Lawyers) and 'Can Do Training' (for conducting regular training on specific OHADA topics, with a particular focus on arbitration). These CADEV projects intensively promote arbitration and mediation across the region. Through COJA, for instance, CADEV is bringing together various organizations of business lawyers and arbitrators from all parts of the OHADA region for arbitration workshops and training. These events take place once a year, in cycles and in different cities.[61] The purpose and focus of this annual meeting is (but not limited) to encourage and support a close network among arbitrators and arbitration institutions. The 'Can Do Training' project holds a special skills-building programme on arbitration, among other courses. Although limited, given the demand, these courses are scheduled once a year and aimed specifically at helping professionals, including arbitrators, in the field.[62] There is no doubt that CADEV offers arbitrators a remarkable opportunity to develop, and build a professional network in the region, and defends the specific interests of their profession, their institution and their clients. But it is also true that

56. Marie-Andree Ngwe is the Chair of the GICAM Permanent Arbitration Committee. Her views were relayed to the author during a telephone interview in preparation for this chapter.
57. GICAM means 'Groupement Inter-Patronal du Cameroun' (in English, the Bureau of Industrial Business Group). It is a regional non-profit organization composed of companies and enterprises operating within the CEMAC (Economic Community of Central African States' and referred to in French as 'Communauté Économique des États de l'Afrique Centrale') region.
58. This information was collected during a Skype conversation with Mrs Marie-Andrée Ngwe, Chair of the GICAM Permanent Arbitration on 9 Mar. 2016.
59. Referred to in French as 'Centre Africain pour le Droit et le Developpement'.
60. A full presentation of CPAM is available at http://www.cadevafrique.org/ [accessed 18 Apr. 2016].
61. Since CADEV launched in 2008, there have been eight editions of COJA and it has trained arbitrators from various cities in the OHADA zone, including Abidjan (Côte d'Ivoire) in 2016; Bamako (Mali) in 2011; Cotonou (Benin) in 2010; Brazzaville (Congo) in 2014; Douala (Cameroon) in 2008, 2009 and 2012; Ouagadougou (Burkina Faso) in 2013; and Yaoundé (Cameroon) in 2015.
62. *Ibid.*

these efforts, most likely due to limited resources, remain difficult to access, both at the local and regional levels.

§8.03 CHALLENGES FACED BY THESE INSTITUTIONS

Arbitration institutions operating within OHADA Member States experience some challenges. These institutionally-related challenges include but are not limited to negative competition with the regional arbitration centre (CCJA), lack of knowledge of the existence of these institutions, lack of qualified and well-trained arbitrators within the region, and lack of cooperation between arbitration institutions located in the same country, as well as in the OHADA zone. Some of these issues are examined below.

[A] Competition between CCJA and other Arbitration Institutions

The CCJA arbitration institution is very often seen as a rival institution by other arbitration institutions within OHADA. As mentioned earlier, this rivalry lies in the community enforcement power of CCJA awards which is not available to awards made under the Rules of other arbitration institutions in the region. Thus, an arbitral award made in an OHADA Member State can only be subjected to exequatur in a domestic court which has jurisdiction with possibility of various appeal processes.[63] Whereas, according to the CCJA Arbitration Rules, an exequatur granted by the CCJA President is subject to compulsory enforcement in all OHADA Member States.[64] As a result, this power, given to the CCJA President to grant an exequatur to CCJA arbitral awards under the above circumstances, is perceived as being fundamentally disadvantageous to awards from the arbitration institutions of Member States.[65]

Therefore, CCJA arbitration appears to be faster and more effective in enforcing its awards and thus, more appealing to users than other arbitration institutions. This truly is an obstacle to the utility and development of ad hoc arbitration. Some scholars have suggested that unfair advantages can only be overturned if there is a reasonably well established balance of power between these institutions.[66] Although the CCJA is a special type of arbitration institution compared to other arbitration institutions which are simply private institutions,[67] it should be possible to extend the same right of exequatur to CCJA's arbitral awards to awards from other arbitration institutions within the OHADA region.[68]

The competition is also extended to the status of arbitrators operating under the Rules of these institutions. Unlike arbitrators in these institutions, the arbitrators from

63. Article 58 UAA.
64. Articles 30.1; 2 CCJA Arbitration Rules.
65. See Sadjo Ousmanou, *Approach Critique du droit et de la pratique de l'arbitrage dans l'espace OHADA*, (unpublished) paper presented at the first African Conference on International Commercial Law, Douala-Cameroon, 2-3 (21 and 22 Jan. 2012).
66. Sadjo Ousmanou, *supra*, at p. 3.
67. See, Gaston Kenfack Douajni, *L'internationalité de l'arbitrage OHADA*, vol. 13 no. 3-4, European Journal of Law Reform, 397(2011).
68. Gaston, Kenfack Douajni, *supra*, at p. 3.

the CCJA list of arbitrators and those designated by parties and confirmed by the CCJA, enjoy diplomatic immunity and privileges.[69] Scholars have argued that this immunity is intended to give to CCJA arbitrators, the same status as senior civil servants employed by the Organization, and to guarantee their freedom and independence. However, arbitrators designated in the list of an arbitral institution are not employees of the institution, which explains why this status and its attendant benefits have been criticized as excessive, unfounded, bias, and an obstacle to the attractiveness of choosing arbitrators from the list of other institutions.

[B] Domestic Law on Arbitration

Another challenge affecting these arbitration institutions is related to the application of the provisions of the UAA, which refer to the 'competent judge of the Member State' on several occasions but do not specify which court is competent. In normal circumstances, the domestic law of the relevant Member State prevails, whenever the uniform law is silent. But the situation becomes more complicated in those Member States that have no arbitration law[70] and have not adopted any new law to supplement the UAA.[71] Table 1 in the appendix contains the list of those OHADA states with no domestic law on arbitration.

[C] Attitude of OHADA Member States to Arbitration

Members States of the OHADA Treaty are considered pro-arbitration jurisdictions, because as mentioned above the UAA contains modern arbitration rules that are similar to the international norms to which most arbitration users and foreign investors are accustomed. However, the restriction of the use of these international norms by a Member State might be considered a less legally secure jurisdiction and thereby may not be selected as a seat of arbitration. An example is the signing by the Democratic Republic of Congo (DRC) of the New York Convention[72] with four specific reservations upon ratification of this Convention.[73] According to the DRC's reservations, only

69. Article 49 OHADA Treaty, from the revised OHADA Treaty by the Conference of Head of States and Governments on 17 Oct. 2008. The previous version of the article provided such privileges only for arbitrators designated by the CCJA.
70. The Democratic Republic of Congo has a domestic law on arbitration supplementing the UAA in Art. 184 of the Code of Civil Procedure, whereby the request for exequatur is to be brought before the lower court chosen by the parties, in accordance with Art. 166 of the same code. Cameroon and Côte d'ivoire have also updated their domestic legislation.
71. Article 35 UAA.
72. The New York Convention entered into force on 3 Feb. 2015 in the Democratic Republic of Congo, following the ratification of Law n° 13/023 dated 26 Jun. 2013, in application of Art. 215 of the Constitution.
73. The Democratic Republic of Congo declared that it will apply the New York Convention (1) on the condition of reciprocity, (2) only in commercial litigation, (3) to arbitral awards rendered after the entering into of the convention and (4) to arbitral awards that concern real estate properties located in the Democratic Republic of Congo. Norway and Tajikistan are the two other countries amongst the party to the New York Convention to have a similar reservation. It is also important to note that very few countries have signed up without any reservation.

commercial matters will be recognized and come within the ambit of the New York Convention and any awards made in the DRC will only be enforced on the basis of reciprocity with other Member States of the Convention. In addition the Convention will apply to awards made after its entry into force and will exclude all disputes related to real estate properties (immovable property or on a right related to immovable property). The last reservation is particularly important in the context of the DRC, where mining falls under immovable property in the domestic law and a large part of the DRC economy revolves around mining activities. As a result of these limitations, foreign arbitral awards will be enforceable in the DRC under the Convention in very limited situations. Therefore, a party seeking enforcement of an award will have to revert to the OHADA regime. Although the signing of the New York Convention by the DRC is itself a positive step toward bringing legal certainty to business operations in the country, the reservations may influence foreign investors who do not trust the OHADA legal system, due to its seemingly lesser notoriety compared with the New York Convention.

[D] Public Awareness of Arbitration Institutions in OHADA

The majority of arbitration institutions (except the CCJA) in OHADA Member States are not well known to either arbitration users or even to each other, both at the national and regional levels.[74] As evidenced from the list under Table 2, some institutions operate without a website[75] and other facilities necessary for improving their visibility to the wider world. It is obvious that these institutions need to embark on an awareness campaign and adopt a proper communications strategy aimed at arbitration users within and outside the OHADA region. These actions will help them communicate their existence and services, their facilities, and list of arbitrators to the wider world. It will also be useful for these institutions to ensure they employ qualified personnel to manage their caseload and enter into partnership arrangements with other institutions to share experience.

To aid this cooperation, it was suggested at the SOAS/AU Addis Ababa conference that arbitration institutions in Africa need a platform both at national and regional levels, to enhance communication and cooperation between themselves. It is my view that such cooperation may address the competition between the CCJA and other arbitration institutions on the one hand, and among these other arbitration institutions themselves. Such interaction will positively impact on the performance of each of these institutions, which will lead to an increase in the arbitration references they administer.

Similarly, another possible solution would be for the CCJA Arbitration Centre and national arbitration institutions to set up a forum to discuss topics on the development

74. When conducting interviews for this piece, I spoke to the legal counsel of two local private companies and three multinational businesses located in three different countries: Cameroon, Cote d'Ivoire, and Benin. Four out of five of these companies did not know about the existence of arbitration institutions other than the CCJA. The company with knowledge of national arbitration institutions had been involved in an arbitration case.
75. This is an example of CAG (Guinee Arbitration Centre) in Guinée; (CENACOM) National Centre for Arbitration, Conciliation and Mediation in the Democratic Republic of Congo.

of OHADA arbitration and to share their experiences of administering arbitration references.[76] It is also my view that such gatherings will provide opportunities for networking between African arbitrators and arbitration institutions. This suggestion will be an appropriate response to the serious criticism of the CCJA made by other arbitration institutions in the OHADA region.[77]

[E] Training for Arbitrators within the OHADA Region

The absence of training on the workings of arbitral institutions and OHADA arbitration laws represents a significant obstacle to the development of OHADA arbitration. After a thorough investigation of several professional training institutions across the OHADA Member States, including ERSUMA (the OHADA Professional School of Magistrates), it is surprising to note that there is no evidence of any official training programme, exclusively dedicated to OHADA arbitration law and practice. It is more surprising to note that several universities in France and Belgium have courses on OHADA arbitration,[78] while universities in the Member States have not yet adjusted their syllabuses to include OHADA arbitration in their law courses. It is important for OHADA to cooperate with Member States' governments to ensure that arbitration courses on, both substantive arbitration law and its administration by arbitral institutions, are included in law schools' syllabuses, university programmes, ERSUMA and other relevant African professional educational institutes. It is my view that the implementation of the OHADA legal system and its arbitration regime, in particular, will never be truly successful without the adequate provision in the region, of training on its instruments and the administration of its institutions.

CONCLUSION

There is a general impression that most, if not all, African jurisdictions concerned by this research have modern arbitration legislation, well-trained arbitrators and the required number of institutions to effectively administer arbitration references in the continent. However, this potential does not correspond to the level of involvement of African practitioners and the participation of the arbitration institutions in these countries, in the development of arbitration, even in disputes emanating from the continent, in practice. French-speaking Member States of the OHADA Treaty are not

76. Three international arbitral organizations, namely the International Court of Arbitration (ICC), the American Arbitration Association (AAA) and the International Centre for Settlement of Investment Disputes (ICSID) have met similarly since 1983 at their joint annual conference to share views on arbitration.
77. Such criticism include that the CCJA overshadows their existence and so acts as an obstacle to their growth.
78. This is the case for example of the Université de Paris II Panthéon Assas with specialized programme for future experts on various areas of OHADA law, including arbitration, available at: http://cfp.u-paris2.fr/16762483/0/fiche___formation/&RH=FORM_AUTRES; see also the Université de Paris 13 with a programme on OHADA with courses on Arbitration, available at: http://www.univ-paris13.fr/dsps/images/stories/pdf/programme-diu-ohada.pdf [both accessed 18 Apr. 2016].

immune to this phenomenon. They are equipped with a toolkit which includes a sophisticated and modern arbitration regime. The choice of two systems for arbitration cases means that they can generate a huge number of arbitration cases with seats in the Member States and under the rules of arbitral institutions within the OHADA Region. And yet, whilst this is plausible in theory, in practice, the results are very different.

If the CCJA, as a regional arbitration institution, is the most visible and most commonly-used seat of arbitration under the OHADA arbitration regime, it is certainly due to its unique powers and privileges. Ad hoc arbitration, on the contrary, faces numerous challenges that make arbitration in the OHADA Member States less appealing and therefore less likely to generate arbitration references. Fortunately, the challenges facing the OHADA arbitration regime are currently being addressed. A study is currently been undertaken by OHADA which will lead to the revision of the UAA and the CCJA Arbitration Rules.[79] Hopefully OHADA will seize this opportunity to equip its Member States, not only with revised instruments that take into account the challenges so far encountered in the initial text, but also with a mechanism and strategy to overcome the practical challenges discussed in this chapter.

79. The assignment in progress intends to achieve the following: to revise and update the UAA and the CCJA Arbitration Rules; to examine the current state of commercial mediation in Member States (inventory of instruments in force, implementation difficulties, and lessons learned); to include commercial mediation in the revised UAA or prepare a new Uniform Act on commercial mediation; to take into account international best practices in the instruments so revised and/or prepared; to offer a guide to arbitration and/or commercial mediation.

CHAPTER 9

Promotion of Arbitration to Domestic Small and Medium Sized Enterprises

Bernadette Uwicyeza

INTRODUCTION

This chapter examines whether arbitration institutions in Africa can play any role in the promotion of domestic arbitration to small- and medium-sized enterprises (SMEs) operating in the countries such institutions are located. It makes the argument that institutions can play such a role and that they are pivotal to the marketing of the process of arbitration to SMEs operating in various African countries. It further argues that such marketing is in practice beneficial to these arbitration institutions primarily because it helps them develop their experience in administering arbitral references.

There is no agreed definition of SMEs. Each country may have its own national definition in line with its policy towards promoting SMEs for economic growth. Multilateral agencies also have their own definition for SMEs. For an arbitral institution concerned with its marketing objective, a simple legal definition under the business association law may be adequate. Notably, many business association laws and regulations may include provisions for other purposes, such as for taxation, financial management procedures or development policies. In Rwanda any company with a turnover less than USD 200,000 is registered as an SME.[1] Data on SMEs are accessible from the Office for Registration of Companies.

Generally in African countries, SMEs constitute a large portion of the domestic market.[2] It is therefore evident that this group comprises a large market for arbitration

1. See the Ministerial Order that defines 'small private company' in Official Gazette no. Special of 8/5/2009 available at: www.primature.gov.rw [accessed 30 Mar. 2016].
2. SME Initiatives available at: http://www.ifc.org/wps/wcm/connect/region__ext_content/regions/sub-saharan + africa/advisory + services/sustainablebusiness/sme_initiatives/sme_initi atives [accessed 30 Mar. 2016].

institutions to promote the use of arbitration for the resolution of their commercial disputes. SMEs are generally registered with the designated companies' registration agency in their country of operation. They are obligated to pay taxes and social security charges and to file annual returns. They have legal personality such that they can sue and be sued in their own name, and therefore able to conclude arbitration agreements. This also means that they are familiar with formalized processes, have an understanding of the working of contracts and can therefore understand the requirements of institutional arbitration in terms of formalities.

Considered in their category, SMEs may have a larger volume of transactions than some large firms in the context of the economies of developing countries. It is these SMEs that supply various component needs of large firms, governments and their affiliated institutions.[3] Therefore, it follows that these transactions numerically generate more contracts which in turn will generate more disputes. In addition, all developing countries have policies and programmes to support the growth of SMEs which provide incentives for sole traders to move from the informal sector of microenterprises. For example, Rwanda has a SMEs Development Policy building on the EAC Industry and SMEs Strategy and the experience of other countries in the region such as Tanzania.[4] Such initiatives also create easy access to data of this category of enterprises which arbitration institutions can obtain for purposes of outreach and to market their dispute resolution services. This chapter argues that it is important (almost a necessity) for arbitration institutions in Africa to consider focusing their marketing initiatives first on the domestic market dominated by SMEs. This is because of the current inability of these institutions to successfully compete in the international arbitration administration market.

This chapter discusses these issues in three sections. Section §9.01 discusses the demand of arbitration services in Africa and argues for prioritization of SMEs in the marketing activities of arbitration institutions. It also analyses the international environment within which African arbitration institutions operate to demonstrate how and why it is difficult for them to compete successfully in the international market for the administration of arbitration.[5] Section §9.02 examines why parties choose a particular arbitral institution; and §9.03 discusses a case study supported by empirical evidence of such marketing activity and its consequence, drawing data from the experience of the Kigali International Arbitration Centre (KIAC) in relation to small- and medium-sized businesses, to show the correlation between such marketing activities and the increase in the use of arbitration by SMEs at KIAC.

Setting up KIAC was the initiative of the private sector in Rwanda. KIAC was set up for the purpose of assisting economic operators resolve their disputes in a timely, efficient and friendly manner. This was important to these economic operators who

3. See *SMES and Growth in Sub-Sahara Africa* (MENON) available at: http://www.norfund.no/getfile.php/Documents/Homepage/Reports%20and%20presentations/Studies%20for%20Norfund/SME%20and%20growth%20MENON%20%5BFINAL%5D.pdf [accessed 30 Mar. 2016].
4. Small and Medium Enterprises (SMEs) Development Policy, 2 Jun. 010, www.minicom.gov.rw.
5. It is this lack of success in the international competition that makes focusing on the domestic market very important.

wish to have their disputes resolved without delays (which is their experience before the courts) but not at exorbitant fees (which is their experience with ad hoc arbitration). The initiative for KIAC received support from the Government of Rwanda as part of its reforms of the investment climate in Rwanda. These reforms focused on the ease of doing business and also sought ways of reducing the costs of arbitration in international arbitral bodies. The idea was therefore to set up in the country the required infrastructure for an efficient and operational international arbitration centre that may be proposed as an alternative to the courts.[6]

§9.01 DEMAND OF ARBITRATION SERVICE IN AFRICA

This section examines the demand for the services of African arbitration institutions. It argues that African arbitration institutions have not recorded major success in competing for clients in the international arbitral market place (§9.01[A]). This therefore makes the case for such institutions to focus first on developing the domestic market (which is dominated by SMEs) and collaborate to grow and deepen the African arbitral market (§9.01[B]).

[A] The Market for International Arbitral Disputes

The business of administering arbitration references is not only a legal service, it is an international market dominated by the 'first arrivals' who are nominated by business parties having negotiation power or knowledge to impose an arbitration clause in their favour. So who are the first arrivals in the market? These are the large international arbitration institutions such as the ICC, LCIA, AAA, CIETAC and the Swiss Centres.[7] For example, while marketing arbitration to professional associations involved in construction contracts, (these include architects, engineers and property developers) KIAC was informed that in many infrastructure projects funded by development partners in Rwanda, arbitration clauses are included in the model contracts proposed by the project funding agencies.[8] KIAC was also informed that generally, the model clause chosen is usually that of one of the 'big four' international arbitration bodies. These are the rules of the ICC, LCIA, AAA and CIETAC.

The challenge remains with the second category of international arbitration users comprised of foreign counterparts dealing with African business partners in Africa. Foreign counterparts dealing with the business community in Africa do not wish to go to the national courts of the relevant African country. They prefer to refer their disputes to arbitration but then choose a seat and arbitration institution outside Africa. This

6. The KIAC was established by Law No. 45/2010 of 14 Dec. 2010. This Law provides for its organization, functioning and competence. KIAC was officially launched in May 2012 and its offices were located in the premises of the Private Sector Federation (PSF) until March 2015 when the Centre moved to its own acquired office facility in Kigali.
7. These arbitration institutions are generally referred to as the traditional institutions.
8. Such agencies include the World Bank Group, IMF, AfDB, and other cooperation agencies and trust funds.

action also has the effect of depriving African arbitration institutions and seats of the opportunity to administer any dispute that may arise from that transaction.

This lack of reference to institutions in Africa is a major challenge for such arbitration institutions and must be remedied. This action also has the effect of depriving African arbitration institutions and seats of the opportunity to administer any dispute that may arise from that transaction. There is a case to be made for such disputes connected to Africa to either have the seat of arbitration in Africa or at the very least for the parties to choose an arbitral institution in Africa to administer the reference where a foreign seat is chosen. This should not be difficult especially since proceedings under the rules of most arbitration institutions in Africa can hold anywhere in the world. For example in the East African Region, Rule 21 of the East African Court (EAC) Arbitration Rules provides that the tribunal may hear witnesses or hold meeting for consultation among its members at any place it deems appropriate, having regard to the circumstances of the arbitration.[9] This meets any perceived needs for convenience for the hearings while the reference is administered by the African arbitration institution. A starting point may be at an African continental level to agree a minimum level of reference to African arbitration institutions. The flip side of this argument is for African arbitral institutions to demonstrate that they offer a minimum level of internationally accepted standard of service for the administration of arbitration for disputing parties.

In the first three years of operation of KIAC, it conducted an intensive campaign for the awareness of arbitration in Rwanda and the East African region. The campaign focused on the advantages of arbitration over litigation and was conducted through various outreach programmes including workshops, road-shows, radio talk shows, seminars with professional associations.[10] The outreach programmes enabled the management of KIAC to build close relationships and networks with the business community involved in cross-border transactions in the region and beyond. Through the same process, KIAC discovered that some local SMEs involved in cross-border transactions had signed contracts with arbitration clauses without understanding the effect and consequences of such clauses. Two examples will demonstrate the challenges some of these SMEs face.

The first example is a Rwandan sub-contractor that signed a contract with a Chinese construction company. The subject matter of the contract was the construction of a retaining wall to protect against erosion action in a locality where there is risk of erosion. The sub-contractor completed the works but was not paid because the Chinese company did not approve the works and corrected on the wall at the request of the supervisor of the main contract. The contract included an arbitration clause providing for arbitration in Singapore. A payment dispute arose between the parties. At a meeting of KIAC with traders of the Southern Province of Rwanda, a presentation was made on

9. In the same vein, s. 18 of the Nairobi Centre for international Arbitration allows the Tribunal with the consent of the parties to hold meetings or hearings in a place other than the seat of arbitration. Also, Art. 23 of the KIAC Arbitration Rules provide that the arbitral Tribunal may hold hearings, meetings and deliberations at any convenient geographical place in its discretion.
10. These are mining, construction, energy developers, architects and engineers, manufactures and bankers associations.

the concept and practice of arbitration. After the session, a trader called to get more advice on if he can sue the Chinese company before the Rwandan Courts to demonstrate that the arbitration clause was inoperative in the context. He explained that the contract was in two copies, one in English for the Chinese company and a second one in Kinyarwanda (local language) for the Rwandan sub-contractor. The Trader explained that the word used in Kinyarwanda for arbitration is very often understood as mediation and 'not this kind of thing that deprived you of your right to sue somebody who is not paying you for the work you did'. The team from KIAC explained to the Rwandan sub-contractors that the practice of the courts is that when this word is used in a dispute resolution clause since it is the word used in the law governing arbitration in Rwanda,[11] the courts enforce the arbitration clause and refer the matter to arbitration. In this example it is clear that requiring a small sized Rwandan business to go all the way to Singapore to resolve a dispute that is in all respects Rwandan defies logic. However, that is precisely what the SME agreed to without proper legal advice. It is debatable if the SME in this case could have negotiated better terms such as arbitration in Kigali (the road construction was in Kigali, payment was in Rwandan currency, and the contract was concluded between the parties in Kigali) with the main contractor which was Chinese, considering the clear power imbalance between the parties.

In the second example another Rwandan SME owner signed a contract for the supply of tyres by a Chinese company. The contract between the parties included an arbitration clause for disputes to be resolved in China using the Chinese language. A dispute about the conformity of the tyres supplied as not meeting the specifications arose. The Rwandan SME owner hired a Chinese lawyer who informed him that they won the case but never sent a copy of the arbitral award. KIAC advised the businessman to try to get a copy of the award from the Chinese lawyer for a translation and identification of the court of enforcement. But, there is no evidence that an award in the Rwandan SME favour exists. In this case, If the arbitration had held in Kigali, the SME will at least have been present at the hearings and have an arbitral award (whether for or against him). But under the arbitration clause in the contract he signed, he had none of these, even after paying a Chinese lawyer in China. If these incidents are happening in Rwanda, then the probability of same occurring in other African countries is also high.

After two years of these outreach programmes by KIAC, the types of inquiries KIAC receives have changed. SMEs in Rwanda are now better informed of what arbitration is and usually now request for information (from KIAC) on how to improve their position when negotiating the details of the arbitration clause. Since KIAC in the first place informed them about the consequences of including an arbitration clause in their contracts, it is only natural that their arbitration institution of first choice is KIAC. This is clear evidence that there is an untapped market which all arbitration institutions in Africa can access to ensure that these businesses are adequately informed about arbitration. Such engagement will build trust between the arbitration institutions and the SMEs within the state they are located. With such trust in place, they will be

11. Law No. 005/2008 of 14 Feb. 2008 on arbitration and conciliation in commercial matters, Official gazette no Special of 6 Mar. 2008 available at: www.primature.gov.rw [accessed 30 Mar. 2016].

arbitration institutions of choice for the SMEs which they can refer to in their negotiations and contracts.

The perception of these SMEs as the market base for arbitration institutions in Africa is a game changer. This is because there are many institutions in Africa allowing for greater choice particularly in intra-regional and international markets. So knowledge of a particular arbitration institution by local businesses is a great boost to the institution when such businesses negotiate with other businesses outside of the particular state of location of the institution. Not only do such SMEs have an awareness of arbitration but also know of an arbitration institution they trust that can effectively administer their dispute. This is an important knowledge to have when negotiating a contract, and arbitration institutions in Africa are well positioned to provide that awareness.

[B] SME focused Marketing

This section examines why African arbitration institutions need to focus their marketing efforts more on SMEs. Users of arbitration institutions in the domestic market are made up of corporations or large firms, multinational corporations, government agencies, individuals and SMEs. In comparison to large firms or corporations, SMEs are more often managed by individuals who also own the business.[12] Generally they cannot afford to hire a permanent legal adviser to advise them on legal matters when entering into contracts. Thus SMEs are in need of basic advice on arbitration which arbitration institutions can provide and in the process encourage the use of their model clauses in their contracts.

The experience of KIAC is that even without the services of a legal adviser, well-informed SMEs are willing to engage in arbitration in order to avoid delays in courts. SMEs and their owners generally have a good understanding of their dispute and ask questions before filing a case and this will be an opportunity for the arbitration institution to advise on the negotiation of arbitration clauses in future contracts. Therefore there is room to build a business and working relationship with SMEs. However, arbitration institutions need to simplify the language of their rules and their procedure and be willing and available to provide further clarification where necessary, to make their services accessible to such parties. For example the language must be clear and simple, when advising on filing a Notice of Arbitration the Case manager must be able to involve the party if so requested and avoid complicated legal vocabulary or explain these where necessary. In any awareness forum such as a seminar, radio or television Talk show, it is always important to keep in mind the targeted audience and tailor the language to their concerns and needs. The need to use simplified language and techniques to reach the audience cannot be over emphasized.

12. Tom Gibson and H.J Van der Vaart in their study on SMEs provide a description of common features of SMEs in comparison with large firms and microfinance. Defining SMES: a less imperfect definition of small and medium Enterprises in developing countries available at: http://www.brookings.edu/~/media/research/files/papers/2008/9/development%20gibson/09_development_gibson.pdf [accessed 30 Mar.] at p. 11.

It is also important to recognize that SMEs conclude contracts with operators such as large firms, government agencies and civil society organizations in the domestic market and beyond, for supply of goods, services and works. Once they understand the advantages of arbitration, in long run they will influence these business partners and more importantly influence their fellow SMEs on the advantages of using arbitration to resolve their disputes.

Another reason to focus on SMEs is that their advisers who are lawyers may not themselves be familiar with arbitration or practice of the courts in relation to arbitration and the advice to their clients may be incorrect. It is always better to take care of both groups although in separate fora. The experience of KIAC is that SME owners prefer to come with their lawyers for advice and very often appear to have a good understanding of what needs to be done and ask the lawyer to formalize their decision to pursue arbitration. SME owners appreciate therefore their proximity and accessibility to the arbitration institution. Such direct engagement with SMEs also serves to demystify the legal language and involve them in building their case.

For these reasons, arbitration institutions in Africa must understand the landscape of arbitration in Africa or at least at regional level and work together to provide correct information to the business community and help them improve their negotiation position. It may be necessary for arbitration institutions in Africa to set up cooperation mechanisms that will help them together to develop the market for arbitration and also collectively share the benefits. Some matters that can be on the terms of reference for such mechanism will be engagement with SMEs, building on their comparative advantages and the creation of joint marketing platforms at least at regional level. These will help to mobilize their collective resources and deepen the arbitration market in Africa for the benefit of all of them.

§9.02 WHY PARTIES CHOOSE A PARTICULAR ARBITRATION INSTITUTION

The continued increase in the number of arbitration institutions in Africa and around the world raises the next question of why disputing parties choose a particular arbitration institution. In deciding which arbitration institution to nominate, parties and their advisers ask themselves a range of questions, answers to which will determine which jurisdiction and institution they will choose. Four of these questions are examined below and a section on suggestions on how arbitral institution can give a positive answer to each question.

[A] Safety of the Jurisdiction

This issue is about the overall legal and physical environment and covers issues such as whether or not the courts respect arbitration agreements and awards. What is important here is what happens in practice. The fact that a country is signatory to the New York Convention or has a pro arbitration national law carries very little weight if the courts in their judgments are not supportive of arbitration. It is therefore important that arbitration institutions work with the judiciary in their jurisdiction to ensure that judges understand and support arbitration. An example from the KIAC operation in this regard is its organization of specific workshops for judges on the legal framework of arbitration in Rwanda and the role of courts in creating an enabling environment for arbitration to flourish. It was an opportunity to explain that if the judiciary is not arbitration friendly and does not respect the outcome of the arbitration process, there is no way to achieve the objective of promoting arbitration in Rwanda. Also if judges do not respect arbitration agreements, KIAC will not meet its mandate. After this first workshop, the Judiciary was invited to allow judges attend the training programme organized for professionals by KIAC. This was to ensure that all legal professionals in Rwanda have the same basic understanding of arbitration. This working relationship and interaction with the judiciary produced tangible results. Some examples of this result are that where there is an arbitration agreement, the courts always give effect to Article 10 of the Law governing arbitration in Rwanda and refer the matter to arbitration.[13] Since these training initiatives, it has been noted that courts refer disputes covered by an arbitration agreement to arbitration. This includes even those with a pathological arbitration clause such as arbitration followed by litigation. To speed up the process of enforcement, the Chief Justice issued in 2012 instructions directing the competent court of enforcement to decide within eight days on any application for the enforcement of arbitral awards in Rwanda. This Direction therefore gives priority of hearing to applications for the enforcement of arbitral award enforcement and do not follow the regular Court Roll.[14] The survey conducted by KIAC in July 2015 on enforcement demonstrated that in three out of the ten awards issued in KIAC arbitration in between September 2013, date of the first award issued and April 2015, the losing parties filed application for setting aside of the awards and all three applications where rejected by the courts.[15]

The physical environment include such factors as visa facilities, assistance offered by the Centre to parties and the arbitral tribunal but also confidence that the arbitration shall be conducted in a safe (in the sense of physical security) environment. These are some of the feedback received from foreign arbitrators and parties involved in KIAC arbitration. It appears these issues are more important than the issue of fees and costs paid. When parties or arbitrators attend a foreign country for a hearing they may have negative perceptions. For example, as it relates to Rwanda, some foreigners still have in mind horrible images of the genocide which they saw on their television sets twenty-two years ago while Rwanda today is quite the opposite: peaceful, stable, increasingly prosperous and facing the legacy of the genocide with courage and

13. Article 10 of the Rwandan Arbitration Act refers to Art. 8 of the UNCITRAL Model Law on the stay of court proceedings before a valid arbitration agreement.
14. Chief Justice Instructions No. 002/2012 of 24 Oct. 2012 determining the competent Court for recognition and enforcement of awards. The instructions were passed to establish the regime of enforcement of arbitral awards pending the amendment to the arbitration Act 2008. The instructions are in process of publication in the official Gazette and are already applied by the Courts.
15. Communication and perception impact end line study on arbitration and other ADR services in Rwanda, July 2015 available online: http://www.kiac.org.rw/IMG/pdf/-28.pdf [accessed 30 Mar. 2016].

optimism.[16] Arbitration institution must appreciate that it matters to people generally how they are received and the safety of their documents in hotels or at the hearing places. Parties and arbitrators are confident of getting these services in well-established arbitral centres in Paris, London, Singapore but for African arbitration institutions, they need to be reassured of these provisions. Therefore African arbitration institutions need to make more efforts to give assurances to foreign users that they operate in a safe environment. Some of these issues are beyond the control of African arbitration institutions. However greater interaction with other economic sector players provides institutions the opportunity to advocate for required changes.

[B] Track Record of the Particular Arbitration Institution

Parties and their lawyers will be reluctant to use an arbitration institution that cannot show a convincing track record of their ability to successfully administer arbitral references. This is why African arbitration institutions need to engage with domestic players to gain experience through the administration of domestic disputes as argued above. In the first international case concluded under KIAC, the counsel was a lawyer who had been involved in KIAC arbitration and advised his client to come and meet the team at KIAC for information on arbitration under KIAC Rules. Lawyers that have been involved in KIAC arbitration either as counsel or arbitrators influence other lawyers in their Law firms and their clients as noted from repeat use by the same law firms for different cases.

[C] Benefits of Institutional Arbitration in Africa

The question of users under this head is what will be the benefit to them of arbitrating under the rules of an arbitration institution in Africa? The answer to this question is particularly important to international parties who have access and familiarity with the major international arbitration institutions. While developing the pricing/cost system for KIAC arbitration, a comparison survey was made of African arbitration institutions to ensure that KIAC arbitration costs are affordable for at least African users and acceptable for arbitrators. Fees aligned to the local market may be an advantage for African arbitration institutions especially for disputes involving SMEs in cross-border transactions. Such disputes are usually not of exceptionally high values and some international arbitrators are willing to offer their services in the African market even for lower fees.[17] In September 2012, KIAC made a call for applications onto the panel of

16. During the Genocide against the Tutsis in Rwanda in 1994, an estimated 1 million people were killed in only 100 days. Rwanda was in ruins and was declared a failed State. Now Rwanda sustains high economic growth of 7.1 % average year on year since 2014 with stable inflation and exchange rate. Rwanda was ranked as the least corrupt country in the East African region, according to the 2012 Corruption Perception Index (CPI) report released by Transparency International. The World Bank Doing Business Survey of 2014 ranked Rwanda as the easiest place to do business in Africa, a position that was previously held by South Africa. Rwanda is among the top three African countries in terms of internet connectivity (Ookla).
17. For such arbitrators, they gain experience and improve their curriculum vitae.

International Arbitrators and received good profiles of renowned international arbitrators in various fields ready to serve for a lower fee than the fees they will receive in large international institutions. This demonstrates that it is possible to find in the international community of arbitration, people with high qualifications open to participate in developing the African market for arbitration for future returns. It is also obvious that such participation is beneficial for such individuals.

[D] Availability of Qualified Professionals

This issue does not only refer to training and certification of arbitrators but extends to practical experience of the individuals to decide the dispute. In developing the domestic arbitral market, arbitration institutions play a key role by giving opportunities to the local community of professionals and lawyers to familiarize themselves with arbitration law and practice. The survey conducted by the KIAC shows that lawyers and arbitrators when asked if they prefer institutional or ad hoc arbitration, answered that they preferred to use both. Ad hoc arbitration for flexibility with the negotiation of fees and institutional arbitration in order to acquire experience and professionalism to serve at the regional and international levels; and also to test the practice under KIAC and advise their clients with confidence.

[E] Some Suggestions

All arbitration institutions in Africa will need to develop appropriate responses to these questions before expecting international parties to take up their services. It is obvious that some of the questions (e.g., attitude of the courts) fall outside the control of institutions but all the factors or issues interconnect and arbitration institutions can positively influence these outcomes through entering into strategic partnerships with other stakeholders playing a key role in creating an enabling environment for arbitration to thrive. This therefore calls for collaboration between arbitration institutions in Africa to engage with their courts and judges, and governments.

To address these needs of arbitrating parties, arbitration institutions in Africa may start by testing in the environment where they are located, their practice and capacity to deliver in the domestic market place where they do not face international competition. It is my opinion that once the local business community becomes familiar with arbitration and its advantages, such businesses will be in a position to negotiate with foreign counterparts for reference to an arbitration institution within their proximity. The word 'proximity' is here very important. It is used to refer to arbitration institutions in the same region (not necessarily in their own country, but one within Africa). Such institutions on their part should also remain open to working with similar institutions at least at the regional level. They need to be willing to advise prospective parties on the available options and on their comparative advantages. For example when KIAC receives a call from a prospective party, for advice on the choice of another African arbitration institution or state as seat of arbitration, it should be possible for KIAC to provide an informed advice, if this addresses the need of the person requesting such information. Arbitration institutions in Africa therefore need to set up a cooperation mechanism that may help to grow the market of arbitration across the continent and aim to together, address the needs of economic operators in cross-border commercial transactions. Such cooperation mechanism may be a platform for activities that increase the branding and visibility of arbitration institutions in the same region; the mobilization of funds for these activities; a procedure that allows these arbitration institutions to address the needs of economic operators in cross-border transactions as it relates to dispute resolution processes; and choice of a seat.

§9.03 THE EXPERIENCE OF KIAC ON THE USE OF ARBITRATION BY SMES

This section draws from the experience of KIAC outreach programmes mentioned above. The first learning point is for arbitration institutions to get to know the organizations (SMEs) located in their place of operation and the particular challenges they encounter with enforcement of contracts. This will assist the arbitration institution target its response and develop appropriate messages to address the identified needs and also to create the appropriate medium for communication with them and in the appropriate language. This will ensure that the arbitration institution is actually meeting the needs of the SMEs.

KIAC worked with professional associations registered with the Rwanda Private Sector Federation, an umbrella of professional organizations in Rwanda.[18] Seminars with various associations of engineers, mining association, energy sector, and architects whose members all fall within the category of SMEs, as defined in this chapter, were organized. Typically during the seminars, a presentation was made by KIAC representative on the concept and practice of arbitration, the distinctions between ad hoc and institutional arbitration, with special focus on KIAC, and the benefits of arbitration for the particular profession. In exchange KIAC also participates in other fora organized by those professional associations as well. These interactions led to the creation of a database of members of professional associations in Rwanda (which is regularly updated) for the circulation of regular information via email and other social media outlets. The experience of KIAC is that this continuous relationship with professional associations has positively influenced KIAC caseload as discussed below.

In addition to the outreach programmes, KIAC used media campaigns such as radio and television talk shows on community and private radio and television stations to reach out to traders who are not yet members of professional associations. It is not unusual for KIAC to receive telephone calls and visits from traders after a television or radio talk show. The types of enquiries usually received include questions on dispute

18. The Private Sector federation is comprised of various associations but KIAC focused on professional associations whose members are likely to conclude contracts including arbitration clauses; architects, engineers and energy developers engaged in contracts of works, microfinance concluding loan agreements, manufacturers association concluding contracts for supply of Goods and services with SMEs, insurance Companies comprising foreign investors familiar with arbitration practice.

resolution clauses in a contract, filing of a case under an arbitration agreement with seat in a foreign country, information on procedural rules, and clarification of dispute resolution clauses. These enquiries lead to the conclusion that it is important for arbitration institutions to have an information desk manned by a well-trained staff, able to provide correct answers to basic questions from interested members of the public. Such interests are generated primarily from the category of SMEs. The experience of KIAC shows that there is a correlation between marketing activities and the increase in the use of arbitration by SMEs in addition to changes in the perceptions of this group in favour of arbitration. This section briefly sets out the main findings from KIAC statistics relevant to SMEs (§9.03[A]); interrogates the correlation between KIAC marketing activities targeted at SMEs and the increase in the use of KIAC arbitration by SMEs (§9.03[B]); and examines the challenging issue of funding such marketing activities (§9.03[C]).

[A] KIAC Statistics and SMEs

Since its official launch in May 2012 until December 2015, KIAC has registered thirty arbitration cases. Parties to these cases are from Rwanda, Kenya, Pakistan, USA, Italy, Senegal and South Africa. Most of these cases involved at least one Rwandan counterpart. This evidently shows that businesses within the location of the arbitration institution may have a stronger impact on case referrals than those completely disconnected from the institution. In terms of market or industry sector, the cases administered by KIAC have been mainly from the construction /engineering/infrastructure sectors which make up 33% of the total caseload of KIAC followed by the service industry (21%) and supply of Goods/equipment (17%).

The portion of this KIAC caseload attributable to parties described as SMEs is very significant. In 83% of KIAC cases, SMEs featured as either claimant or respondent. In the first year of operations, June 2012-June 2013, KIAC registered five cases all involving SMEs as claimants. In the second year, July 2013-June 2014, KIAC registered twelve cases including seven cases involving SMEs as claimants but with a small change on the part of the respondents. In four cases, the respondents were also SMEs. From July 2014, SMEs involvement in KIAC statistics became more significant. Of the thirteen cases registered, twelve cases involved a domestic SME and in half of these cases, both claimant and respondent were SMEs.

It should be noted that in total, 56% of parties involved are domestic SMEs, although KIAC communications and marketing included outreach activities targeted at all types of audiences in Rwanda, East Africa and beyond. For the limited involvement of large firms in KIAC arbitration,[19] some reasons may be proffered. One reason may be that large firms pay for the services of law firms (usually paid on a monthly basis) for legal representation in courts and have always integrated the cost of disputes in their risk management plans which is not the case for SMEs who cannot afford to pay

19. Only two large firms have been parties to KIAC arbitration as at the end of 2015.

lawyers a retainer basis. This is especially important in the face of delays in the judicial system with the availability of more than one level of appeal.

It should also be noted that the number of SMEs involved in KIAC arbitration increased from year on year. For example, there was an increase from five SMEs in 2012 to eleven SMEs in 2013 and eighteen SMEs in 2014. These increases did not suddenly happen. There is a very clear correlation between KIAC marketing activities and these increases in its caseload. However the most important (and gratifying) change is the more positive perception by the SMEs in favour of arbitration as an effective mechanism for the resolution of commercial disputes.

[B] Link between Marketing and the Use of Arbitration by SMEs

From 2012, KIAC management embarked on an intensive programme or campaign for the promotion of the effective use of arbitration through various media including training of professionals; lawyers, judges, engineers, architects, urban planners, procurement officers or project Managers and agents. The training programme not only aimed at creating local capacity in arbitration but also was seen as the best way of promoting a culture of arbitration, thus a marketing and communication platform. In addition, to training, KIAC organized seminars with professional associations, public education through various media outlets and training sessions for journalists and editors.

A first series of training sessions was launched in December 2012 linked to the requirement for admission onto the KIAC panel of arbitrators. For admission to the domestic panel, Annex III to the KIAC Arbitration Rules include having undertaken a recognized course of study in law and practice of arbitration, and/or having been qualified for the Associate Membership level of the Chartered Institute of Arbitrators or any comparable professional arbitration Institute, as criteria to be satisfied. Many professional individuals enrolled on this training programme to qualify for admission to the KIAC panel of arbitrators.[20] For those who have already trained in arbitration with other providers or have experience through practice in arbitration, it was an opportunity to refresh their knowledge. For KIAC, it was important to offer the opportunity to everyone to discover and learn about arbitration concepts and practice.[21] Each session of the training was reported in the media and a documentary was produced with participants in order to associate the public to this learning process.[22] In addition to the training sessions, KIAC has organized a series of seminars with professional associations to reach those who have not been able to attend the training

20. About 277 professionals enrolled in the capacity building programme undertaken by KIAC for the introduction to arbitration leading to associate Member CIArb, a half continued with the second level leading to Member CIarb.
21. This training over the years has attracted over 500 participants primarily engineers, architects, lawyers, accountants, energy developers and consultants.
22. Documentary on KIAC achievements are available online, for example: https://youtu.be/cMiogOvi6f0 [accessed 30 Mar. 2016]; and https://youtu.be/7d9CsjsMMqg [accessed 30 Mar. 2016].

programmes. In this first series, seminars were organized for the period of January-March 2013 with energy developers, mining association, architects and engineers associations, construction association and media practitioners playing a key role in public education.[23] This awareness campaign has continued.

The survey conducted in July 2015, on the impact of marketing and communications activities, demonstrated changes in perception of arbitration on the domestic market between 2013 and 2015, which also explains the increase in the use of arbitration by SMEs.[24] The 2015 survey included among other specific objectives: (i) the review of the content of the communication tools produced and to find out what messages target groups retained from the communication, if accurate and if it contributed to the level of awareness of KIAC services; (ii) whether the target groups receiving the messages and tools used understand the messages and to find out if their perceptions of arbitration are changing; (iii) if there is a behaviour change in the target groups. The method used in the 2015 survey involved collecting information from a sample of 500 respondents among those interviewed during the 2013 survey. The users were divided into two categories: (a) Users, primarily those who attended KIAC events, seminars, workshop, conferences, symposium or trainings; and (b) Agents, comprised of advocates and Judges, those who influence users of arbitration in one way or another. SMEs comprised of members of professional associations (such as construction industry, energy developers, mining association) constituted the largest proportion of respondent users at 25% followed by government agencies at 18%. Also a separate mini survey questionnaire on client satisfaction was conducted targeting parties that already participated in KIAC arbitration, predominantly SMEs either claimants or respondents in KIAC arbitration.

The main and general conclusion from the impact evaluation was that the intensive communication campaigns conducted and messages delivered by KIAC had a positive impact on perceptions of arbitration and other ADR services among these SMEs in Rwanda. Perceptions and awareness of KIAC increased from 72.2% (in 2013) to 96.4% in 2015. In addition, the number of respondents who indicated they did not know about KIAC reduced from 27.8% (in 2013) to 3.4% in 2015.

A large number of respondents (84%) indicated that arbitration messages delivered by KIAC was accurate, and helped them become aware of KIAC and its arbitration services in general (91.1%). This showed that there was a change of respondents' perceptions, awareness and attitude towards arbitration as a result of the campaigns by KIAC. Change in attitude may not translate into behaviour change since behaviour change takes time but in this case, there is a change of behaviour that can be measured by the progressive increase of the number of cases involving SMEs filed before the KIAC.

---

23. Following this campaign in 2013, in April 2013 a dispute involving an SME was registered at KIAC. The claimant was an SME owned by an engineer who had attended the seminar with energy developers.
24. Communication and perception impact end-line study on arbitration and other ADR services in Rwanda, July 2015 is available online at: http://www.kiac.org.rw/IMG/pdf/-28.pdf [accessed 30 Mar. 2016].

It is recognized that the behaviour change may also be influenced by the level of satisfaction with services of KIAC. The mini survey with people who have used KIAC arbitration showed that generally, clients had a positive experience and were satisfied with KIAC administration of their arbitration reference. Clients of KIAC, majority of who are SMEs indicated that the overall quality of the services rendered by KIAC during their arbitration was very good and a large number indicated that they would put KIAC arbitration in their future contracts.

It is therefore important for any arbitration institution in Africa, not only to reach out to potential users through an appropriate marketing strategy; but to also ensure they deliver the right message to the right people; and also to deliver high quality services in terms of case administration and management. Institutions must also measure the impact of their activities so that these are evidence based. However, it must be noted that marketing and communication activities cost a lot of money which may limit the type and numbers of such activities arbitration institutions in Africa can undertake.

[C] Funding the Marketing Activities

From the experience of KIAC, for an arbitration institution to achieve a significant increase in its caseload, there is a need to invest a lot of funds into marketing and communication activities. The cost of communication and marketing activities may be a challenge for some arbitration institutions in Africa, particularly those starting without any support either from their host government, or the private sector such as an organization, or with membership funds. One of the common features of well-established institutions such as the ICC, AAA, LCIA, HKIAC and SIAC is that their finances are not dependent solely upon revenues from case administration activities. Both AAA and LCIA have significant paying membership base. The ICC is part of the International Chamber of Commerce and receives some funding from its parent organization. Singapore and Hong Kong have received support from their home governments or the private sector.

Even in cases where there is support, one of the important lessons arbitration institutions in Africa can learn from these better established international institutions is that, it takes many years for an arbitration institution to create demand.[25] Therefore the sustainability of an arbitration institution in Africa depends on its capacity to mobilize funds either from the government or from the private sector for its business development. KIAC invested a lot of funds in marketing activities particularly during the first three years of its existence. During this period marketing and communications expenditures amounted to 60% of its total expenditure, that is an average of USD 300,000 each year, an amount largely beyond the income generated by KIAC through its caseload.

25. Singapore International Arbitration Centre has published a table on statistics of international Centres and the SIAC itself showing the slow increase of cases in the first years: www.siac.sg/index.php?.

CONCLUSION

Arbitration institutions in Africa can play a major role in promoting the use of arbitration by SMEs located in their states of domicile and operation. It is a necessity for these arbitration institutions to grow their domestic market and promote the use of arbitration by SMEs. As evidenced by the experience of KIAC, once SMEs start participating in arbitration, this will influence other groups contracting with them at the local, regional and international level, and lead to an increase in the caseload of these arbitration institutions.

Focusing on the domestic market implies providing better arbitration related support to the local business community. At the regional level, arbitration institutions in Africa need to collaborate better and build on their respective comparative advantages, growing the market together and sharing the benefits together. This requires that each arbitration institution must think about how to mobilize funds for its business development since funding remains the major challenge for many of them. Finally an African initiative should be created to support arbitration institutions in Africa based on set of standards and harmonized marketing activities.

Appendices

APPENDIX I

African Countries: Arbitration Laws and Conventions*

No	*Country*	*National Legislation*	*New York Convention*	*ICSID Convention*
1	Algeria	Arbitration Law No 08-09, 2008	8 May 1989	22 March 1996
2	Angola	Voluntary Arbitration Law 2003	-	-
3	Benin Republic	OHADA UAA; Civil Procedure Code 2008	14 Aug 1974	14 Oct 1966
4	Botswana	Arbitration Act, 1959	19 Mar 1972	14 Feb 1970
5	Burkina Faso	OHADA UAA	21 June 1987	14 Oct 1966
6	Burundi	Civil Procedure Code 2004	21 Sept 2014	5 Dec 1969
7	Cameroon	OHADA UAA	19 May 1988	2 Feb 1967
8	Cape Verde	Arbitration Law of 2005	-	26 Jan 2011
9	Central Africa Republic	OHADA UAA	13 Jan 1963	14 Oct 1966
10	Chad	OHADA UAA; Civil Procedure Code	-	14 Oct 1966
11	Comoros	OHADA UAA	27 July 2015	7 Dec 1978
12	Congo, Republic of	OHADA UAA; Civil Procedure Code.	-	14 Oct 1966

* The information provided in Appendix I is as of April 2016.

No	*Country*	*National Legislation*	*New York Convention*	*ICSID Convention*
13	Cote d'Ivoire	OHADA UAA; Law 93-671 of 1993	2 May 1991	14 Oct 1966
14	Democratic Republic of Congo	OHADA UAA	3 Feb 2015	29 May 1970
15	Djibouti	Code of International Arbitration 1984	27 June 1977	-
16	Egypt	Arbitration Law 1994 (amended 1997)	7 June 1959	2 June 1972
17	Eritrea	Book IV, Civil Procedure Code 1965	-	Signed 21 Sept 1965
18	Ethiopia	Civil Procedure Code of 1991	-	Signed 21 Sept 1965
19	Equatorial Guinea	OHADA UAA	-	19 Nov 1978
20	Gabon	OHADA UAA; Civil Procedure Code.	15 Mar 2007	14 Oct 1966
21	Gambia	ADR Act 2005	-	26 Jan 1975
22	Ghana	ADR Act 2010	8 July 1968	14 Oct 1966
23	Guinea	OHADA UAA; Code on Economic Activities; Code of Civil, Economic and Administrative Procedure.	23 April 1991	4 Dec 1968
24	Guinea-Bissau	OHADA UAA	-	Signed 4 Sept 1991
25	Kenya	Arbitration Act 2005 amended 2009	11 May 1989	2 Feb 1967
26	Lesotho	Arbitration Act No 12 of 1980	11 Sept 1989	7 Aug 1969
27	Liberia	Arbitration Law, Chapter 7 Commercial Code 2010	15 Dec 2005	16 July 1970
28	Libya	Code of Civil Procedure 1953	-	-
29	Madagascar	Arbitration Law 98-019 of 2 Dec 1998	14 Oct 1962	14 Oct 1966
30	Malawi	Arbitration Act of 6 Nov 1967	-	14 Oct 1966

No	Country	National Legislation	New York Convention	ICSID Convention
31	Mali	OHADA UAA; Civil Procedure Code.	7 Dec 1994	2 Feb 1978
32	Mauritania	Code of Arbitration No 2000-06	30 April 1997	14 Oct 1966
33	Mauritius	International Arbitration Act No 37 of 2008	17 Sept 1996	2 July 1969
34	Morocco	Code of Civil Procedure 1947 (modified in 2007)	7 June 1959	10 June 1967
35	Mozambique	Law on Arbitration, Conciliation and Mediation No 11/99 of 8 July 1999	9 Sept 1998	7 July 1995
36	Namibia	Arbitration Act No 42 of 1965	-	Signed 26 Oct 1998
37	Niger	OHADA UAA	12 Jan 1965	14 Dec 1966
38	Nigeria	Arbitration and Conciliation Act 1988	15 June 1970	14 Oct 1966
39	Rwanda	Arb & Conciliation in Commercial Matters Law No 005 of 2008	29 Jan 2009	14 Nov 1979
40	Sao Tome & Principe	Voluntary Arbitration Law No 9 of 2006	18 Feb 2013	19 June 2013
41	Senegal	OHADA UAA; Law 98-30 of 1998 on Contracts; Decree 98-492 of 1998.	15 Jan 1995	21 May 1967
42	Seychelles	Commercial Code 1977 & Code of Civil Procedure 1920	-	19 April 1978
43	Sierra Leone	-	-	14 Oct 1966
44	Somalia	Civil Procedure Code, Book III, 1974	-	30 Mar 1968
45	South Africa	Arbitration Act No 42 of 1965	1 Aug 1976	-
46	South Sudan	-	-	18 May 2012
47	Sudan	Arbitration Act 2015	-	9 May 1973
48	Swaziland	Arbitration Act No 24 of 1904	-	14 July 1971

No	*Country*	*National Legislation*	*New York Convention*	*ICSID Convention*
49	Tanzania	Arbitration Act 1931 revised 2002	11 Jan 1965	17 June 1992
50	Togo	OHADA UAA; Decree 82-50 of 1982; Law 89-31 of 1989.	-	10 Sept 1967
51	Tunisia	Arbitration Code, Law No 93-42, 1993	15 Oct 1967	14 Oct 1966
52	Uganda	Arbitration & Conciliation Act 2000 (amended 2008)	12 May 1992	14 Oct 1966
53	Zambia	Arbitration Act No 19 of 2000	12 June 2002	17 July 1970
54	Zimbabwe	Arbitration Act No 6 of 1996	28 Dec 1994	19 June 1994

OHADA UAA = OHADA Uniform Arbitration Act 11 March 1999
Riyadh Convention 1983 African member states: Tunisia, Algeria, Djibouti, Sudan, Somalia, Libya, Morocco, and Mauritania.
Sources: https://arbitrationinafrica.com/countries/; http://www.uncitral.org/uncitral/uncitral_texts/arbitration.html; https://icsid.worldbank.org/apps/ICSIDWEB/Pages/default.aspx; http://ohada.org/.

APPENDIX II

African Countries: List of Arbitration Institutions*

No	Institution/Centre	Country
1	Algerian Chamber of Commerce & Industry, Algiers Web: http://www.ccis-agadir.com/pages/c_arbitrage.php	Algeria
2	Annaba Mediation & Arbitration Centre, Annaba	Algeria
3	Centre for Extra Judicial Resolution of Disputes (CREL)	Angola
4	Arbitration, Mediation and Conciliation Centre of the Chamber of Commerce & Industry of Benin Web: http://www.ccibenin.org/	Benin Republic
5	Conciliation and Arbitration Chamber of the Cotton Inter-professional Association of Cotonou	Benin Republic
6	Ouagadougou Arbitration, Mediation & Conciliation Centre of the Chamber of Commerce & Industry Web: http://www.camco.bf/	Burkina Faso
7	Burundi Centre for Arbitration & Mediation	Burundi
8	Centre d'Arbitrage du GICAM (Groupement Interpatronal du Cameroun), Douala Web: http://legicam.cm/	Cameroon
9	Centre d'arbitrage du CPAM, Yaounde Web: http://www.cadevafrique.org/	Cameroon
10	Centre d'Arbitrage, de Mediation et de Conciliation de Centrafrique (CAMC-CA), Bangui.	Central Africa Republic
11	Centre de Mediation et d'arbitrage, Ndjamena (project launched in March 2016)	Chad

* The information provided in Appendix II is as of April 2016.

No	Institution/Centre	Country
12	Centre d'Arbitrage et de Mediation attached to the Brazzaville Chamber of Commerce, Industry, Agriculture and Jobs, Libreville. Web: www.cciambrazza.com	Congo
13	Centre de mediation et d'arbitrage au Congo (CEMACO)	Congo
14	Le Centre d'Arbitrage du Congo (CAC) Kinshasa Web: www.cac-rdc.org	Democratic Republic of Congo
15	National Centre for Arbitration, Conciliation & Mediation (CENACOM), Kinshasa Web: http://www.cenacom.cd/	Democratic Republic of Congo
16	Intergovernmental Authority on Development (IGAD) Business Arbitration Centre	Djibouti
17	Cairo Regional Centre for ICA (CRCICA) Web: http://www.crcica.org.eg	Egypt
18	Sharm El Sheikh International Arbitration Centre Web: http://www.shiac.com/	Egypt
19	Dr A Kheir Law & Arbitration Centre (AKLAC) Web: http://www.kheirlaw.com.eg	Egypt
20	Addis Ababa Chamber & Sectorial Association Arbitration Institute Web: http://www.addischamber.com/	Ethiopia
21	Centre d'Arbitrage, de Mediation et de Conciliation (CAMC-GA)	Gabon
22	Ghana Arbitration Centre Web: http://www.ghanaarbitration.org/	Ghana
23	Ghana Association of Certified Mediators & Arbitrators (GHACMA), Accra Web: http://www.ghacma.org/	Ghana
24	Arbitration Centre Chambre d'Arbitrage de la Guinée, Conakry	Guinea
25	Arbitration Centre Chambre d'Arbitrage de Cote d'Ivoire Web: http://www.caci.ci/	Ivory Coast
26	Common Court of Justice & Arbitration of OHADA Web: http://www.ohada.org/ccja.html	Ivory Coast
27	Chamber of Commerce & Industry of Ivory Coast, Abidjan Web: http://www.cci.ci	Ivory Coast
28	Dispute Resolution Centre, Nairobi Web: http://www.disputeresolutionkenya.org/	Kenya
29	Nairobi Centre for International Arbitration Web: http://ncia.or.ke/	Kenya
30	The Directorate of Dispute Prevention & Resolution Web: http://www.ddpr.org.ls	Lesotho

No	Institution/Centre	Country
31	Libyan Centre for Mediation & Arbitration	Libya
32	The Libyan International Arbitration Commercial Centre Web: http://odysseia.ly/portfolio-items/the-libyan-international-arbitration-commercial-center/	Libya
33	Arbitration Centre of Madagascar Web: http://www.camm-mada.org/	Madagascar
34	Centre d'Arbitrage et de Conciliation du Mali (CECAM) Bamako Web: www.ccigabon.com	Mali
35	Permanent Court for Arbitration at the Mauritius Chamber of Commerce & Industry Web: http://www.mcci.org/en/	Mauritius
36	LCIA-MIAC Arbitration Centre, Ebene Web: http://www.lcia-miac.org/	Mauritius
37	Euro-Mediterranean Centre for Mediation & Arbitration, Casablanca	Morocco
38	Rabat International Mediation & Arbitration Centre (CIMAR) Web: http://www.cimar-maroc.org/	Morocco
39	CCIS, Agadir Web: http://www.ccis-agadir.com/	Morocco
40	Centre for Arbitration Conciliation & Mediation (GACM) Maputo Web: www.cacm.org.mz	Mozambique
41	Centre de Mediation et d'Arbitrage de Niamey (CMAN) attached to the Niger Chambre de Commerce, d'Industrie et d'Artisan Web: www.camco.bf	Niger
42	Regional Centre for ICA Lagos (RCICAL) Web: http://www.rcicalagos.org/	Nigeria
43	Maritime Arbitrators Association of Nigeria (MANN) Web: http://maanigeria.org/	Nigeria
44	Lagos Court of Arbitration Centre Web: http://www.lagosarbitration.org/	Nigeria
45	International Centre for Arbitration & Mediation, Abuja (ICAMA) Web: http://www.icama.com/	Nigeria
46	Lagos Chamber of Commerce International Arbitration Centre Web: http://www.laciac.org/	Nigeria
47	Janada International Centre for Arbitration & Mediation, Abuja Web: http://www.jicam.org/	Nigeria

No	Institution/Centre	Country
48	Kigali International Arbitration Centre (KIAC) Web: http://www.kiac.org.rw	Rwanda
49	Arbitration Centre of the Dakar Chamber of Commerce, Industry and Agriculture Web: http://www.cciad.sn/	Senegal
50	Dakar Arbitration & Mediation Centre	Senegal
51	Arbitration Foundation of Southern Africa Web: http://www.arbitration.co.za	South Africa
52	Equillore Group Web: http://www.equillore.com/wp/	South Africa
53	Africa Alternative Dispute Resolution (Africa ADR) Web: http://www.africaadr.com/	South Africa
54	The Association of Arbitrators Web: http://www.arbitrators.co.za/	South Africa
55	Commission for Conciliation, Mediation & Arbitration (CCMA) Web: http://www.ccma.org.za/	South Africa
56	Tokiso Dispute Settlement Pty Ltd	South Africa
57	South Sudan Chamber of Commerce, Industry & Agriculture, Juba Web: http://www.southsudanchamber-commerce.org	South Sudan
58	Arab Centre for Arbitration	Sudan
59	International Chamber of Arbitration	Sudan
60	The Sudanese Centre for Conciliation & Arbitration Web: http://sudanesearbitration.com/	Sudan
61	Conciliation, Mediation and Arbitration Commission (CMAC) Web: http://www.cmac.org.sz/	Swaziland
62	The National Construction Council, Dar es Salaam Web: http://www.ncc.or.tz/index.html	Tanzania
63	East African Court of Justice (Arbitration Institution) Arusha Web: http://eacj.org/	Tanzania
64	Tanzania Institute of Arbitrators (TIA), Dar es Salaam	Tanzania
65	Arbitration Court CATO, Lome Web: http://www.ccit.tg/	Togo
66	Centre for Conciliation & Arbitration of Tunis (CCAT)	Tunisia
67	Al Insaf Centre, Tunis	Tunisia
68	Centre for Arbitration & Dispute Resolution, Kampala	Uganda
69	Zambia Centre for Dispute Resolution	Zambia

No	*Institution/Centre*	*Country*
70	Commercial Arbitration Centre in Harare	Zimbabwe
71	Africa Institute of Mediation and Arbitration, Harare Web: http://www.aima.org.zw/	Zimbabwe

APPENDIX III

Participation of African Parties, Cities and Arbitrators in ICC Arbitrations: 2000-2015

Year	*Parties*	*Cities*	*Arbitrators*
2000	89	2	9
2001	74	3	12
2002	74	7	13
2003	79	6	28
2004	72	2	18
2005	68	8	23
2006	81	-	27
2007	50	3	16
2008	87	2	34
2009	126	14	39
2010	122	9	40
2011	174	12	52
2012	127	6	23
2013	174	9	27
2014	163	8	38
2015	48	3	32
TOTAL	**1608**	**94**	**431**

Bibliography

2013 ICC Statistical Report, vol. 25 no. 1 ICC Bulletin 5 (2014).

USA International Business Publications, Burundi Mineral & Mining Sector Investment and Business Guide: World Strategic and Business Information Library 128 (Int'l Business Publications, 2013).

LCIA Statistics: LCIA Registrar's Report 2013 at: http://www.lcia.org/LCIA/reports.aspx [accessed 13 March 2016]. See also to the same effect, ICSID statistics, available at: https://icsid.worldbank.org/apps/icsidweb/resources/pages/icsid-caseload-statistics.aspx [accessed 13 March 2016].

MIAC 2010 Book (Government of Mauritius, 2010).

SMES and Growth in Sub-Sahara Africa (MENON), available at: http://www.norfund.no/getfile.php/Documents/Homepage/Reports%20and%20presentations/Studies%20for%20Norfund/SME%20and%20growth%20MENON%20%5BFINAL%5D.pdf [accessed 30 March 2016].

Tanzania, Arbitration in Africa, 5 June 2007, available at: http://www.nortonrosefulbright.com/files/tanzania-25762.pdf [accessed 7 April 2016].

USA International Business Publications, Burundi Mineral & Mining Sector Investment and Business Guide: World Strategic and Business Information Library 128 (Int'l Business Publications, 2013).

LCIA Statistics: LCIA Registrar's Report 2013 at: http://www.lcia.org/LCIA/reports.aspx [accessed 13 March 2016]. See also to the same effect, ICSID statistics, available at: https://icsid.worldbank.org/apps/icsidweb/resources/pages/icsid-caseload-statistics.aspx [accessed 13 March 2016].

MIAC 2010 Book (Government of Mauritius, 2010).

SMES and Growth in Sub-Sahara Africa (MENON), available at: http://www.norfund.no/getfile.php/Documents/Homepage/Reports%20and%20presentations/Studies%20for%20Norfund/SME%20and%20growth%20MENON%20%5BFINAL%5D.pdf [accessed 30 March 2016].

Asian-African Legal Consultative Organization, *Report on the AALCO's Regional Arbitration Centres*, AALCO/51/ABUJA/2012/ORG 3.

Asouzu, A.A., *Arbitration in Africa: Agenda for Reform*, ADR L.J. 343-436 (1997).

Asouzu, A.A., *Some Fundamental Concerns and Issues about International Arbitration in Africa*, vol. 1 African Development Bank Law Development Review 81, 86 (2006).

Anyebe, P., *Towards Fast Tracking Justice Delivery in Civil Proceedings in Nigeria*, available at http://www.nials-nigeria.org/journals/Peter%20Anyebe-%20Towards%20Fast%20Tracking.pdf [last accessed on 18 May 2016].

Baghdadli, I. et al. (eds), *Breaking the Cycle: A Strategy for Conflict-sensitive Rural Growth in Burundi: Main Report.*

Bentham, J. and Woodd-Walker, *The Rise of Arbitration in Africa* (Simmons & Simmons, Power Point Presentation dated 10 December 2015), available at: http://www.elexica.com/~/media/Files/Training/2015/12%20December/The%20Rise%20of%20Arbitration%20in%20Africa.pdf [accessed 9 April 2016].

Blackaby, N. et al., *Redfern and Hunter on International Arbitration* 58 (6th ed., Kluwer Law International/OUP, 2015).

Born, G.B., *International Commercial Arbitration* (Wolters Kluwer, 2009).

Bosman, L., *The PCA's Contribution to International Dispute Resolution in Africa*, vol. 25 Stellenbosch Law Review 308 (2014).

Boseman, L. (gen ed.), *Arbitration in Africa: a Practitioner's Guide*, (Kluwer Law International, 2013).

Bosman, L., *The PCA's Contribution to International Dispute Resolution in Africa*, 25 Stellenbosch Law Review 308 (2014).

Carbonneau, T. E., *Arbitration in a Nutshell* 287 (2nd ed., West 2009).

Candide-Johnson, C.A. and O. Shasore, *Commercial Arbitration Law and Practice in Nigeria* 27 (LexisNexis, 2012).

Castellani, L.G., *International Trade Law Reform in Africa*, vol. 13 no. 3-4 European Journal of Law Reform 480 (2011).

Chikwanha, A.B., *The Anatomy of Conflicts in the East African Community (EAC): Linking Security With Development*, keynote speech to Development Policy Review Network-African Studies Institute, Leiden University, The Netherlands, Theme for 2007-Development Policy and the Security Agenda for Africa: Reassessing the Relationship, available at: https://www.issafrica.org/uploads/EACANNIE.PDF [accessed 27 January 2016].

Cosmas, J., *The State of International Commercial Arbitration in Tanzania: A Comparative Critique And Call For The Reform*, vol. 12 US-China Law Review 513-529, 521 (2015).

Cosmas, G.L., *Critical Analysis on the Challenges Facing Legal and Institutional Frameworks on Recognition and Enforcement of Foreign Arbitral Awards in Tanzania*, vol. 39 Journal of Law, Policy and Globalization 165-177, 172 (2015).

Cresswell, P., *International Arbitration: Enhancing Standards* 10, 10-13 (The Resolver, Chartered Institute of Arbitrators, 2014).

Daele,K., et al., *Country Q&A: Tanzania*, in Cross-Border Handbooks: Arbitration, 2010/11, available at www.practicallaw.com/arbitrationhandbook [accessed 20 March 2016].

Degos, L. and D. Akchoti, *The Democratic Republic of the Congo Joins OHADA and Its Arbitration Mechanisms* (K&L Gates Publication).

Dickerson, C.M., *The Common Court of Justice and Arbitration: Exogenous Forces Contributing to its Influence*, vol. 79:63 no. 1 Law and Contemporary Problems 63 (2016).

Douajni, G.K., *L'internationalité de l'arbitrage OHADA* vol. 13 no. 3-4, European Journal of Law Reform 397 (2011).

Drahozal, C.R. and R.W. Naimark, *Towards a Science of International arbitration: Collected Empirical Research* 27 (Kluwer Law International, 2005).

Dutta, A., *Origin of Alternative Dispute Resolution System in India* 87, available at: https://www.academia.edu/4371674/ORIGIN_OF_ALTERNATIVE_DISPUTE_RESOLUTION_SYSTEM_IN_INDIA [accessed 8 April 2016].

Ecobank, *Africa 8 Insight 6 – Intra-Africa Investments,* available at: http://ecobank.com/africa8/insight6.html#africa8_main [last accessed 6 May 2016].

Economic Times, *Top FPIs Raise Concerns with Sebi over Mauritius Treaty, GAAR and Participatory Notes*, available at: http://articles.economictimes.indiatimes.com/2015-08-14/news/65524781_1_tax-treaty-mauritius-treaty-capital-gains-tax [accessed 13 March 2016].

Fouchard, P., (ed) *Relationships Between the Arbitrator and the Parties and the Arbitration Institution,* December, ICC Bulletin, paragraph 13, 15 (1995).

Franck, S.D., *The Role of International Arbitrators,* available at: https://international-arbitration-attorney.com/wp-content/uploads/Microsoft-Word-ILW-ILSA-Article.docsfranck2.pdf [accessed on 7 April 2016].

Gaillard, E., *Freshfields Lecture on Sociology of Arbitration* (26 November 2014), available at: http://embed.buto.tv/kQJnL#play [accessed 20 April 2016].

Herbert Smith Freehills Dispute Resolution, *Burundi becomes 150th state party to the New York Convention*, available at: http://hsfnotes.com/arbitration/2014/09/03/burundi-becomes-150th-state-party-to-the-new-york-convention/ [Accessed 8 April 2016].

IBA Report, *The Current State and Future of International Arbitration: Regional Perspectives- IBA Arb 40 Subcommittee*, 20-21 September 2015.

ICC, *ICC Arbitration: A Ten-Year Statistical Overview,* vol. 9 no. 1 ICC Bulletin 51-63 (2008).

IDEAS Report, *Political Stability: Crucial for Growth,* available at: http://www.lse.ac.uk/IDEAS/publications/reports/pdf/SU004/shepherd.pdf [accessed 13 March 2016].

Ikome, F.N., *Africa's International Borders as Potential Sources of Conflict and Future Threats to Peace and Security.*

Jahnel, A.W., *Assessment Report of Arbitration Centres in Côte d'Ivoire, Egypt and Mauritius,* available at: http://www.afdb.org/fileadmin/uploads/afdb/Documents/Procurement/Project-related-Procurement/Assessment_Report_of_arbitration_centres_in_C%C3%B4te_d%E2%80%99Ivoire__Egypt_and_Mauritius.pdf, [accessed 20 April 2016].

Joshi, M., *The Role of Arbitration Institutions in the Development of Arbitration in Africa,* (unpublished) delivered at the conference on the Role of Arbitration Institutions in the Development of Arbitration in Africa, African Union Commission, Addis Ababa, 23 July 2015.

Kakooza, A.C.K., *Arbitration, Conciliation and Mediation in Uganda: A Focus on the Practical Aspects*, (2009) vol. 7 no. 2 Uganda Living Law Journal 268, 272 (December 2009).

Kapinga et al., *Getting the Deal Through,* Arbitration 406-412 (2014), available at: http://www.academia.edu/9872218/Getting_the_Deal_Through_-_Arbitration-_Tanzania_Chapter_2014 [accessed 7 April 2016].

Lawton Kirtley, W., *Bringing Claims and Enforcing International Arbitration Awards against Sub-Saharan African States and Parties,* vol. 8 The Law and Practice of International Courts and Tribunals 143,143 (2009).

Lee, J., *Mauritius: Its Creole Language* (3rd ed., Merlin Press, 2008).

Lew et al., *Comparative International Commercial Arbitration* 237 (Kluwer Law International, 2003).

Mashamba, C.J., *Alternative Dispute Resolution in Tanzania: Law and Practice* 125 (Mkuki na Nyota Publishers, 2014).

Maury, F., *Guinée. Ces honoraires qui coûtent très chers à GETMA, Jeune Afrique,* available at: http://www.jeuneafrique.com/mag/292443/economie/guinee-honoraires-coutent-tres-cher-a-getma/ [accessed 9 March 2016].

Maury, F., *Port de Guinée. la Port de Guinée. la condamnation de la Guinée annulée,* available at: http://www.jeuneafrique.com/283427/societe/port-de-conakry-la-condamnation-de-la-guinee-annulee/ [accessed 9 March 2016] de la Guinée annulée, available at: http://www.jeuneafrique.com/283427/societe/port-de-conakry-la-condamnation-de-la-guinee-annulee/ [accessed 9 March 2016].

McLaughlin, J.T., *Arbitration and Developing Countries,* vol. 13 no. 2 The International Lawyer 211, 212 (1979).

Melis, W., *Function and Responsibility of Arbitral Institutions,* vol. 13 Comparative Law Yearbook of International Business 107, 109 (1991).

Mercadal, B. et al., *Code Pratique Francis Lefebvre OHADA: Traité, Actes uniformes et Règlements annotés* 126-127 (2nd ed., Editions Francis Lefebvre, 2014).

Meyer, P., Professeur de Droit à l'Université de Ouagadougou (Burkina Faso), *Droit de l'arbitrage,* p. 10, doc. ERSUMA, October 2009.

Muigua, K., *Role of the Court under Arbitration Act 1995: Court Intervention Before, Pending and After Arbitration in Kenya,* Kenya Law Review 2 (2008-2010).

Muigua, K., *Natural Resources and Conflict Management in East Africa,* paper presented at the 1st NCMG East African ADR Summit held at the Windsor Golf Hotel, Nairobi on 25 and 26 September 2014.

Muigua, K., *Making East Africa a Hub for International Commercial Arbitration: A Critical Examination of the State of the Legal and Institutional Framework Governing Arbitration in Kenya,* available at: http://www.kmco.co.ke/attachments/article/114/Making%20East%20Africa%20a%20Hub%20for%20International%20Commercial%20Arbitration.pdf [accessed 8 April, 2016].

Muigua, K., *Promoting International Commercial Arbitration in Africa,* available at: http://www.kmco.co.ke/attachments/article/119/PROMOTING%20INTERNATIONAL%20COMMERCIAL%20ARBITRATION%20IN%20AFRICA.pdf [accessed 5 April 2016].

Nairobi Centre for International Arbitration, *First Arbitration Conducted at the NCIA Boardroom,* available at: http://ncia.or.ke/index.php?option = com_phocagallery&view = category&id = 1:first-arbitration&Itemid = 1263 [accessed 20 March 2016].

Ngotho, P., *Pathological Arbitration Clauses in Ad Hoc Arbitrations: Kenya's Experience*, paper, available at: http://www.ngotho.co.ke/PathologicalArbitration Clauses.8.8.14.pdf [accessed 8 April 2016].

Nsekela, H.R., *Overview of the East African Court Of Justice*, paper, available at: http://eacj.huriweb.org/wp-content/uploads/2013/09/Overview-of-the-EACJ.pdf [accessed 5 April 2016].

OECD, *OECD Investment Policy Reviews: Mauritius* 92-93 (OECD Publications, 2014).

Olatawura, O.O., *Stay of Proceedings in Nigerian Law of Arbitration: Analysis of its Functions, Applications and Problems*, vol. 28 no. 4 Arbitration International 689-720 (2012).

Onyema, E., *Regional Arbitration Institution for ECOWAS: Lessons from OHADA Common Court of Justice and Arbitration,* IALR 99-111 (2014).

Onyema, E., *The New Ghana ADR Act 2010: A Critical Overview* vol. 28, no. 1 Arbitration International 101-124 (2012).

Oppong, R.F., *Legal Aspects of Economic Integration in Africa* 240 (Cambridge University Press, 2011).

Ousmanou, S.D., *Approach Critique du droit et de la pratique de l'arbitrage dans l'espace OHADA,* (unpublished) paper presented at the first African Conference on International Commercial Law, Douala-Cameroon, 2-3 (21 and 22 January 2012).

Peeroo, J. et Guilmain A., *Pour une réforme du droit mauricien de l'arbitrage international en matière de reconnaissance et d'exécution des sentences* vol. 3 The New Bar Chronicle (Mauritius), 9-14 (November 2011).

Prime Minister of Mauritius, *Mauritius International Arbitration Conference 2010 Speech,* available at: http://itcoach.intnet.mu/portal/goc/pm/file/miac.pdf [accessed 13 March 2016].

Queen Mary University of London, *International Arbitration Survey on Choices in International Arbitration 2010,* available at http://www.arbitration.qmul.ac.uk /research/index.html [accessed 13 March 2016].

Queen Mary University of London, *2013 Survey on Corporate Choices in International Arbitration,* available at http://www.arbitration.qmul.ac.uk/research/index. html [accessed 13 March 2016].

Sarkodie, K., *Arbitration in Ghana – The Alternative Dispute Resolution Act 2010* (Mayer Brown Practice Notes, 2011), available at: https://m.mayerbrown.com [accessed 29 March 2016].

Thaddeus Sory, *The International Arbitration Review,* Chapter 20, 1-12 (6th ed., June 2015).

Sutton and Gill (eds), *Russell on Arbitration,* paragraph 3-046 (22nd ed., Sweet & Maxwell, 2003)

Tetteh, K., *Civil Procedure: A Practical* Approach [full publication data].

Torgbor, E., *Opening up International Arbitration in Africa*, vol. 1 no. 1 LCA Dispute Resolution Journal 1-20 (2014).

Tumnde, M.S., *OHADA as Experienced in Cameroon: Addressing Areas of Particular Concern to Common Law Jurists*, in C. Dickerson Moore (ed.), *Unified Business*

Law for Africa: Common Law Perspectives on OHADA, *supra* 72 (GMB Publishing, 2009).

World Bank, World Bank Doing Business Report 2016, available at: http://www.doingbusiness.org/~/media/GIAWB/Doing%20Business/Documents/Annual-Reports/English/DB16-Full-Report.pdf [accessed 13 March 2016].

Yakubu, J. A., *Community laws in International Business Transactions*, in C. Dickerson (ed.) *Unified Business Law for Africa: Common Law Perspectives on OHADA*, 4 (GMB Publishing London, 2009).

Table of Cases

Attorney General v. Balkan Energy Ghana Ltd & Others [2012] 2 SCGLR 998, 124, 125, 126, 142
BCM Ghana Ltd v. Ashanti Goldfields Ltd [2005-2006] SCGLR 602, 132
Centre Canadien d'Arbitrage Commercial v. Garantie des Baltiments Residentiels Neuf de l'APCHQ Inc, [2005] QCCA 728, 30
Ceskolowenska Obchodni Bank AS (Cecobank) v. ICC (1986) *rev* Arb (1987) 367 No. 1 Medt & Mid. East Arb Qtly 3 (1987), 30
Cruz City 1 Mauritius Holdings v. Unitech And Others [2014] SCJ 100, 104
George Kodua v. Interbeton B.V. Suit No. H1/53/2004 dated 26 November 2004 Court of Appeal (unreported), 132
Glencore Grain Ltd v. T.S.S.S Grain Millers Ltd [2012] eKLR, 89
Khoury v. Khoury [1962] 1 GLR 98, 132, 147
Klimatechnik Engineering Limited v. Skanska Jensen International [2005-2006] SCGLR 913, 137
Mitsubishi Motors Corp. v. Soler Chrysler-Plymouth, Inc., 473 U.S. 614 (1985), 76
Oxenham v. France Maritime Agency Ltee (FMA) 2016 SCJ 10, 101
Ras Pal Gazi Construction Company v. Federal Capital Development Authority [2001] 5 SC (pt II) 16, 137
Republic v. High Court, Accra, ex parte Asakum Engineering and Construction Ltd. [1993-94] GLR 643, 128
Republic v. High Court, Tema; Ex parte MY Shipping PVT Limited (Dee Jones Petroleum & Gas Limited & MV MY Arctic Interested Parties) [2011] 1 SCGLR 237, 133
Rockson v. Ghana Football Association [2010] SCGLR 443, 128
Skanska Jensen International v. Klimatechnik Engineering Ltd [2003-2004] SCGLR 698, 133
Societe Opinter France v. Sarl Dacomex Rev Arb (1987) 475, 30
State Insurance Corporation Takoradi v. Badu [1965] GLR 105, 126, 132
Sulamerica CIA Nacional De Seguros SA and Others v. Enesa Engenharia SA and Others [2012] EWHC 42 (Comm) and on appeal [2012] EWCA Civ 638, 105
W Limited v. M SDN BDH [2016] EWHC 422 (Comm), 40

Table of Legislations

Kenya

Mauritius

Nigeria

Rwanda

Tanzania

Uganda

UK

Zimbabwe

Arbitration Rules

International Bar Association Documents

Index

I

J

K

L

M

N